Reaching Every Reader: Promotional Strategies for the Elementary School Library Media Specialist

Pat Miller

A Publication of THE BOOK REPORT & LIBRARY TALK
Professional Growth Series

Linworth Publishing, Inc.
Worthington, Ohio

"Human Tic-Tac-Toe," pages 40-41 was first published as "Getting to Know You: Tic-Tac-Toe" in the February, 1999 issue of *School Library Media Activities Monthly*. Reprinted with permission.

Chapter 7: **Tender Loving Care** is expanded from an article "Build Library Support with TLC" from *Library Talk*, Volume II Number 3, Copyright © 1998 by Linworth Publishing, Inc. All rights reserved.

Library of Congress Cataloging-in-Publication Data

Miller, Pat, 1951-
    Reaching every reader : promotional strategies for the elementary school library media specialist / Pat Miller.
        p. cm. -- (A Publication of the Book report & Library talk professional growth series)
    Includes bibliographical references and indexes.
    ISBN 1-58683-001-5
        1. School libraries--Activity programs--United States. 2. Instructional materials personnel--United States--Handbooks, manuals, etc. I. Title. II. Professional growth series.

    Z675.S3 M375 2000
    027.8'0973--dc21

                                                    00-061815

Published by Linworth Publishing, Inc.
480 East Wilson Bridge Road, Suite L
Worthington, Ohio 43085

Copyright©2001 by Linworth Publishing, Inc.

Series Information:
        From The Professional Growth Series

ISBN 1-58683-001-5

5 4 3 2 1

Dedication

For John, who kept the home fires burning,
and for Sandy Henson, who kept the library fires burning
With love and gratitude

Acknowledgements

My family is my fan club, and I am grateful for their support. Thanks to my children, Chris, Marty, and Bonnie, for many encouraging e-mails. I appreciate the backing of my patient husband, John, and my sister, Tereasa, who was my constant rah-rah girl. Thank you, Mom and Dad, for raising me to be a reader. My special thanks go to you who read this book. I often thought about you in the year I was writing it.

Table of Contents

Table of Contents *(continued)*

Table of Contents *(continued)*

Figures

List of Figures

Reproducibles

List of Reproducibles

Introduction

Two fourth-grade students were at our computer terminals looking up Internet sites for blue whales. Next to them, a fifth grader was trying to reserve the latest Harry Potter book on our automated catalog. As I went to assist them, a second-grade girl stopped me. "My mom gave a book to the library when I was in kindergarten. I want to check it out again," she said, looking up into my face hopefully. "I can't remember the name of it, but I brought my friend who thinks he remembers what it was about."

As I was sidetracked by this challenge, I saw my fifth-grade class walking in noisily. I needed to move them to the instructional area for a lesson on almanac usage. Before I could meet them, a freckle-faced first grader stopped me with a detailed note from his teacher requesting books. "She said I should wait for an answer," he said firmly.

At that moment, my office phone rang. One of the fourth graders using the Internet called for help. The first grader and her friend jogged alongside me. "I'm not sure if the book was about a dog or a cat, but I am sure the cover was green," the friend said helpfully.

Before I could reply, the fire alarm went off.

About This Book

This book is the result of thirteen years of experience in several library media centers. It is for overextended librarians and for those who are looking for fresh approaches to what they have been doing for years. These ideas will help you whether you are planning lessons with minimal cooperation from your teachers or have achieved the pinnacle of collaborative planning. They can be adapted for various elementary grades and used to inspire teachers.

Because we are always pressed for time, these lessons are based on picture books and easier nonfiction books; they can be read and the lesson completed in one class period. The lessons can be used independently or as station activities in library centers. At the end of chapter eight, for example, a lesson in outline form is presented for center use, followed by a detailed plan from which to select activities to teach as a group lesson.

Many of the lessons can be taught without teacher assistance, and all can be taught in cooperation with classroom teachers. Sometimes I begin a lesson in the library that the teacher will complete in the classroom. If your teachers don't stay with their classes, plan these partnership activities in advance so they will know what to do when the children return to the class.

Grade levels mentioned are representative, and the activities can be adapted using your own ideas and curriculum. I did not include time limits,

because time depends on how you use the activity. Some of the activities in this book lend themselves to a 15-minute storytime, others to lessons you teach with teachers, and longer ones to collaborative teaching during a flexibly scheduled time.

Using This Book

My intent is to incorporate traditional techniques, such as storytelling and puppetry, with the use of technology, particularly the Internet. Many different learning styles are incorporated to reach every reader.

Chapter One presents numerous ideas and examples of working with teachers to plan cooperative lessons. This is one of the most important jobs we have as educators in the library.

Chapter Two is about storytelling techniques, especially using some attention-getting but simple props. This is intended for beginners as well as more experienced tellers. There are also tips for booktalking a variety of books, particularly those that are shelf-sitters.

Chapter Three will show novice puppeteers how to begin and provide old hands with new ideas. Examples and ideas for a variety of stages and lesson correlations also are presented.

Chapter Four describes how to adapt traditional games to a variety of skills. All games are easily and inexpensively made, and will add fun to the learning in your library. Games are suited to all abilities, all learning strengths, and all curricular areas.

Chapter Five contains numerous songs related to the curriculum. Musical intelligence is underused in the library. Tap this ability by using chants and songs with a variety of lessons.

Chapter Six discusses ways to get out of a lesson rut by using creative dramatics and out of the walls of your library with virtual field trips for all topics.

Chapter Seven gives you lots of ways to brighten the days of your faculty and staff. Spread some kindness with these easily implemented ideas and see how good you feel in the process. Don't be surprised to see an increase in library usage as well as goodwill.

Chapter Eight packs a treasure chest of ideas, lessons, and center activities. Whether you need an activity for Groundhog Day for younger students or some research methods for older ones, you will find them in this chapter. Twelve learning topics are extended through a variety of center and group activities that are easy to use and require few special materials. Activities were developed to appeal to the multiple intelligences researched by Dr. Howard Gardner. All chapters contain Internet extensions and sites you will use again and again. Pick and choose, adapt and extend. These ideas are going to jazz up your library program!

Objectives and Standards

The lessons in chapter eight can be correlated to a variety of standards, including your local ones. You can find the national standards for various curricular areas on the Internet. Check these sites to match your academic activities with state or national standards.

English Language Arts: The National Council of Teachers of English and the International Reading Association have written the *Standards for the English Language Arts* at <www.ncte.rg/standards>.

Look for *The Nine Information Literacy Standards for Student Learning* from the American Library Association and the Association for Educational Communications and Technology in Appendix A.

Mathematics: Use *Principles and Standards for School Mathematics* from the National Council of Teachers of Mathematics at <www.nctm.org/standards2000>.

Science: The National Academy of Sciences has their *National Science Education Standards* on the Internet at <www.nap.edu/readingroom/books/nses/html>.

Social Studies: For guidelines, check the *Standards and Position Statement* of the National Council for the Social Studies at <www.ncss.org/standards>.

Technology: The International Society for Technology in Education has developed *The National Educational Technology Standards Project* that you can access at <cnets.iste.org>.

Rubrics

Each lesson has an evaluation component. At our school, we are evaluating more often with rubrics that have been explained to children before the assignment. In many instances, children have a say in the writing and administering of the rubric.

Whether you are new to writing rubrics or experienced and looking for additional ideas, you will find two Web sites especially useful. The first is *Ideas and Rubrics* at <intranet.cps.k12.il.us/ Assessments/Ideas_and_Rubrics/idea_and_rubrics. html>. This site features a bank of rubrics arranged by subject and articles on creating your own. The site is maintained by the Chicago Board of Education for use in their school district; you can benefit just as readily. The second is a site from the Huron Perth (Australia) Catholic District at <www.odyssey.on.ca/~elaine.coxon/ rubrics.htm>. It includes hundreds of rubrics, including those for making graphs, group presentations, varieties of student writing, and many others. The site also provides an extensive list of Internet sites for the use and creation of your own library rubrics, or to help teachers write their own.

Web Sites

At press time, the Web sites in this book were functioning. If they aren't working when you go to access them, here are a few things you can try.

First, backtrack in the Web address to the root, or basic, address. If the site you are looking for is <www.TexasMarine.fishing.bass.edu>, try deleting the secondary part of the address until you have only <www.TexasMarine.edu>. This page may be a home page with a listing of other sites, including the bass fishing tips for which you are searching.

Second, try searching for the Web page's title in a mega-search engine, such as Dog Pile at <www.dogpile.com>. If you want to find the site, *Cowboy Clothing of the 1800s*, type that title, enclosed by quotation marks, into the search window. You may find the new address for the site.

Last, you may realize the site has disappeared. This happens frequently and without warning on the Internet. If you can't find the site about writing haiku that is listed in this manuscript, go to a search engine, such as Yahoo, and search by topic. You may find other fine sites not listed here.

A Final Note

Here is how I have dealt with problems of semantics: throughout the book, I have randomly used either he or she when I needed a third person pronoun. Librarians have a variety of titles these days, including teacher-librarian, information and media specialist, and cybrarian. I have tended to use the term *librarian* to include all those titles. The same transition has been going on with the term "library." I realize that libraries now are the heart of the school, have virtually no walls, and include equipment, Internet connections, computers, and closed-circuit television. I intend to include all this when I use the term *library*. After all, libraries are the places to which students go for information, attention, and "that book with the green cover."

Working with Teachers

When I began as a school librarian thirteen years ago, collaborating with teachers was basically a parallel kind of teaching. Every grading period, teachers gave me a list of topics they were planning to teach. I developed objectives and lessons to complement this list, but rarely touched base with teachers again regarding instruction.

Within a few years, our district added computers to each campus, and the American Library Association and the state adopted new teaching standards. As technology increased and a more demanding curriculum was implemented, collaboration between teachers and librarians became essential.

The roles of the librarian have been expanded to include teacher, instructional partner, information specialist, and program administrator. These roles are guided by a vision based on collaboration, leadership, and technology. Librarians definitely have several big jobs to perform.

Collaboration: A Standard of Excellence

In 1998, the American Association of School Librarians and the Association for Educational Communication and Technology published the second edition of *Information Power: Building Partnerships for Learning* (ALA, 1998). It contains "Nine Information Literacy Standards for Student Learning" that outlines what students should be able to do by the time they leave our library pro-

grams. See Appendix A for details of the literacy standards.

ALA lists eight "Learning and Teaching Principles of School Media Programs" (see Appendix B). The third principle is "The library media program models and promotes collaborative planning and curriculum development" (ALA, 1998, p. 58). As anyone who has taught will testify, the workload of teachers is more than one person can do well. Teachers rely on their teaching team members, on professional magazines and books, and—hopefully—on their librarians for ideas and support. We need to become an important part of their support team. We can help to integrate information literacy, curricular objectives, and resources into their teaching plans. We also can help to teach and to assess student achievement of the standards included in our collaboratively planned lessons.

Planning with Teachers

What planning means to me in my daily library life is that I steal time to meet with teachers as they plan. When we had a totally fixed schedule, we met during lunch or twice a month at weekly planning sessions. Our goal was to collaboratively plan one unit or lesson per month for each grade.

As our joint units proved successful, more teachers asked to plan with me. Some of our first units included Puppets and Fairy Tales, Knowledge

Quest in the Middle Ages, and How to Recognize a Folktale. Collaboration became so successful at our school that we were able to move to a more flexible library schedule to allow more time for teaching and planning integrated units.

Sometimes collaboration involves simply listening to the teacher explain her unit, and supplying resources (including Web sites) and perhaps some lesson suggestions. Teachers can then choose from the resources I pull for them and include my ideas if desired. This approach is non-threatening and is sometimes best with teachers who are reluctant to share teaching with me.

Partner Teaching with Poetry

Collaboration on poetry produced a unit on reading and writing poetry, and we promoted it during Children's Book Week. After perusing our collection, we selected five themes and filled baskets with books related to them. (See the bibliography at the end of this chapter.)

Along with the books, I sent information about the Poetry Writing Workshop with Jack Prelutsky from the Web site at <teacher.scholastic.com/writewit/poetwit/index.htm> and professional books on helping students to write poetry. We also used the ideas from Caroline Feller Bauer's book *The Poetry Break* (Wilson, 1995). Bauer explains how to interrupt classes (with permission) to announce a poetry break, then proceed to read or perform a poem and leave. After reading Bauer's ideas, we decided to emphasize poetry for the upcoming Children's Book Week and to recruit the two fifth-grade classes that were studying poetry to be the "Poetry Breaksters."

Poetry Break!

At the appointed time (though students were unaware), I broke into Joyce Baysinger's fifth grade class and said in a loud voice, "Poetry break, poetry break, stop what you're doing for a poetry break!" I carried a large sign proclaiming POETRY BREAK, proceeded to the front of the room, and waited a dramatic moment. Students looked at me with curiosity. I read the Charles Wilkins' poem, "Successful Pancakes," from the book *Never Take a Pig to Lunch* (Scholastic,

1988). After reading the poem, I said, "Thank you," took a slight bow, and left amid flabbergasted silence.

Outside the classroom, I donned a tall pointed cap made from a poster board. Iridescent blue streamers cascaded from the top, making the hat resemble something from the Middle Ages. The hat was covered with stick-on vinyl letters to form words such as *poetry, 811, rhymes*, and *imagery*.

Back into the classroom I went, again pronouncing loudly, "Poetry break, poetry break, stop what you're doing for a poetry break!" This time the students smiled as I unrolled a scroll and read the poem, "Books Go Everywhere," by Naomi Shihab Nye. The poem was on a bookmark produced by The Children's Book Council, Inc.

After my second exit, I waited in the hall ten minutes to build suspense. Then I interrupted the class a third time, beginning with the poetry break chant. This time, students joined in the refrain. For the last poem, I wore a simple apron from the craft store to which were attached various stickers of books and vinyl letters spelling *Poetry Break*. I opened a box covered with purple and silver fabric and encrusted with fake jewels. I removed the poem from the box and read Eloise Greenfield's poem, "Harriet Tubman," in a serious and dramatic voice. The poem, found in *Pass It On: African American Poetry for Children* (Scholastic, 1993), raised goose bumps on my arms as I read it and caused a thoughtful hush over the class. After my last "thank you" and bow, students burst into applause.

This third time, I stayed and explained how the students could become Poetry Breaksters. Each student was asked to make three decisions:

1. Choose a poem to perform or read. Find at least three excellent poems. Write a bibliography card for each poem and the reasons you think it's best.
2. Decide how to present the poem. You may read it from the book or write it on a scroll, poster board, prop, or use your own idea.
3. Design a sign, hat, T-shirt, apron, or other way to designate yourself as a Poetry Break student. Decide whether to write a jingle, a song, or a poem to introduce the break.

We announced the deadline for the first rehearsal date. I supplied the poetry books, and the teacher supplied the schedule, time, and encouragement as students searched for poems.

Two days after students had begun the poetry search, I returned to explain some tips (from ideas in Bauer's book) to help as they read or performed their poems. In "Methods of Presentation," Bauer explains how to read poetry aloud, how to introduce the poem, and how to perform a poem with puppets, props, or a partner.

Dress rehearsal amazed me. Students had selected poems—mostly humorous ones—that they had written on scrolls, in boxes, on posters, and even on a T-shirt. Most carried signs, but one dressed as the Poetry Knight in shining (foil) armor. Some students spoke as a team, alternating verses. Two boys did a version of "Fireflies" from Paul Fleischman's *Joyful Noise* (HarperCollins, 1988) that demonstrated much practice.

During Children's Book Week, the fifth graders caused all 40 of our classes to take several poetry breaks. They even interrupted the library's book fair and entertained speechless buyers. Because the much-admired fifth graders seemed to be having so much fun with poetry, younger students checked out nearly our entire poetry collection. Poetry was no longer considered "uncool."

The week was a success, as was our fifth-grade poetry unit. Students learned writing techniques from poet Jack Prelutsky, shared poetry aloud with numerous classes, and compiled their own poetry into a class book. As we all know, one enthusiastic teacher is the best ambassador for library collaboration; it wasn't long before other fifth-grade teachers wanted to do units with me.

Picture Books for Older Readers

Another collaborative effort involved using picture books with fifth graders. Their teachers wanted to have mixed ability groups read and discuss books.

Using grade level books was not working. One reason was that they were so long that students could read only one or two. That limited their ability to compare a number of books. Another reason was that fifth graders have such a wide range of reading levels that reading the same class novel was not effective. Our jointly planned unit was based on thematic groups of picture books.

The advantages were apparent. Everyone in class could read the books and could read several

in a week's span. Then they could discuss and compare books based on plot, characters, illustrations, or other points suggested by the teacher. Some groups of books were chosen to feature authors, such as Bill Peet, Patricia Polacco, and Byrd Baylor. By using the more challenging picture books, students could read a good body of the work of a single author. They could more readily track themes, style characteristics, and other story elements.

This project was successful in many ways. It gave 11-year-olds an excuse to get books from the E section, which they usually shunned on principle. It circulated good E books that were not chosen by younger readers because of the increased amount of text. It was also another successful collaborative effort with teachers.

Brain Appeal

Once you get in the habit of looking at picture books with older readers in mind, you will be amazed by how many are appropriate for use with 9- or 10-year-olds. Here are some connections I made while perusing recent picture books in our local book company's warehouse.

Treeman (Peachtree, 1993), by Carmen Agra Deedy, is a story about a toucan, a sloth, and a boa constrictor that discover a card meant for Santa that fell from a plane bound for the North Pole. Seeing the cover of Santa sitting by a Christmas tree surrounded by gifts makes the animals mistakenly think that the man in red gives trees in return for gifts. As dark smoke rises over the rain forest, the animals think of gifts they can give in exchange for a tree. The ecological message is quietly stated and fits with our fifth graders' spring drive to raise money to purchase acreage in the rain forest to protect trees. Students can rewrite the story as a Readers' Theater and perform it for other grades as the kickoff for their fund raiser.

One Duck Stuck (Candlewick, 1998), by Phyllis Root, appears at first glance to be a counting book for younger readers. But the rhyming rhythm and onomatopoeias make it a definite fit with the fourth-grade curriculum that requires such writing. Interestingly, the book is printed in Belgium. You might instigate a "Where in the World" search for books printed elsewhere in the world. Students can pinpoint a world map with book titles and featured books. They can see how many they can collect. They can go online to write the publishing companies and ask why the books are not printed in the United States. While they are making inquiries, students might want to find out why the prices for Canada are higher. See Appendix C for the Web pages of the most popular children's publishers.

Look-Alikes (Little, Brown, 1998), by Joan Steiner, is an interesting alternative to the Eye Spy series. It presents three-dimensional pictures created with the use of matchsticks, broccoli, zippers, and over 1,000 other everyday objects. Students are challenged to find a certain number of objects, listed in the back, along with particularly difficult ones to see. This is a great book for productive thinking: Can students construct a similar picture?

Mailing May (Greenwillow, 1997), by Michael Tunnel, is historical fiction based on the true story of a child who was mailed under the livestock mailing provision in 1914. It can be used with other "based on true" stories. We used it with our Laura Ingalls Wilder unit to show what life was like for people who lived in the later years described in her books. It also can be tied with a service project we do in fourth grade. At Christmas and Valentine's Day, we operate a post office for the week before the holiday.

Cooperatively with teachers, we do a letter-writing unit with correct address on letter and envelope, and "mail" them to other students and teachers in the building. *Mailing May* talks about sorting mail and delivering it to small towns by rail. Each day, different fourth graders pick up, sort, and deliver mail from each of our 40 classrooms.

The Three Little Pigs (Morrow, 1997), by Steven Kellogg, is not your ordinary retelling—it's based on waffles! This story contains great vocabulary (*barrage, bombarded, flabbergasted*), and visual puns for older readers ("Say Yes to Thugs," written on a background banner). It demonstrates that a true adaptation changes at least three major elements in a story. Grades 3 and 4 write adaptations; this book serves as a perfect example.

How Santa Got His Job (Simon & Schuster, 1998), by Stephen Krensky, is a good choice any time of the year to illustrate foreshadowing.

Students who know the folklore of Santa will quickly figure out the story. A young, slim man named Santa is fired from his job as chimney sweep because he always stays clean, no matter how hard he works, and no one believes he's done a good job. He loses his job at the post office because he likes to make deliveries in the night to avoid traffic. Santa is a good worker at the zoo, but his favoritism to the reindeer causes jealousy among the other animals, and Santa is let go. Children will enjoy being in on the suspense because they know how it ends, though it's funnier than students will anticipate.

Autumn: An Alphabet Acrostic (Clarion, 1997) is an incredible book. Beautiful woodcuts by Leslie Evans illuminate the acrostic verses of Steven Schnur that feature autumn words from A to Z. What could become a contrived or cutesy group of poems instead makes some startling observations. These poems will inspire young poets to write acrostics on any theme or topic that you are studying. One of my favorites is for frost (p. 10):

> "**F**rom the window the
> **R**ows of
> **O**range pumpkins
> **S**eem clothed in
> **T**hin white shawls."

I Love You, Stinky Face (BridgeWater, 1997), by Lisa McCourt, is similar in premise to *The Runaway Bunny* (Brown, 1942), but has more snap and humor. A child challenges his mother to say what she would do if he were a super smelly skunk or a bug-eating green alien from Mars. She lovingly replies that she would bathe and powder and hug her "Stinky Face," or would buy clothes that complement his green skin and would leave affectionate notes in his insect-filled lunch box.

Have students write the mother's possible responses to the what-ifs. How would the mother reply if her son said, "What if I were an alligator with big, sharp teeth that could bite your head off?" Each idea should be accompanied with an illustration. Though they will never admit it, older elementary students, whose behavior can often be irritating, still like to read about parents who cherish their child no matter what.

There Was an Old Lady Who Swallowed a Trout! (Holt, 1998), by Terri Sloat, can be used to teach students to work with indexes. This humorous book portrays animals of the Pacific

Northwest being swallowed in progressively larger stages. Have students list the animals next to two columns labeled yes and no. The question to research is, "If this were an example of a food chain, would the succeeding animal really eat the one before it?" The emphasis is on using an index to locate specific information, but the task would interest students.

Another book to use as a model for beginning research, even for as old as fifth grade, is Harriet Ziefert's book *Polar Bears Can Swim: What Animals Can and Cannot Do* (Penguin Putnam, 1998). Though it is a Viking Science Easy-to-Read at Level 2, the premise is one that students can imitate, whether researching explorers, animals, or planets. The author lists three things an animal can do and one it cannot. That is followed by an animal that can do what the previous one can't, plus two more and one it can't in a repetitive pattern. For example, Ziefert writes, "A bat can sleep upside down. A bat can catch 600 insects in an hour. A bat can fly in the dark without bumping into things. But a bat can't fly backward. A hummingbird can fly backward…" Each sentence is accompanied by the appropriate illustration. This is an inspiring model for older students to put their facts into a more original context and would be a good way to avoid copying from sources. Another idea is to use the same formula for a class book on famous African Americans.

Picture book artwork is an important way to connect with readers. Most recent picture book publishers mention the art media used in the book's artwork on the verso page, usually near the Cataloging in Publishing. Connect your 8- to 11-year-olds with today's beautiful picture books and give them the excuse they need to enjoy the literature and the art: "She made me do it!"

Getting Personal

The most carefully selected books will not leave the shelves if students don't know about them. A lot of our energy is spent promoting books through displays, booktalks, and bibliographies. The most effective way to get my students to read a book is to show them my own enthusiasm for the book. Students willingly tackled challenging books such as Gail Levine's thick *Ella Enchanted* (HarperCollins, 1997) and Karen Hesse's *The*

Music of Dolphins (Scholastic, 1996) because I explained why I love them. Both have uninspiring covers, so I read excerpts to give them an enticing sense of the books. I described Mary Downing Hahn's ghost story *Wait Until Helen Comes* (Clarion, 1986) as the scariest children's book I've ever read. My daughter made me promise to warn them to not read the book before going to sleep. Students were so intrigued that we did not have to shelve our multiple copies until the last weeks of school.

The same thing happened when I booktalked Louis Sachar's *Holes* (Farrar, Straus and Giroux, 1998) by simply reading the first chapter. *Holes* has one of the most captivating first sentences. It would be a good kick-off to a "First Sentence Contest." Children turn in the title, author, and first line of a book they think is a great "grabber." Winners are selected by the librarian, based on her opinion, or by a drawing. Hopefully, such a contest will engage your verbal or introspective learners in reading books they might not otherwise choose.

Spur student reading in *Scholastic Reading Counts* or *Accelerated Reader* by including yourself and teachers as readers. One of our fifth-grade teachers, Michelle Durbin, suggested this idea: "If I expect my students to read books and answer questions each grading period, I should be the first to do so to set an example."

She challenged her students to read for more points than she did. She gave them a six weeks' head start. As she began to earn points, her students were motivated to read more difficult books to stay ahead of her. The teacher set aside time to talk about what she was reading and to encourage them to do the same. Her students were reading more and were proud to brag that they were ahead of their teacher. She provided a picnic lunch for all her students who "beat" her. The success came about because she had found a way to make reading personal.

Art Appreciation

In art class, the art teacher showed the students examples of various art media, such as acrylics and watercolor, and examples of work done with them. She taught them about realistic and abstract art.

When students came to the library, I used art transparencies to have them rate the pictures based on degree of realism. They used a subjective ranking system of holding up fingers (from five, which was photographically realistic, to one, which was recognizably abstract). This brought about some interest, as children saw the disparity of rankings among the students.

Next the students examined a pile of books on their tables. I had selected them because the books mentioned the art media used in the illustrations on the verso page.

Artistic Media

These are the types of media we discussed:

▲ Acrylics—pigments mixed with a plastic resin, quick-drying
▲ Collage—made with bits of paper, fabric, and real objects attached to the page
▲ Colored Chalk
▲ Colored Pencil
▲ Digital Illustrations—drawn on a computer
▲ Gouache (rhymes with squash)—pigments mixed with water and liquid gum
▲ Oil Paints—pigments mixed with linseed oil
▲ Pastels—pigment mixed with gum and formed into crayons
▲ Pen and Ink
▲ Photography
▲ Tempera Paint—pigments mixed with casein or egg yolk
▲ Watercolor—pigments mixed with water
▲ Woodcuts—carved wood with ink washed over surfaces

Students completed the Picture Book Evaluation Form (see full size on page 229) on several books of their choice. Then they wrote a brief paragraph about the one that they liked the best.

Name_____ Teacher _____

PICTURE BOOK ILLUSTRATION EVALUATIONS

1. Title of book: _____

   Art media used (look on copyright page): _____

   Scale of realism (Circle one, 1 is least, 5 is most):   1   2   3   4   5

2. Title of book: _____

   Art media used (look on copyright page): _____

   Scale of realism (Circle one, 1 is least, 5 is most):   1   2   3   4   5

3. Title of book: _____

   Art media used (look on copyright page): _____

   Scale of realism (Circle one, 1 is least, 5 is most):   1   2   3   4   5

4. Title of book: _____

   Art media used (look on copyright page): _____

   Scale of realism (Circle one, 1 is least, 5 is most):   1   2   3   4   5

5. Title of book: _____

   Art media used (look on copyright page): _____

   Scale of realism (Circle one, 1 is least, 5 is most):   1   2   3   4   5

   The illustration I like best is_____

   because _____

In the art room, students replicated several styles of realism that were displayed in the halls. I ended our look at illustrators' art by bringing in children's book illustrator Jim LaMarche from California. His books, including *The Rainbabies* (Melmed, Lothrop, 1992) and *The Carousel* (Rosenberg, Harcourt Brace, 1995), were done with watercolors. Jim explained the steps in illustration from idea to sketch to "art draft" to finished product ready for reproducing in a book.

▶

Mrs. Rose Shows You is a Web site that teaches how to do art projects such as Ukrainian eggs, clay animation, masks, and drawing. Find detailed instructions at <www.homestead.com/mrsroseshowsyou/map.html>. *The @rt Room* at <www.arts.ufl.edu/art/rtroom/index.html> has six art centers:
Sparkers—Twelve different art projects, such as how to draw hands
@rtrageous Thinking—How to "think like an artist"
@rt Gallery—View art from children worldwide
@rtifacts—Historical facts and trivia from the world of art
@rt Library—Reviews of children's art books
@rt Links—Sites dedicated to children, art, and education

Media In Illustrated Books

Our art teacher asked for a list of books that would correlate with some of the media that she was teaching students to use. Here are some of the books we suggested:

Acrylics

Mixing powdered color with water-based plastic makes this paint.
Bunting, Eve. *Smoky Night.* (acrylic paintings set against mixed media collage backgrounds)
Hodges, Margaret. *Saint George and the Dragon.* (India ink and acrylic)
McPhail, David. *Edward and the Pirates.*
Musgrove, Margaret. *Ashanti to Zulu: African Traditions.* (acrylics combined with pastels and watercolors)
Ringgold, Faith. *Tar Beach.*

Collage

Textured pictures result from the illustrator's use of paper, fabric, feathers, and other three-dimensional objects.
Carle, Eric. *Hello, Red Fox.* (cut paper collage)

DeZutter, Hank. *Who Says a Dog Goes Bow-Wow?* (tissue paper collage)
Ehlert, Lois. *Snowballs.* (collage includes real objects)
Steiner, Joan. *Look-Alikes.* (three-dimensional collages from found objects)
Wisniewski, David. *Rain Player.*

Colored Pencil

Anderson, Laurie Halse. *No Time for Mother's Day.* (pen and ink, colored pencil and watercolors)
Aylesworth, Jim. *Teddy Bear Tears.*
Janovitz, Marilyn. *What Could Be Keeping Santa?* (colored pencils and watercolors)
Krull, Kathleen. *Lives of the Presidents: Fame, Shame (and What the Neighbors Thought).* (pencils and watercolors)
Lyon, George Ella. *A Traveling Cat.*

Digital Illustrations

Illustrations are created using computer software and a draw tablet.
Pelletier, David. *The Graphic Alphabet.*
Wood, Audrey. *Bright and Early Thursday Evening: A Tangled Tale Dreamed by Audrey Wood.*
_____. *The Red Racer.*

Gouache

This is paint made by mixing the powdered color with an opaque white.
Macaulay, David. *Black and White.* This story is told in four panels per page, and each panel is done with different media. ("Udder Confusion"—gouache, "A Waiting Game"-gouache and watercolor, "Seeing Things"—watercolor, and "Problem Parents"—ink line and wash)
Moss, Lloyd. *Zin! Zin! Zin! a Violin.*
Murphy, Shirley Rousseau. *Tattie's River Journey.* (gouache applied over colored inks)
The Firebird and Other Russian Fairy Tales. Edited by Jacqueline Onassis.

Oil Paints

The oil mixed with the powdered color is made from linseed.
Burleigh, Robert. *Black Whiteness: Admiral Byrd Alone in the Antarctic.* (oil and vinyl paint)
Blake, Robert. *Akiak: A Tale From the Iditarod.*
George, Kristine O'Connell. *Old Elm Speaks: Tree Poems.*

Kirk, David. *Miss Spider's ABC.*
Medearis, Angela Shelf. *Too Much Talk.* (oil paint on wood)

Pastels

The media looks like chalk but is oilier. It is made with powdered color, white chalk, and binding liquids.
Cooney, Barbara. *Ox Cart Man.*
Irving, Washington. *Legend of Sleepy Hollow.* Illustrated by Gary Kelley.
Van Allsburg, Chris. *The Wreck of the Zephyr.*

Pencil

Lobel, Arnold. *Frog and Toad Are Friends.*
Peet, Bill. *Bill Peet: An Autobiography.*
Van Allsburg, Chris. *Jumanji.*

Pen and Ink

Gag, Wanda. *Millions of Cats.*
Neuschwander, Cindy. *Amanda Bean's Amazing Dream: A Mathematical Story.*
Viorst, Judith. *Alexander and the Terrible, Horrible, No Good, Very Bad Day.*
Yagawa, Sumiko. *The Crane Wife.* (pen and ink on textured paper)
Yolen, Jane. *Owl Moon.* (pen and ink, watercolor)

Photography

Ballard, Robert D. *Ghost Liners.*
Hoban, Tana. *So Many Circles, So Many Squares.*
Robbins, Ken. *Autumn Leaves.*
Wegman, William. *Cinderella.*
Wick, Walter. *Optical Illusions.*

Scratchboard

The illustrator scratches the illustration onto a board that has been layered first with color, then with black. The color shows through the lines drawn with a sharp instrument.
Kennedy, Richard. *Song of the Horse.*
San Souci, Robert D. *The Faithful Friend.*
_____. *Sukey and the Mermaid.*

Tempera

This mainstay of the art classroom is made from powdered color and a colloidal medium. It is mixed with water before use.
Eric Carle. *The Very Hungry Caterpillar.* (Carle uses tempera paint to paint large sheets of paper. He then cuts them up and uses them as collage pieces to illustrate his books.)
Rylant, Cynthia. *Dog Heaven.*

Watercolor

One of childhood's earliest mediums, watercolor paint is made with powdered color mixed with gum arabic and glycerin. It is combined with water just before use.
Browne, Anthony. *Willy the Dreamer.*
Carlstrom, Nancy. *Northern Lullaby.*
Isadora, Rachel. *Caribbean Dream.*
Tafuri, Nancy. *Counting to Christmas.*
Vail, Rachel. *Over the Moon.*

Woodcuts

A picture is drawn on wood. The artist cuts away the areas around the design, then rolls ink on the raised surface. Color prints require a different woodblock for each color.
Bowen, Betsy. *Antler, Bear, Canoe: A Northwoods Alphabet Year.*
Emberley, Barbara. *Drummer Hoff.*
Falls, C. B. *ABC Book.*
Haley, Gail. *A Story, A Story.*
Tejima, Keizaburo. *Fox's Dream.*

Other Art Techniques

Fleming, Denise. *Mama Cat Has Three Kittens.* (colored cotton rag fiber poured through hand-cut stencils)
Sabuda, Robert. *Cookie Count.* (painted collage illustrations on paper-engineered pop-ups. Some illustrations include clear plastic or colored gold foil.)

Books Used in the Poetry Workshop

See the bibliography at the end of the book for complete bibliographic information

Basket 1—World Famous Poets

Brooks, Gwendolyn. *Bronzeville Boys and Girls.*
Carroll, Lewis. *The Walrus and the Carpenter.*
Frost, Robert. *Stopping by Woods on a Snowy Evening.*
Hughes, Langston. *The Dream Keeper and Other Poems.*
Lear, Edward. *Daffy Down Dillies.*
_____. *Owls and Pussycats.*
Sandburg, Carl. *Poetry for Young People.*
Service, Robert. *The Cremation of Sam McGee.*

Basket 2—From a Different View

Agard, John. *No Hickory, No Dickory, No Dock: Caribbean Nursery Rhymes.*

Angelou, Maya. *Soul Looks Back in Wonder.* (African-American)

Hand in Hand: An American History Through Poetry. (historical events in poetry) Selected by Lee Bennett Hopkins.

Inner Chimes: Poems on Poetry. (world poems) Selected by Bobbye S. Goldstein.

Bryan, Ashley. *Sing to the Sun.* (African-American)

Cassedy, Sylvia. *Red Dragon on My Shoulder: Haiku.* (Japanese)

Home: A Collaboration of Thirty Distinguished Authors & Illustrators of Children's Books to Aid the Homeless. (poems to benefit the homeless) Selected by Michael Rosen.

Pomerantz, Charlotte. *The Tamarindo Puppy and Other Poems.* (Hispanic)

Sleep Rhymes Around the World. (world poems) Selected by Jane Yolen.

Basket 3—Just for Fun

Bagert, Brod. *Let Me Be the Boss: Poems for Kids to Perform.*

Dahl, Roald. *Dirty Beasts.*

Fleischman, Paul. *Joyful Noise: Poems for Two Voices.*

Lillegard, Dee. *Do Not Feed the Table: Lots of Limericks.* Selected by Myra Cohn Livingstone.

Rosen, Michael. *Walking the Bridge of Your Nose.*

Singer, Marilyn. *It's Hard to Read a Map With a Beagle on Your Lap.*

Snuffles and Snouts. Selected by Laura Robb.

Viorst, Judith. *Sad Underwear and Other Complications: More Poems for Children and Their Parents.*

Basket 4—Poetry to Compare and Contrast

a. humor

Florian, Douglas. *Bing Bang Boing: Poems and Drawings.*

Silverstein, Shel. *Falling Up.*

b. school—related poetry

I Thought I'd Take My Rat to School: Poems for September to June. Selected by Dorothy M. Kennedy.

School Supplies: A Book of Poems. Selected by Lee Bennett Hopkins.

Winters, Kay. *Did You See What I Saw? Poems About School.*

c. Weather

Winter Poems. Selected by Barbara Rogasky.

Yolen, Jane. *Weather Report: Poems.*

d. Color poems

O'Neill, Mary De Luc. *Hailstones and Halibut Bones: Adventures in Color.*

Oram, Hiawyn. *Out of the Blue: Poems About Color.*

Basket 5—Anthologies

A. Nonny Mouse Writes Again! Selected by Jack Prelutsky.

For Laughing Out Loud: Poems to Tickle Your Funnybone. Selected by Jack Prelutsky.

Moore, Lillian. *Sunflakes: Poems for Children.*

Pass It On: African American Poetry for Children. Selected by Wade Hudson.

Poem Stew. Selected by William Cole.

Sing a Song of Popcorn: Every Child's Book of Poems. Selected by Beatrice de Regniers.

Small Talk: A Book of Short Poems. Selected by Lee Bennett Hopkins.

Storytelling and Booktalking

Storytelling is one of the most powerful things you can do with your young readers and nonreaders. Before there was recorded history, there were stories. Early people told stories to recount their histories, to remember their battles and triumphs, and to entertain. Since the days of troubadours and bards, storytelling has been an honored profession. This ancient art has been a part of the librarian's repertoire and has enjoyed a popular resurgence in recent years.

I started telling stories because I was embarrassed into doing it. In May of 1996, Christine McNew, children's librarian at the George Memorial Library, came to our school to tell stories and to explain the summer reading program. When her performances were over, I recommended a book she might enjoy telling. I explained how my students loved hearing about Anansi's tricks in Eric Kimmel's book *Anansi and the Moss-Covered Rock* (Holiday House, 1988). When we looked on the library shelf, the book had been checked out. By then Christine was intrigued and

asked, "Why don't you just tell me the story?" Well, tell it I did, mainly because I didn't want to admit that I had never told a story. She loved the trickster tale. With her encouragement, I was hooked.

Storytelling has an important place in the school curriculum. It appeals to several of the different multiple intelligences, including auditory, visual/spatial, and kinesthetic.

Hearing carefully selected tales without benefit of visuals strengthens students' auditory intelligence. Storytelling provides them with tales of their cultural heritage. Time spent sharing oral stories can create a powerful, positive classroom or library climate as you spin a story that students will continue to hear in their auditory memories.

Visual intelligence is stimulated as storytelling ignites the picture-making ability of the listeners, an important exercise for the imaginations of students raised on television and computer games. The ability to visualize is built upon the power of the imagination. Storytelling affords students who aren't skilled at visualization a chance to develop it.

Drawing a picture of what they imagined immediately after hearing a story stirs students' auditory recall and kinesthetic intelligence. It also offers insights into their thoughts for teachers and the students themselves. Ask students to explain their illustration to the class. After listening to *Anansi and the Moss-Covered Rock*, students drew the scene that most appealed to them. Surprisingly, my students had no trouble drawing

The National Storytelling Association can give you much support and encouragement. Their bimonthly magazine contains helpful articles for the beginning and advanced storyteller. The NSA Web page gives details about the National Storytelling Festival, the National Storytelling Conference, and a schedule of events around the country. Their *Storynet* is at <www.storynet.org>. The links include storytelling links and a Story Net Cyber Café where you can discuss storytelling topics. Membership information also is available. If you prefer, you can contact the National Storytelling Association by letter: 116 West Main Street, Jonesborough, TN 37659; phone: 800-525-4514; fax: 423-753-9331; or e-mail: mwhited@naxs.com.

the Sky God or the Fairy-Whom-No-Man-Sees. The more often students hear and then draw stories, the more detailed the drawings will become.

It helps some learners to have a starting point for imagining. Years later, *Anansi and the Moss-Covered Rock* is still my favorite story to tell. I found a perfect rock in a burr-infested field and covered it with simulated moss (peel-and-stick felt). Now when telling the story, I use the rock as the focus, and even the youngest feels the dismay of each forest animal as Anansi sets his wicked but clever trap. (See Topic #8, p. 135)

Grabbing Attention

A storytelling prop also can set the mood or help the teller remember the tale. An Anansi tale by Gail Haley, *A Story, A Story* (Aladdin, 1970), explains how Anansi won all the stories from the sky god Nyame and brought them to earth. The students are dazzled by the king's treasure box—an old cigar box decorated with sequined, royal purple fabric. The box also keeps them from noticing the tiny cheat sheet attached to the back of the box to help me tell the story.

An eye-catcher for your storytime can range from something as simple as a ring to an elaborate prop, such as a complete costume. Whatever you choose, remember that no prop should overshadow or distract from the most important element—the story.

When a class comes to the library, time is short in which to include a book exchange and story or lesson. So I like to have an "attention-getter" that will launch the theme or lesson immediately. One way to do that is with a simple prop. Twenty-five years ago, a fellow student teacher named George walked to the front of the class with an orange maple leaf on his head and began to talk about autumn. Not only did he snag my attention, but to this day I remember his explanation of why leaves appear to change color. His prop was simple and effective.

George taught me that an unusual bit of attire can jump-start a lesson. I began a class one warm winter Texas morning wearing a mitten on one hand and a glove on the other. Because it rarely snows in our Houston area, the students were intrigued. With a flourish, I opened the pages of our big book wearing the colorful knitted items. The kindergartners couldn't stand it and began asking why I was wearing different gloves. "Glad you asked, because our story today just happens to be about a mitten, and do you know the difference between gloves and mittens?" I had captured their attention and aroused their curiosity.

Other quick introductions are as close as your closet. Once you see how a little fashion adds interest to your storytelling or other lessons, you will discover interesting bits of finery at department stores, resale shops, and even toy stores.

Many stories contain a ring, a necklace, or other piece of jewelry that can be used to introduce the story. In Joan Lowery Nixon's *Search for the Shadowman* (Delacorte Press, 1996), a horseshoe nail bent into a circle and hung on a leather thong proves the key to exonerating a family member who died 120 years ago. It would be easy to make a replica to lead students into the story.

Rings figure in numerous books and often have magical powers. For older students, there is the Tolkien trilogy, beginning with *The Fellowship of the Ring* (Ballantine, 1993). For younger students, there is the Irish whopper by Teresa Bateman called *The Ring of Truth* (Holiday House, 1998). In this tale, a leprechaun punishes a boastful liar with a ring that forces him to always tell the truth. The story contains much humor, especially when the arrogant Patrick O'Kelley is compelled to compete in the Donegal blarney contest and cannot tell a lie! It is great fun to tell, and the ending will give students a satisfying surprise.

Before telling *The Ring of Truth*, you will need a gaudy ring, the

▶ Phillip Martin spent years in Liberia, West Africa, as a Peace Corps volunteer. He has compiled a wonderful resource called *Deep in the Bush, Where People Rarely Ever Go: Use Folk Tales to Bring Africa Alive in the Classroom* at <members.nbci.com/Pmartin/Bush/bushhomepage.htm>. It contains Liberian folktales, recipes, links to African sites for student research, and detailed lesson plans for teachers. Visit the site for directions on playwriting, performing folktales, and catering to the interpersonal, verbal, and kinesthetic intelligences of your students.

◀ A wonderful Web site for St. Patrick's Day, or whenever you study Irish folklore or history is *Customs and Traditions of St. Patrick's Day* at <wilstar.com/holidays/patrick.htm>. At this site, you can read about the customs and traditions of this day, as well as listen to audio clips of traditional Irish music and songs, learn Irish children's games. Or try Shamrock La at <www.fi.edu/fellows/fellow7/mar99>. At this site, you can read Irish limericks or take a virtual tour of Ireland.

bigger the stone the better. Mine came from the dress-up section of a local toy store. You can make one by gluing a huge green plastic gem from your craft store to any flat-faced costume ring. Call attention to the ring before starting the story, telling children that it once belonged to leprechauns and at one time had an amazing magical power. If they listen carefully, they will discover what that power was.

The Appeal of Rituals

Research has shown that children enjoy and even need rituals. Beginning every storytime with the same poem, the same location, or the same sequence of activities gives students a sense of comfort.

My friend Dorothy McMahon has made a jester's head on a dowel rod and decorated it with elaborate ribbons, glitter, and shiny foil. Every time she begins a storytime, she twirls the story-teller figure over the children like a wand and recites the same rhyme about traveling to story land. Then Dorothy has a child come to the front to open the elaborately decorated magic story chest. Inside is an object that relates to the book that is going to be read. Sometimes it is obvious, such as a doll's quilt for *Geraldine's Blanket* by Holly Keller (Mulberry, 1988). It can be less obvious, such as a bluejay feather for Tomie dePaola's *The Legend of the Bluebonnet* (Putnam, 1983). The volunteer removes the mystery item from the box, and the class tries to guess the subject of the story. A second child comes to the front, pulls the velvet cloth "bottom" from the box, and displays the hidden book. Children can then modify their guesses based on the cover and title. After the story is read, students talk about whether they were correct or what the introductory prop had to do with the story.

More Books and Props

Prop	Title	Author
small feather-covered bird	*The Emperor and the Nightingale*	Hans Christian Andersen
small jar with a little water in it	*Teddy Bear Tears*	Jim Aylesworth
gaudy ring in a gift box	*The Ring of Truth*	Teresa Bateman
large dog biscuit	Any dog book	
small doll quilt	*The Quiltmaker's Gift*	Jeff Brumbeau
clean artist's paintbrush	*Liang and the Magic Paintbrush*	Demi
tattered, dirty book	*Petunia*	Robert duVoisin
small drum	*Drummer Hoff*	Barbara Emberley
small cat figurines	*Millions of Cats*	Wanda Gag
red neckerchief	*Ranch Dressing*	Jean Greenlaw
rubber fly	*I Know an Old Lady Who Swallowed a Fly*	
clipboard	*The Music of Dolphins*	Karen Hesse
toy cooking pot	*The Wolf's Chicken Stew*	Keiko Kasza
three beans	*Jack and the Beanstalk*	Steven Kellogg

More Books and Props

Prop	Title	Author
cantaloupe	*Anansi and the Talking Melon*	Eric Kimmel
small pair of boxer shorts	*Froggy Gets Dressed*	Jonathan London
postcard to the class	*Amelia Writes Again*	Marissa Moss
bottle of syrup	*If You Give a Pig a Pancake*	Laura Numeroff
tree leaf	*Old Elm Speaks: Tree Poems*	Kristine O'Connell
color sample strips from the paint store	*Hailstones and Halibut Bones: Adventures in Color*	Mary de Luc O'Neill
pair of wire-rimmed glasses	*Pink and Say*	Patricia Polacco
ginger snap	*Cookie Count*	Robert Sabud
shark's tooth	*Sharks* *Punia, King of the Sharks*	Seymour Simon Lee Wardlaw
valentine candy box	*Somebody Loves You Mr. Hatch*	Eileen Spinelli
large soup spoon	*Tiger Soup: An Anansi Story from Jamaica*	Frances Temple
brown package wrapper with canceled stamps	*Mailing May*	Michael Tunnel
pair of boy's underpants	*Captain Underpants*	Dav Pilkey
pea	*Princess and the Pea*	Harriet Ziefert

My friend Julie Cowan closes her storytimes by having some members of her audience feed a carrot to her storytime mascot. The mascot is a large, lap-sized rabbit puppet named Chomper. Julie makes a funny display of the rabbit chomping the carrot and "accidentally" grabbing a few fingers in the process. Children love the finish and know storytime is over.

Robin Krig, another Texas librarian, used a large girl puppet with a weakness for suckers. At the end of the story, Robin selected a child to give Penelope a sucker from a jar. These were large, all-day suckers. The ritual came to be such a favorite that children made or found suckers for Penelope, and she soon had a collection for every occasion.

Thematic Dressing

Students are intrigued and charmed by the many thematic outfits Ms. Frizzle wears in the *Magic School Bus* series. I wanted to tap into that popularity, but had neither the time to sew nor the budget to buy such interesting outfits. Instead, I bought a simple vest pattern that takes less than one hour to make. Now I have reversible vests for nearly every theme. If you don't sew, vests are readily available, especially at holiday times, in most discount and department stores. Fabric stores sell vests by the yard. Just cut on the dotted lines for your size, then stitch, and you have a colorful visual. If you prefer ties, you could wear a thematic tie on occasion, like Mr. Slinger in Kevin Henkes' *Lilly's Purple Plastic Purse* (Greenwillow, 1996).

A basket of apparel and accessories for storytelling and performing should be in every elementary classroom and library. They can be just the ticket for tapping the interpersonal and logical intelligences by providing opportunities for impromptu skits, story re-enactments, or role-playing activities. Some items to include are various kinds of gloves, glasses without lenses, assorted ties, gaudy jewelry, a feather boa, a fancy vest, a top hat, a stethoscope, a lorgnette, an apron, a shawl, a crown, a veil, a cape, and a wand.

You can use any vest to tell Phoebe Gilman's story *Something from Nothing* (Scholastic, 1992). In this story, a thrifty tailor remakes a blanket, as it wears out, into successively smaller kinds of clothing (including a vest) until he has merely a cloth-covered button and then only the story itself. (See Topic 5, p. 110) This can be a good introduction for a recycling unit. I used the story as an introduction to storytelling when training a fifth-grade Storytelling Troupe. It also is the folktale that is the basis for the 2000 Caldecott Winner, *Joseph Had a Little Overcoat*, by Simms Taback (Viking, 1999).

Top Off Your Lesson

Dr. Seuss knew there was not just a cat in that hat—there was also magic. A red and white striped top hat is the trademark for his wonderful silliness. A delightful way to introduce a unit on hats is by sharing Rita Gelman's *Hello, Cat, You Need a Hat* (Scholastic, 1979). The variety of hats makes it perfect for Career Day or a study on clothing.

Follow up this story with a participation version of Esphyr Slobodkina's classic *Caps for Sale* (HarperCollins, 1947). I tell this story while students wear colored caps. As the story progresses, students act out their parts by hat color. Culminate the story with a relay race. Line students up in two or three rows facing you. At a signal, the first student passes his hat behind him without turning around. He then runs to the end of the line. The second person does the same. The relay ends when the last person in the original line has passed her hat and run to the end of the line. Students will enjoy this rousing, kinesthetic end to storytime.

► Hats can be a problem if you [ar]e concerned about lice. Try plastic [ha]ts that can be wiped down with [alcoh]ol. You can buy them by the dozen [in] a variety of colors from Oriental [Tra]ding Company at <www.oriental. [...]com>. Look for the ones called "gangster hats."

Ideas at Your Fingertips

Gloves and storytelling go hand in hand. I slip on long, black evening gloves before putting on puppets. Against the black curtain of the puppet stage, my arms disappear, leaving the puppets to act as if by magic. Put on gloves that represent a character in your story, such as heavy work gloves for telling John Henry's story, and make an instant costume. Slip on gardening gloves before telling or reading the story of *Miss Rumphius* (Viking, 1982) by Barbara Cooney.

Any time of year is good for the participation story *The Mitten* (Putnam, 1989), by Jan Brett. In this folktale, a child loses a mitten in the forest, which becomes the overcrowded home for numerous animals until the mouse squeezes in and causes the bear to sneeze. Then all the animals make an explosive exit, and the boy's grandmother is left to wonder why the boy returns home with one huge mitten! We use *The Mitten* when our kindergartners are studying woodland animals in the fall (see Topic #6, p. 117).

◄ Put the Velcro buttons with the soft loop side on the apron pockets. When you fold up the apron, it won't stick to itself. The pictures will have the hook side, but when pictures are stacked faceup, they will not cling together.

Storytelling Apron

Aprons can help when you are telling a story. Use a craft store apron or make one, and stitch on pockets to make a wearable stage. Add a stick-on Velcro button to the top edge of each pocket and attach the hooked side of the button to the back of laminated storytelling pictures.

The apron works well with any story that has an event sequence that can be represented by pictures. I've used it for repetitive picture books and for nonfiction that features a life cycle, such as that of the frog or the apple tree (see Topic #2, p. 89). Use the figures from Topic #10 (p. 151) to retell *Are You My Mother?* by P. D. Eastman (Random House, 1960).

Velcro buttons

Storytelling apron

Hide each picture facedown in the pockets in correct sequence. Stand in front of your group and tell the story. Remove the picture from the pocket as you mention it in the story and attach it to the Velcro button. The story sequence is vividly displayed as you wear and tell the story. Other stories that lend themselves to this approach are Kathy Parkinson's *The Enormous Turnip* (Albert Whitman, 1986), Audrey Wood's *The Napping House* (Harcourt Brace, 1984), or any story written in the pattern of *The House That Jack Built*.

Winter on the Line

Because we have mild winters in Texas, we provide videotapes, prints, pictures, and lots of books about winter for our students. Many have never seen snow, and it is not uncommon to wear shorts into December.

While teaching the winter unit, I bring in winter clothing courtesy of Ohio relatives. We research how the clothing is used and read stories about snowy winters. One of the students' favorites is *Froggy Gets Dressed* (Viking, 1992) by Jonathan London. Froggy keeps forgetting important items of winter clothing in his eagerness to get out and play in the snow instead of hibernating with his family. Another fun story we do for sequencing and winter wear is *The Jacket I Wear in the Snow* (Greenwillow, 1989) by Shirley Neitzel.

► Craft or discount stores sell tiny clothespins that are useful for clipping sequence pictures to a clothesline, as we do in the lesson for *The Jacket I Wear in the Snow*. See Topic #4, p. 103.

Other Fashionable Props

► Lilly's purse can be purchased from Merry Makers, Inc., San Francisco, CA 94104 (ISBN 1-579-820301). The purse has a picture of Lilly on the front and plays "Twinkle, Twinkle, Little Star" when opened. It is purple, plastic, and comes with a strap. You have to supply the quarters and the movie star glasses. At my local bookstore, the purse was $17.95.

A great story for connecting with units on school, cause and effect, emotions, or even writing letters is *Lilly's Purple Plastic Purse* (Greenwillow, 1996) by Kevin Henkes. Lilly's impulsive actions draw a smile from students in all grades through 5.

To introduce the story, use a purple plastic purse containing the articles in Lilly's purse (movie star glasses with glittery chain and three shiny quarters). You may find purple plastic "purses," packed with travel toiletries, at a reasonable price in the bath shops. If you can't find a purple one, any color will do. After using the purse to introduce the story, merely mention that Lilly's purse happened to be purple and was special because it played music when opened. For centers based on this book, see Topic #11, p. 157.

◄ In your library, you might want to establish an uncooperati▮ chair and a Lightbulb Lab, like M▮ Slinger's, and introduce them with ▮ story. For my students, a visit to t▮ uncooperative chair gives them ▮ moment to rethink before returning to the group.

Another Kind of Book Jacket

Booktalking is a time-honored tradition with librarians. Booktalking is to books what MTV is to music. The book is a mute masterpiece, filled with an author's hard work and insights, with imaginative prose or heartfelt poetry. Though the illustrations may speak a thousand words, books often leave the library with a reader only after the librarian puts her voice to the book. Some of the best booktalks are the ones given by students to their peers. Don't overlook the value of teaching your students how to perform a booktalk.

The booktalk can include reading or telling part of the story, reading the book jacket, giving an opinion of the book, and any other verbal persuasions to get the book off the shelf and into the hands of a reader. For these reasons, booktalks will greatly appeal to the verbal intelligence.

Pass around the featured books or make them accessible so students can examine the cover art and flip through the books. This will help readers who are strong in the visual and kinesthetic intelligences, and rely on these strengths to make book judgments.

As with storytelling, props can grab and focus students' attention during a booktalk. At the beginning of the year, new students are sometimes ill at ease. Don a red windbreaker or jacket to read the first chapters of Barbara Park's *The Kid in the Red Jacket* (Knopf, 1987). The humor breaks the ice, especially the first time the class comes to the library.

A quilted Jacket with Oriental closures transforms you into a travel agent as you take students to China for Chinese New Year. Wear it to share a story that has Chinese or Japanese protagonists, such as Demi's two books, *The Empty Pot* (Holt, 1990) and *Liang and the Magic Paintbrush* (Holt, 1983), or Hans Christian Andersen's tale of *The Emperor and the Nightingale* (Troll, 1979).

A down jacket can be a lure to hook students on a winter theme or book. Use it to introduce Shirley Neitzel's *The Jacket I Wear in the Snow* (Greenwillow, 1989) or Gary Paulsen's *Brian's Winter* (Delacorte, 1996). Use a long muffler or woolen throat scarf before you booktalk *Jeremy's Muffler* by Laura Nielsen (Bradbury, 1994). Before you do the booktalk, have a child stand in front of the group and wrap the muffler mummy-style around and around his neck. Your students will laugh and be clued that this is a humorous book.

Telling With Sign Language

Combine word smarts with body smarts when you tell a story using sign language; it's an interesting change for your storytimes. An excellent resource is *Beyond Words: Great Stories for Hand and Voice* by Valerie Marsh (Alleyside Press, 1995). The book includes 20 stories, such as *The Three Bears, Henny Penny, and The Three Billy Goats Gruff*. The stories are only about a page long and are followed by discussion activities. No story has more than 12 clearly drawn hand signs.

I used this book to learn *The Little Red Hen* with signs. Marsh shows the signs for key words, such as *wheat, little, red, hen, duck, cat, dog,* and *did not help*. My students enjoyed learning the signs and doing them with me as I told the story. Because the story is repetitive, the students and I used the same signs over and over. They liked the sign for dog, which is patting the thigh twice, then snapping the fingers twice, as if calling a dog. We also discovered that the sign for "r" is the same one we use to indicate a child would like to go to the restroom.

Sparking Interest in "Boring" Books

Some books are more difficult to booktalk than others, such as books on language and poetry. I lure readers into trying these books by using a game or participatory exercise rather than a traditional narrative. The goal is the same: "Try it, you'll like it!"

Language books get overlooked because it doesn't occur to students to read them. Whether they are books on the parts of speech or books that teach words in other languages, all can be sent home with readers if you pique their interest. Young people are curious about other languages. It is not uncommon in most of our schools to find that our students speak numerous languages.

With English grammar books, students often can be hooked just by hearing you read parts of the book. Authors who delight in word usage and wordplay find a ready audience once their words are voiced. Such actions greatly appeal to the verbal intelligence.

Use the big book versions of Ruth Heller's books to share her enthusiasm and magnificent illustrations for verbs, nouns, adjectives, and even prepositions. Parts of speech have never been so much fun. Read aloud from the palindrome books of Jon Agee. The wordplay books of Marvin Terban are fun to read and thought-provoking as well. You might begin with his book *Funny You Should Ask: How to Make Up Jokes and Riddles with Wordplay* (Clarion, 1992). See the book list at the end of this chapter for more titles.

To introduce students to our variety of foreign language books, I use two books. One is Marc Robinson's *Cock-a-Doodle-Doo: What Does It Sound Like to You?* (Stewart, Tabori & Chang, 1993), which details not only written sounds for animals but also sounds for a train's whistle and for water dripping. The second is Hank DeZutter's *Who Says a Dog Goes Bow-Wow?* (Doubleday, 1993), which lists the sounds an animal makes as perceived in several languages. Students are surprised to realize that onomatopoeias are not the same in every language. For example, our students think dogs say, "bow-wow," but French children think they say, "wah-wah," and Russians know their dogs say, "how-how." The sound of a cat, which English-speaking children always thought was "meow," is "me-yong" in Indonesian, "nyan-nyan" to the Japanese, and "yaong-yaong" in Korean.

Besides having these two books, you need to prepare for a lesson in foreign languages by pulling a variety of foreign language books and displaying them in your teaching area. Also ahead of time, you will need a cassette tape of animal sounds. Make one by taping your dog barking, a bird singing, or your own voice mimicking these sounds. Only three sounds are needed.

To begin the lesson, play one of the taped animal sounds and have students write the approximate spelling of the sound. Repeat the sound as often as needed. Compare what students have written for each sound by writing student responses on the board. Students will be amused by the differences.

Then explain that people of all countries have different spellings for animal sounds, though animals all over the world make the same sound. Share the two books mentioned above. After telling the stories and sharing the sounds, remind students that different countries have different words for the same items. Point out that they can find out what these words are by checking out the books on display.

Pass the Poetry

Sometimes all it takes to get students to read poetry is to tell them poems you have memorized or to read them aloud. Share all kinds of poems, from funny to serious and from classic to contemporary poets. Read haiku, jingles, and limericks. Keep commentary to a minimum and let the poem work its own magic.

Encourage each student to find a poetry book. Explain to them that a week from now will be Traveling Poem Day. On the designated day, students arrive at school with a poem neatly handwritten or typed on a 5 x 8 inch card provided by the library. The card includes the title, author, book from which the poem was taken, and the poem itself. Students may choose to write their own poem. To track the poem's travels, you might write on the back of the poem: "Write your name and grade on the lines below. By 3:00 today, please return it to (originating student) in (room number or teacher's name)."

Students begin the day by sharing the poem with a friend. The friend reads it aloud, signs the back, then passes it to another child. Through the day, students will be reading and passing numerous poems. Include several grades in the Traveling Poetry Day. The student who has the poem at 3:00

returns it to its owner. Then students can see how far their poems traveled, and they will have a fun souvenir for this special day.

Another simple way to get students into poetry is to pile books on tables or on the floor. Have students sit in a circle around the pile of books. Each of them should take a book and read it for about four minutes. At the end of the time, ask for a volunteer to share a poem that she likes. Then have students pass the books to the left until you say, "Stop!" Again students read for four minutes, and a volunteer shares. Repeat the procedure until students have read and heard at least five poems.

Another idea to share poetry is to use large plastic eggs. Type poems on small pieces of paper, fold them, and insert each into an egg. Then pile the eggs into a basket and ask, "Who is willing to crack into poetry?" The volunteer chooses an egg and reads the poem. An alternative idea is to write the title of a poem, the title of the book in which it is found, and the page number. Then students at tables try to see if that poem is in a book on their table. The finder can read the poem aloud.

Wordplay Book List

Agee, Jon. *Go Hang a Salami! I'm a Lasagna Hog? and Other Palindromes.*
_____. *So Many Dynamos! and Other Palindromes.*
Heller, Ruth. Behind the Mask: *A Book About Prepositions.*
_____. *A Cache of Jewels and Other Collective Nouns.*
_____. *Fantastic! Wow! And Unreal! A Book About Interjections and Conjunctions.*
_____. *Kites Sail High: A Book About Verbs.*
_____. *Many Luscious Lollipops: A Book About Adverbs.*
_____. *Merry-Go-Round: A Book About Nouns.*
_____. *Mine, All Mine: A Book About Pronouns.*
_____. *Up, Up, and Away: A Book About Adverbs.*
Terban, Marvin. *The Dove Dove: Funny Homograph Riddles.*
_____. *Eight Ate: A Feast of Homonym Riddles.*
_____. *Funny You Should Ask: How to Make Up Jokes and Riddles with Wordplay.*
_____. *Guppies in Tuxedos: Funny Eponyms.*
_____. *In a Pickle and Other Funny Idioms.*
_____. *It Figures: Fun Figures of Speech.*
_____. *Mad as a Wet Hen! and Other Funny Idioms.*

Storytelling Book List

DeSpain, Pleasant. *Thirty-Three Multicultural Tales to Tell.*

Harrison, Annette. *Easy-to-Tell Stories for Young Children.*

Justice, Jennifer. *The Ghost & I: Scary Stories for Participatory Telling.*

MacDonald, Margaret Read. *The Storyteller's Start-Up Book.*

Maguire, Jack. *Creative Storytelling: Choosing, Inventing, and Sharing Tales for Children.*

The National Storytelling Association. *Tales as Tools: The Power of Story in the Classroom.*

Sierra, Judy and Robert Kaminski. *Multicultural Folktales: Stories to Tell Young Children.*

Puppetry

One of my favorite first-grade memories is working the Turkey Lurkey puppet for our class rendition of the old folktale *Chicken Little.* Our puppets were pictures stuck on Popsicle sticks, and the stage was a long table turned on its side, behind which we crouched. But for me, it was magic, and the feeling has stayed with me all these years.

That experience gave me the misconception that to use puppets you have to have a stage and a lot of actors. From necessity, I now realize that all you need to "do puppets" is a hand, a puppet, and an audience. The magic is still there even with this minimal set.

This truth became apparent when a focus was needed for a pet unit that I was planning with kindergarten teachers. Because the logistics of live pets in a short library class was too difficult, I decided to substitute stuffed animals. I lined up an assortment of toy dogs, cats, and rabbits in my story area, where they looked as exciting as couch pillows with ears. How could I inject some life into this pet project without the real thing? Inspiration came in the form of a dog puppet purchased as a souvenir of Las Vegas.

That puppy puppet began a new phase for me. I slipped the dog on my hand and used it to tell pet riddles to kindergartners before our nonfiction booktalk on pets. Though the children could clearly see my hand stuck in the puppet, and I was using my normal speaking voice, the children were enchanted. I was amazed that they talked to the puppet, and the riddle interaction and laughter were directed solely to the furry fabric on my fingers. I had become invisible; the puppet had taken over.

That experience taught me that puppets can be simple and the puppeteer inept, but if the adult is willing to suspend disbelief, the children willingly go along for the magic. Puppets can introduce a lesson, draw students into performing a story, or help them relate to an experience through the safety of a puppet persona. Full-stage productions are fabulously fun but rare at my library. And no one seems to mind.

Lesson Integration with Puppets

Puppets integrate well with technology and the curriculum because they are adaptable and user-friendly. They are inexpensive to purchase, or you and your students can make them. Puppets support storytelling and reading text, and can be used in all areas of the curriculum. I've used a paper plate shark to gobble pompom finger fish as an introduction to an ocean unit and to *Punia, King of the Sharks* by Lee Wardlaw (Dial, 1997). Stick puppets help us do a noisy and satisfying performance of Ann McGovern's *Too Much Noise* (Houghton Mifflin, 1967). A hippo hand puppet introduces a lesson on nonfiction vs. fiction and provides a focus for our discussion of this mammal.

Children have little difficulty becoming puppeteers. Puppets free their tongues and their imaginations, and allow them to put their words into action.

Puppets are a great way to encourage writing and active learning. Have students make their own puppets and write or adapt their own scripts.

Puppet Stand-ins

Children and adults retain new information better when it is linked to previous knowledge. Using a realistic puppet can give students a visual image of the animal you are studying and is a fun way to play with that image. We introduce a compare and contrast lesson with a hippo puppet that looks realistic. A picture could be used, but a moving, "talking" hippo focuses young children's attention more readily and helps them connect new information with a child-friendly puppet.

Folkmanis makes finger puppets that come in habitat groups. After the habitat unit, one project may be to have a small group write a puppet story that incorporates facts about these animals.

Working together to plan, and to share and reinforce knowledge utilizes the interpersonal intelligence. Puppetry also draws out the shy child because attention is focused on the puppet rather than on the child.

Getting Personal with Puppets

Over the years, I've collected enough hand puppets to let a class help me act out "Old McDonald Had a Farm." Use wild animal puppets so young students can rewrite the verses to accommodate Old McDonald's Zoo. Encourage students to build their musical talents by writing new words to old songs. The new song should be one that can be acted out with the animal puppets.

Trace the gingerbread man puppet pattern (page 236) on brown felt and stitch up enough hand puppets for your whole class to act out the Jim Aylesworth version of the classic story *The Gingerbread Man* (Scholastic, 1998). We also use these "anybody puppets" to practice puppet moves. Students practice having their brown, faceless puppet skip, limp, dance, walk as though sad, and other puppet movements. Then when we perform, our puppets aren't just hopping up and down.

Gingerbread Man Puppet Pattern

Creating Puppets

When fourth-grade teachers and I were planning a fairy tale unit, we decided that the culminating activity would be for students to make a puppet of their favorite fairy tale character. My parts of the unit were to explain the characteristics of a fairy tale vs. a folktale and to teach students to make puppets.

Teachers read fairy tales to students and had each student read at least two others. They discussed plots, described characters, and read adaptations of fairy tales. Comparisons and contrasts were drawn (see Fairy Tale Analysis worksheet page 223). Then students selected a favorite character to make into a puppet. I again became involved and showed students 15 puppets that could be made easily from materials they had at home. The puppets were made from socks, gloves, milk cartons, envelopes, sticks, unstuffed animals, and other simple materials. Many puppet ideas came from *Storytelling with Puppets* by Connie Champlin (ALA, 1998). I also showed them slides of last year's puppets, grouped by type. Students had two weeks to complete their puppets and prepare them for exhibition in our library Puppetry Museum.

In our museum, puppets were grouped by type and displayed with the books they represented. Signs marked the Sock Puppets, the Stick Puppets, and even the Recycled Puppets. Each puppet had a tent sign with the student's name, the character's name, and the title of the book.

After the display was arranged, we sent invitations to the other classes and put a parent invitation in the library newsletter.

Before disbanding the exhibit, I took slide pictures of the puppets to show to next year's group.

They also can be scanned into a program such as *HyperStudio* as each student completes a "how to" sheet on the puppet (see Fairy Tale Puppet worksheet page 28). Then the Puppetry Museum can be a permanent reference tool on your library's computer.

full page at page 223

Name_____ Date _____

FAIRY TALE ANALYSIS

Check off the appropriate characteristics for the fairy tales you read or hear.

Title, Author, Copyright	Conflict between good and evil	Conflict resolved	Use of three	Royalty	Happy ending	Magical powers

Name_____ Date _____

FAIRY TALE PUPPET

Name of fairy tale:

_____

Name of puppet:

_____

Type of puppet:

_____

I made my puppet using:

_____

_____

_____

_____

Explain on the lines below the steps I take to make your puppet. Use the back of the page if needed. Be specific. When you complete the instructions, try following them to see if you can make another puppet from the directions as you wrote them.

_____

_____

_____

_____

_____

_____

_____

_____

_____

Worldwide Stages

Third-grade teachers asked me to work with them on their social studies units. Each grading period, they took a continent and explored the countries. My contribution was to present the folktales from countries on the continent. I also wanted to do the presentations in ways that could be imitated by the students so they could do something similar for their unit projects.

Continent	Folktale	Technique
North America	*The Bossy Gallito* (Cuba) by Lucia Gonzalez (Scholastic, 1999)	Flannel board
Asia	*Bony Legs* (Russia) by Joanna Cole (Four Winds Press, 1983)	Shadow puppets
Africa	*The Crocodile and the Ostrich* (Kenya) retold by Verna Aardema (Scholastic, 1984)	Storytelling
Australia	*What Made Tiddalick Laugh* retold by Joanne Troughton (Blackie and Son, 1977)	Readers' Theater
South America	"The Two Parrots" from *Jump the World* by Sarah Pooley (Dutton Children's Books, 1997)	Hand puppets on stage
Europe	"The Hungry Cat" (Norway) from *Multicultural Folktales: Stories to Tell Young Children* by Judy Sierra (Oryx, 1991)	Magnetic board puppets

Use the following list for ideas for culminating products for your own students or as ways for you to present stories.

I booktalked a number of folktales for each continent, then performed one of the stories. After the tale, I explained to students how I did the shadow play, made the magnetic or hand puppets, learned the story, or wrote the Readers' Theater script. To help with their projects, I loaned the students my flannel board, magnetic board, shadow stage, and hand puppet stage for their performances.

For those who learned stories for Africa, I showed them an easy way to make a *dashiki,* an African robe-type outfit with only two seams and no snaps, buttons, zippers, or other tricky sewing techniques. One year, an entire class made dashikis from old bed sheets. We first painted them with African designs, then sewed the seams by hand. We caused quite a sensation when we all went to lunch in our African outfits.

Make Your Own Stage

The stages I made were inexpensive and easy to make. Caroline Feller Bauer told me how to make a large, inexpensive, magnetic flannel board. Purchase a large, metal drip pan that is used under a car when changing oil. You can buy one from an automotive or large discount store. Cover the dish side with felt, edge it with a jazzy trim, and you have a magnetic flannel board that measures 2 x 4 feet. I covered the reverse side with blackboard-surfaced adhesive paper. The adhesive paper is available at most large teacher supply stores. That side also is your large magnetic board.

To make the shadow stage, use a large frame that is normally used to stretch fabric before it is framed. Stretch part of an old, white sheet or piece of light fabric tightly over the wooden frame and use flat metal thumbtacks to secure it every four inches on the backside of the frame. Stack a pair of bookends together at each end so the stage is sandwiched between them. Fasten a pair of clip lamps to the top, on the performing side, and students are ready to perform.

The formal stage that I loaned to my students will house four children simultaneously. It was built from the pattern in Joanne Schroeder's *Fun Puppet Skits for Schools and Libraries* (Teacher Ideas Press, 1995). When I use it to perform, there is room for two folding tables on which to put my props and puppets. If you make it, add a platform to the front edge of the stage on which to set props; as pictured in Schroeder's plans, a place is not provided on which to set furniture, scenery, or props.

In *How to Do "The Three Bears" with Two Hands* (ALA, 2000), Walter Minkel has detailed plans for a stretched cloth stage and a PVC (polyvinyl chloride) pipe stage. Both conceal the performer, and include lights to spotlight the stage and places to temporarily store puppets while off-stage.

Using a Mascot Puppet

Some librarians use a mascot puppet to pull the day's storybook out of a basket or treasure chest. The puppet can give students clues about the book so they can guess the title. The puppet becomes an old friend, and students know when they see it that a good read is on its way.

You can use a puppet to introduce the book you plan to read. A puppet also can model library behaviors you want students to use. We told our youngest readers, "After you check out your books, go sit in the story area and read your book until everyone has their books." Because most of these little ones cannot read, some would spend the time talking or playing. I wanted to show students how to "read" the pictures in a book even if they could not read the words.

A large bear or child puppet from Folkmanis is just the thing to introduce nonreaders to the proper way to "read" a book. The puppet I use is a large bear that sits in my lap. I slip my arms and hands into its furry ones and can gesture, hold books, and hide his eyes with his paws.

We use the big book version of Brinton Turkle's wordless book *Deep in the Forest* (Puffin, 1987) to model how to read the pictures and tell a story. Kippy Joe, our puppet, gets enthused and shows students how to make up the story as I turn the pages. He gets a bit out of hand and gets the children giggling. I correct and encourage Kippy Joe and show him how to read without disturbing others. This way, the students know what to do without being corrected themselves, and the whole exercise looks like fun.

Sources for Inexpensive Puppets

Once you and your students are puppet-minded, you'll be surprised at the places you can find puppets. While searching for vitamins at the local drugstore, I found well-made animal puppets that were three for $10. At that price, I could buy enough for group participation. A local pet store chain had puppets, possibly to appease children whose parents refused to buy them one of the live pets. I've bought puppets at our local Puppetry Festival's store, toy departments, and bookstores. A bath shop had soap mitts that looked just like foam animal puppets, but cost only a few dollars each. A vendor was even selling puppets at the Houston Livestock Show and Rodeo.

◄

Ann McCarthy crochets exquisite but inexpensive finger puppets. You can purchase all five animals for Harriet Ziefert's version of *Little Red Hen* (Puffin, 1995) for $6, the nine characters in *Know An Old Lady Who Swallowed a Fly* (Holiday Hou 1990) for $10, and numerous other story and Mother G characters for equally reasonable prices. I bought a clas of a wolf and chick puppets for the 100th day of scho when we read and acted out Keiko Kasza's *The Wolf Chicken Stew* (Putnam, 1987). Get a price list by writing to McCarthy at Route 7, Box 7590A, Palestine, TX 75801 or call 903-549-3281.

The Oriental Trading Company catalog offers wonderful, inexpensive plush puppets, including dinosaurs and other reptiles. In October 2000, OTC offered 24 plush hand puppets for $2.95 each. These included a kangaroo with a baby in its pouch, a lion, a giraffe, a shark, and other wild and domestic animals. OTC also sells finger puppets of dinosaurs and sea animals for $3.60 per dozen. You could get enough for everyone in the class to perform a participation rhyme or to accompany their reports and stories about the animals. Order them at <www.oriental.com>.

Puppets with a Large Group

The first puppets I used with a whole class were stick puppets, one per child. I used the Ellison diecut machine to cut out five colors of cats and attached each to a craft stick. I prepared gray cats for the hundreds, black for thousands, and white, brown, and tan for the higher numbers. They were great assistants as we practiced place value with Wanda Gag's *Millions of Cats* (Coward McCann, 1928). As I read, students raised their cats at their part of the refrain, "Hundreds of cats, thousands of cats, millions and billions and trillions of cats." Attentiveness increased as students waited their turn to participate. Because the puppets were so inexpensive, we allowed students to take them home as souvenirs, where many retold the story to their families.

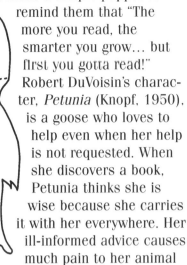

We have students make a simple puppet to remind them that "The more you read, the smarter you grow… but first you gotta read!" Robert DuVoisin's character, *Petunia* (Knopf, 1950), is a goose who loves to help even when her help is not requested. When she discovers a book, Petunia thinks she is wise because she carries it with her everywhere. Her ill-informed advice causes much pain to her animal friends, until an explosion helps Petunia realize she has to *read* the book to get smarter. We make a Petunia puppet from a clothespin (page 212) to use as a bookmark, because now Petunia loves to read and frequently asserts that she is "glad to help!" After our puppets are made, we have a practice session. All squeeze their clip-mouth puppets as we say, "The more you read…"

Petunia Bookmark Puppet, full size at p. 212

You can initiate more elaborate group participation using any story with multiple characters, especially if they are farm or zoo animals. These are the easiest puppets to collect. You might begin with Kathy Parkinson's version of *The Enormous Turnip* (Whitman, 1986), Jan Brett's rendition of *The Mitten* (Putnam, 1989), or The Grimm Brothers' *The Bremen Town Musicians* (North-South Books, 1998). Stand students at the front to act out the story as you read. To involve the whole class, have multiples of each character. Form students into seated groups on your story carpet and have them participate as you read. When the bear enters the mitten in Brett's story, several bears will climb into several mittens as each group participates simultaneously.

Before the performance, teach the players how to hold their puppet friends when they are performing and especially when they are not. Our young actors know that puppets are to be kept behind their backs when not "on stage" so as to not distract the audience, and to be held up at just

below the chin when they are performing. Allow younger children a minute to get acquainted with their puppet before beginning the performance. This will decrease the temptation to "fool around" with their puppet during the story.

Glove Puppets for Math Instruction

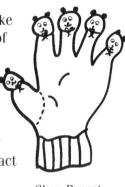

Soft cotton gardening gloves make great finger puppets. Stuff the tips of each with a wad of fiberfill or other stuffing. Tie a thin ribbon or a piece of yarn tightly at the "neck" (just below the tip) of each finger. Add faces with fabric paints, markers, or googly eyes. A family of five, with pompom ears added, can act out Eileen Christelow's *Five Little Monkeys Jumping on the Bed* (Clarion, 1989).

Glove Puppet

Attaching self-adhesive Velcro "buttons" to each fingertip can make another quick and versatile glove puppet. Glue or sew the hook-half of the buttons to the glove, and the loop-half to the back of laminated pictures, diecut figures, or small three-dimensional figures. With this kind of glove, you can use a variety of finger puppets to introduce a story or a lesson.

◄

Lynda Roberts has written *Mitt Magic: Fingerplays for Finger Puppets* (Gryphon House, 1985) with dozens of fingerplays based on the number five, arranged by animal or special occasion. Instructions and patterns for mitt and finger puppets are included. They allow for practicing adding and subtracting to five for your youngest students, as well as practicing manual dexterity.

Shadow Puppetry on the Overhead Projector

The easiest way to do your first puppet show that involves a cast and scenery is on the overhead projector. Choose a simple story and cut characters from tagboard. Tape a narrow straw to each silhouette and lay it on the glass stage to perform the action. For backgrounds, draw scenery on transparencies with colored markers and move puppets across the backgrounds. If you draw several backgrounds, you can quickly accomplish scene changes.

Projector puppetry is a dramatic form of theater because the characters are enlarged on the

David Wisniewski, award-winning author of *Golem* (Clarion, 1996) and *Rain Player* (Clarion, 1991), has written a detailed book on shadow puppetry called *Worlds of Shadow: Teaching with Shadow Puppetry* (Teacher Ideas Press, 1997). His plays and tips are useful for overhead projection and for a shadow stage.

screen and perform in a spot-light from the projector.

Also, you don't have to be an artist to do the puppet outlines. If you don't draw hands or faces well, you don't have to worry about this with shadow puppets.

The Baba Yaga story that is retold by Joanna Cole as *Bony Legs* (Four Winds Press, 1983) can be told on either the overhead projector or the shadow stage. My students have made their own puppets and acted them in groups on the overhead. Use the patterns to make your own. (See pages 208-211)

Baba Yaga   *Cat*

Comb

Dog   *Sasha*

House on Chicken Feet   *Gate*

For the overhead projector, tape a thin coffee stir stick to each figure so it can be manipulated across the glass. Or, you can attach a strip of transparent plastic. For the shadow stage, open a paper clip into an "L" shape. Tape one end to the back of the puppet. Lay the other end snugly against the eraser end of a pencil or wooden skewer and wrap that end with tape to attach it. When you hold the stick or pencil, the puppet will fit flush against the cloth screen.

Students enjoy making these puppets them-selves, and such a performance can be done in lieu of a book report or as a cooperative project between upper and lower classes. We had fifth graders who read a story and planned the pup-pets. Then they partnered with first graders to make the puppets. At the performance, the older child read or told the story, and the first grader manipulated the puppets on the overhead. The applause from the classes they entertained made both young and older students feel like profession-al puppeteers.

Older students enjoy Readers' Theater, and you can involve more students if you have readers *and* puppet performers. Readers stand to one side of an impromptu stage, and others perform with pup-pets held before them as the readers verbalize the parts. Their puppets can be homemade or store-bought, and the group effort can be performed before an appreciative audience. As we did when I was in first grade, you can flip a long table on its side for a stage. You can make another impromptu stage with a curtain hung on a spring rod at shoul-der height in a doorway. For guidance on a variety of puppets, scripts, and tips for performances, refer to one of the following books:

Anderson, Dee. *Amazingly Easy Puppet Plays: 42 New Scripts for One-Person Puppetry* (ALA, 1997). Each of the scripts comes with a list of suggested books and instructions to make inex-pensive puppets.

Bauer, Caroline Feller. *Leading Kids to Books Through Puppets* (ALA, 1997). The book is filled with ideas for using puppets to entice kids into reading good literature.

Schroeder, Joanne. *Fun Puppet Skits for Schools and Libraries* (Teacher Ideas Press, 1995). Got your puppets? Now use this book for fun, short, and easily performed puppet plays with a variety of children's stories.

Rump, Nan. *Puppets and Masks: Stagecraft and Storytelling* (Davis Publications, 1996). Rump details puppets, scenery, and scripts that are imaginative yet simple.

Sierra, Judy. *Fantastic Theater: Puppets and Plays for Young Performers and Young Audiences* (H. W. Wilson Company, 1991). Puppet plays are based on 30 nursery rhymes, folktales, myths, songs, and poems. Chapters include how to make rod and shadow puppets and how to use them on stages you make.

Wright, Denise Anton. *One-Person Puppet Plays* (Teacher Ideas Press, 1990). Book includes scripts, directions for making puppets, and hints on using them for putting on successful one-person plays.

Now You See It...

What place does magic have in the library media center? The LMC is definitely a place to come to satisfy one's curiosity, and nothing makes children more curious than watching a magic trick. Caroline Feller Bauer has written an entire book on the benefits of magic in the library. In *Leading Kids to Books Through Magic* (ALA, 1996), she explains how to use sleight of hand to correlate with numerous books. The tricks are clearly explained and require no fancy supplies.

In one trick, the librarian shows the audience a banner that reads "FRESH FISH SOLD HERE." As the librarian tells a story, he tears one word after another from the sign. But at the end of the story, he magically restores the banner to its original words!

After the trick, Caroline suggests sharing David Day's *The Walking Catfish* (Macmillan, 1992), Patricia McKissack's *A Million Fish... More or Less* (Knopf, 1992), Cathy Wilcox's *Enzo the Wonderfish* (Ticknow & Fields, 1994), and others.

A trick I learned as a child can be used to introduce any story in which coins play an important part. Some that come to mind are Vera Williams' *A Chair for My Mother* (Greenwillow, 1982), Amy Axelrod's *Pigs Will Be Pigs* (Simon & Schuster, 1994), or Robin Tzannes story of *Sanji and the Baker* (Oxford University, 1998). As you are preparing to tell the story, interrupt your introduction to say, "You know, this book reminds me of a magic coin trick. Would you like to see it?" Of course they do.

Here's what you do: Form the children into a close circle. Show them four quarters or four foreign coins, if appropriate to the story. Tell them that you are going to close your eyes while they pass a coin around the circle and put it back with the other three. Then you are going to shake them up and tell them which coin was sent around.

Have a child serve as the magic assistant. He should note which year (or other identifying mark) is on the coin. He also verifies that all four coins are the same size but different years. Without telling you, he writes the date of one coin in large numbers on a piece of construction paper, shows it to the class, and turns it facedown.

Close your eyes or—for more drama—be blindfolded. The students pass the coin from hand to hand around the circle. Every now and then say, "Stop! Hold the coin in your hand while thinking about the year. I am trying to read your mind." Then tell them to continue a while before repeating the stop gambit.

The magic assistant adds the coin that's been passed to the other three coins and places them in your hand. Still with your eyes closed or blindfold on, ask the class to think of the year as you dramatically handle each coin. When you announce the correct coin, the students think you have read their minds! The secret? The coin that has been passed and held will be warm when it comes to you. Keep track of that coin as you proceed with your magic patter. This simple trick is sure to cause attention to focus on you and the book as you prepare to read it.

Try simple magic with your students. You may not have anything up your sleeve, but you will have a lot on your mind as you plan your integration with the time-honored skill of magic.

◄ Many sites on the Internet can teach you to perform tricks. *The Conjuror* illustrates 15 simple tricks by Neil Alexander. Find them at <www.conjuror.com/magictricks>. At *Diamond Jim's Interactive Magic* site at <www.diamond-jim.com>, you can see magic done virtually before your eyes. You choose from five online card tricks, which are performed on the computer as you participate. You will still find yourself saying, "How did he do that—and over the Internet?"

Games

Over the years, I have played a lot of games with my classes. I try to choose games that will appeal to a variety of abilities. The best are often the simplest. Most require few supplies and are easy to make. Often we play for no prizes. Sometimes we use marshmallows or small candies for card markers. Getting to eat these at the end of the game seems to be enough reward. On other occasions, we allow winners to check out an additional book. Surprisingly, this is a privilege they really like, and it costs us nothing. It also is a sneaky way to encourage more reading! This chapter describes many of the games my students enjoy as a class. Near the end of the chapter, you will find suggested software and Internet games for individuals and small groups.

Planning For Play

In planning to play, first specify your objectives. Second, think of a game that will reach those objectives. Last, decide if you will purchase the game or make it, perhaps with the help of your students.

Keep in mind that numerous games can help you reach the same objective. These can include simulation games, action games, games adapted from traditional children's games, and strategy games involving cards, a board, dice, or other game pieces.

For example, suppose you want children to be able to identify the title, author, illustrator, dedication, publisher, copyright, and other parts of the book, such as the spine, contents, and index. Students can practice by playing any of the following games:

CARDS: Students try to collect a full set of book parts. Play the game like *Go Fish*, including the following cards in four different colors: Author, title, publisher, and illustrator. In four other colors, include title page, table of contents, index, and glossary. After students know the meanings of each book part, have them play to get the most sets by color.

BOARD GAME: Use a path that includes stars indicating the card students must pick up. The cards review all parts of a book, referring to the stack of library books that you provide. Students roll a die, move, select a card, and follow directions. For example, a card could read, "Choose the top book from the stack. Name the author of this book." Correct answers advance the player two squares. Wrong answers take the player back one square.

DICE GAME: Question cards are used with the dice. A student who rolls an even number must answer a question. If correct, the student keeps the card. The winner is the student with the most cards at the end of the game. Or, you could play it with a stack of books. Dice numbers = a certain book part that must be named about the book on the top of the stack, for example, 2 = title, 4 = author, and so on.

SIMULATION GAME: Student teams have cards listing all parts of a book. They pretend they are editors and stack the pages in the order they would be found in a book. Some pages will not be needed, depending on the type of book. Book types are drawn and include reference, picture book, chapter book without illustrations, nonfiction about cheetahs, and so on.

ACTION GAMES: Use this chart, written on the board or projected on the board with a transparency and overhead projector.

mation at random on their cards. After cards are filled, play in the same way as bingo, calling out the correct answers instead of bingo numbers. This is a game to review previously taught skills.

ADAPTED TRADITIONAL GAME: Play this version of "Paper, Rock, Scissors." Instead of these terms, use title, author, publisher. Publisher outranks author that beats the title. Title bests the publisher.

Games appeal to a variety of learning styles. They break up your library routines and provide

Team 1	Team 2	Book Part	Team 2	Team 2
		Author		
		Title		
		Illustrator		
		Publisher		
		Copyright		
		Call Number		
		Dedication		

Provide strips simulating the parts of a book. Give each student on a team a book part strip with a magnet on the back. At a signal, team members hurry to the board, place their book part in the appropriate place, and hurry back to the next team member, who either draws another book part from the pile or corrects the part placed by the person before her. The team with the most correct parts first wins.

QUESTION AND ANSWER GAME: Set up a Jeopardy-type game with the categories of titles, authors, publishers, copyright dates, indexes, and tables of contents. Students use real books to supply answers to the questions uncovered behind each money card. Correct answers earn the student that amount of money. For example, under Publishers for $100, the question might be, "Who is the publisher of the fiction book in your stack?"

BINGO GAME: Give each student a bingo card with 16 or 25 bingo squares (see pp. 47 and 48 for templates). Hold up a book and say, "The title of this book is *Make Way for Ducklings*. Write this title anywhere on your card." Do the same for various books, naming their publisher, author, illustrator, or copyright date. Students write this infor-

fun for you as well as your learners. Try them for many objectives, especially when rote memory is required. Involving the emotions will improve memory. In addition, when students are having fun, they tend to relate more positively to the subject matter.

Traditional Games for Information Literacy

The simplest games, such as tic-tac-toe, are still loved and played and adapted by teachers today. Games can appeal to all abilities and intelligences. Examine this list for examples:

Linguistic: Hangman
Mathematical: *Yahtzee* (Milton Bradley)
Spatial: *Pictionary Junior* (Milton Bradley)
Kinesthetic: Charades
Musical: Name That Tune
Team games: *Outburst* (Parker Brothers)

A variety of higher level thinking skills are used in many commercial games. These are the skills that are being tested more frequently on state tests. In *Clue* (Parker Brothers), players use logic to deduce the identity of the killer. Players pay fines, make change, and buy, sell, and trade property in *Monopoly* (Parker Brothers). The game of *Risk* (Parker Brothers) has players planning battle strategy, grouping numbers of armies, and adding and subtracting forces. Card games of all kinds involve strategy, point counting, and keeping score.

In the library, many traditional games can be adapted to teach information literacy skills or incorporated into jointly-planned curricular lessons to help teachers with instruction. The emphasis should be on skill attainment, not on competition. Prizes are not necessary.

▶ Books that explain traditional children's games can be adapted for information skills or integrated with a lesson. Look for these titles:

Gallery of Games by Catherine Marchon-Arnaud (Tichnor & Fields, 1994). This is a fully illustrated instruction book for making games such as checkers, roulette, peg solitaire, battle, and Chinese checkers.

Games by Godfrey Hall (Thomson Learning, 1995) explains numerous games that are played around the world, many of which will be familiar to students.

Sidewalk Games Around the World by Arlene Erlbach (Millbrook, 1997) can easily be played on the hardtop or sidewalks at school, or using tape on tiled floors.

Hopscotch Around the World (Morrow, 1996) and *Jacks Around the World* (Morrow, 1992) by Mary Lankford will show your students variations of these childhood staples.

Fairy and Folktale Tic-Tac-Toe

A tic-tac-toe format can be used as an alternative in the question and answer game format. On an overhead screen, lay thick yarn or ribbon to form a 3 x 3 inch grid on the glass. Number the squares of the grid to make it easy for students to tell you the square in which to place their marker. Use large X's and O's cut from tagboard and laminated. You will need five of each.

Divide the class into two teams. You may provide them with a list of possible answers. Give the following clues about each folk or fairy tale. Team One supplies its answer. If it is correct, they get to place an X. If the answer is incorrect, give Team Two a chance to "steal" but do not repeat the clue. If the second team is correct, it places an O in a square, then gets its own team question.

Clue	Title
Cat in footgear	*Puss in Boots*
Not awake, not ugly	*Sleeping Beauty*
Trio of small hams	*Three Little Pigs*
Girl from the ashes	*Cinderella*
The lovely and the ugly one	*Beauty and the Beast*
Small carmine-caped girl	*Little Red Riding Hood*
Guy and the climbing vine	*Jack and the Beanstalk*
Girl pale as winter	*Snow White*
Unattractive swimming fowl	*Ugly Duckling*
Royalty and the vegetable	*The Princess and the Pea*
Long-haired ladder girl	*Rapunzel*
Blonde and the hairy forest dwellers	*Goldilocks and the Three Bears*
Royalty's fresh attire	*The Emperor's New Clothes*
Little folks and the footwear specialist	*The Elves and the Shoemaker*
Scrawny limbs	*Bony Legs*

What's My Book?

Many of your learners will delight in problem solving of all kinds, and riddles are one kind of problem to solve. Riddles are also a fun way to promote sections of the library. Feature a section each week or month, and highlight it daily with riddles. Use this promotion as a contest format, putting riddles on slips to be answered and entered in a drawing.

For the 398.2 section: "I could not sleep for nights because there was something hard in my bed. I could feel it even though I piled 100 mattresses on my bed! Who am I?" (The princess from *The Princess and the Pea*)

For the fiction section: "I've been raised by dolphins since I went overboard in a boating accident. Now I'm a prisoner of scientists who want to learn how I can speak to dolphins. What's my book?" (*Music of the Dolphins* by Karen Hesse, Scholastic, 1996)

For biographies: "Flying was my passion, and it didn't matter to me that most folks thought flying was just for men. My final dream was to be the first woman to fly around the world. My story is found in the biography section. Who am I?" (Amelia Earhart)

For picture book section: "My dream was to marry royalty or at least a mayor. When my fairy godmother didn't show, I married the farmer next door. It wasn't until we had several children—including twins—and the house burned down, and we struggled to run a farm together that the fairy godmother showed up. What book can you read about me?" (*Fanny's Dream* by Caralyn Buehner, Dial, 1996)

A fun way for the whole school to enjoy the riddles is to read them as part of the morning announcements. Students can help you write the riddles and can take turns reading them each morning. Allow classes to submit a class answer. Each correct class earns a point. At the end of the designated time, the winning classes receive a special bookmark or other reward for each student. Sometimes, just announcing which class was the most clever is enough reward.

Try Something New

Readers often get into ruts, and booktalks guide them to areas of the library in which they rarely choose to read. A nonverbal way to encourage children to try a new genre or Dewey section involves clip art, some 4 x 6 inch note cards, and a little ingenuity. You can make the cards or involve students in the activity. Select clip art (enlarge if necessary) that represents genres or areas of your collection, and mount one on each card.

Students select a card at random and try to find a book they think would match the symbol. For example, for a hammer, the student might select a book on building birdhouses, a book about John Henry, or a book on architecture. Any reasonable match would earn the student a bookmark to place in the book after she checks it out. An alternative is to supply the clip art card to each child and have each come up with three books from different parts of the library. Encourage students to read at least 10 pages of the book they select—they may find it good enough to finish! This activity encourages use of the catalog, as well as spurring discussions and suggestions from classmates.

You might want to use the following list for more ideas:

Clip Art	Picture Book Title	Fiction Title	Nonfiction Title
candle	*The Christmas Candle* Evans, 1998	*House on Haunted Hill* Prince, 1998	*Colonial Days* King, 1998
bucket	*Max Found Two Sticks* Pinkney, 1997	*The Mopwater Files* Erickson, 1997	*There's a Hole in My Bucket* Schubert, 1998
wheat plant	*The Little Red Hen* Galdone, 1973	*Out of the Dust* Hesse, 1997	*From Wheat to Pasta* Egan, 1997
snake	*The Day Jimmy's Boa Ate the Wash* Noble, 1980	*Cam Jansen and the Scary Snake Mystery* Adler, 1997	*The Singing Snake* Czernecki, 1995
dog	*Henry and Mudge* Rylant, 1987	*Sounder* Armstrong, 1969	*Buddy: The First Seeing Eye Dog* Moore, 1996
newspapers	*Black and White* Macaulay, 1990	*Alice Rose & Sam* Lasky, 1998	*Deadline! From News to Newspaper* Gibbons, 1987
gift box	*Somebody Loves You, Mr. Hatch* Spinelli, 1991	*Herbie Jones and the Class Gift* Kline, 1987	*Making Gift Boxes* Hendry, 1999

Clip Art	Picture Book Title	Fiction Title	Nonfiction Title
gift box	*Somebody Loves You, Mr. Hatch* Spinelli, 1991	*Herbie Jones and the Class Gift* Kline, 1987	*Making Gift Boxes* Hendry, 1999
quilt	*The Quiltmaker's Gift* Brumbeau, 2000	*Bess's Log Cabin Quilt* Love, 1996	*The Names Project* Brimner, 1999
brick	*Little Lumpty* Imai, 1996	*The Junkyard Dog* Tamar, 1995	*The Three Little Pigs* Kellogg, 1997
apple	*Cinderella* Perrault, 1999	*The Just Desserts Club* Jurwitz, 1999	*Johnny Appleseed* Kellogg, 1997

The Quiltmaker's Gift by Jeff Brumbeau is a treat for the math-savvy student. Inside the book jacket is a puzzle poster in which students can find 250 quilt patterns hidden in the picture. Patterns are listed in the margins. The answer key is at <www.Quiltmakers Gift.com>, along with other activities.

Card Games

Card games can be played to reinforce a variety of skills. Formats can involve collecting a set of cards, playing cards with points, and using cards in a memory or matching game.

Cards can be made from 5 x 8 inch index cards. Cut through the center of the card in a distinctive pattern so pieces can be matched. Use the halves to match names with the word illustrator or author, for example, or to match titles with authors or genres.

Practice nonfiction and fiction concepts with a matching card game. Students match the title of a book with a matching fiction or nonfiction card. Play in the usual card fashion, dealing five cards to each player and placing the rest in the center for a draw pile. Students can draw from the center or from another player to try to make a match. One player can be the judge, using the answer key to make sure players are correctly matching cards. Use your collection to make the cards. Students may be inspired to find the book to read after playing the game.

Memory is a card game in which students match cards from a grid of cards placed facedown. For a "parts of book" *Memory* game, make two cards of each of the following: author, title, illustrator, copyright date, spine, table of contents, glossary, index, publisher, place of publication, title page, verso page, flyleaves, and dedication page. Also have two WILD CARD cards that will match any card.

Students place cards facedown in a 4 x 4 inch array. They take turns exposing two cards. If the cards match, the player keeps the pair, replacing them with cards from the draw pile, and takes another turn to match. If the cards don't match,

the player replaces them in their original places. The student with the most pairs is the winner.

For additional ideas and games, refer to these books:

Collis, Len. *Card Games for Children.* Barron's, 1989. Included are games for one to four players that can be played by children of all ages.

Goodwin, Jude. *Let's Play Cards: Great Card Games for Kids.* Devyn Press, 1989. Many of these games can be adapted for instructional use.

Longe, Bob. *The World's Best Card Tricks.* Sterling Publishing Co., Inc., 1991. Card tricks appeal to both the logical/mathematical and kinesthetic intelligences. Use this book in one of your centers.

Board Games

Games based on a track around the board are readily available for the classroom or library media center. One that has been adapted from a popular family game is *Intermediate Science Trivial Pursuit* (Good Apple, 1992). You can adapt *Candy Land* (Milton Bradley), *Monopoly* (Parker Brothers), or *Game of Life* (Milton Bradley) to library or curricular concepts. With student help, adapt the game by covering the squares with new information and supplying rewritten game cards (such as Chance cards).

Many books of game ideas are available at teacher supply stores, and in curricular guides, teacher's guides, and your own library collection. Get more ideas from Ruth Oakley's *Board and Card Games* (Marshall Cavendish, 1989). Her book provides games for older students to play and to use as inspiration to design their own.

You might also look at Carol Lee's book

57 Games to Play in the Library or Classroom (Alleyside Press, 1997). These games are simple to play and easy to make. All game boards, patterns, and directions are included. Topics range from book care, parts of a book, and call numbers to genres and reading promotion. Some games can be played with kindergarten students, and others can be played through grade 5. Store the game pieces in a manila folder or envelope, and attach the directions to the front. Place the games in centers in the library or loan to classes.

Question and Answer Games

To get their students to use the library reference materials more effectively, Myram Tunnicliff and Susan Soenen developed the question game in the book *The Reference Information Skills Game* (Libraries Unlimited, 1995). On Monday, post one of the questions and one clue. Each day, reveal another clue that makes it easier to determine the title of the book. Participants complete a form showing the steps in their search, the correct answer, and the source. End the game any day and award every participant, or put winning names in a drawing for the week.

Following are other books that contain questions and answers:

Gerberg, Mort. *Geographunny: A Book of Global Riddles*. Clarion, 1991. Students use a knowledge of geography to solve a variety of riddles.

Gleason, Karen. *Factivities*. Good Apple, 1991. This contains a variety of question and answer games for grades K-5.

Heller, Robert J. *How to Win at Trivial Pursuit and Other Knowledge Games*. Rinehart & Winston, 1984. This title is appropriate for grades 4 and up.

Human Tic-Tac-Toe

Fifth grade does a biography unit every February that the teacher and I plan and teach. Each student reads a biography and then dresses like the character to tell a first person 10-minute history of that person. The other students take notes. This is an excellent way to encourage critical listening. Students may bring these notes with them to the review game we play in the library and may use them as they take the biography unit test. Our review game is based on the people the students researched, so the questions vary each year. You can write your own for each character or require that each student submit two questions and answers as part of their project.

To play with the students as game markers, you will need nine floor pillows or chairs arranged in a 3 x 3 foot grid. Mark five sheets of two colors of construction paper with X's and O's. Each team selects a spokesperson. Students may confer with their teams for the answer, but only the spokesperson may answer for each team. If the team answer is correct, the spokesperson appoints someone to sit in the grid, holding the colored sheet chin high. If the answer is incorrect, the other team gets to answer as a bonus question, but the question is not repeated. They would then receive another question as their team question.

The first team to complete a tic-tac-toe earns a point. New spokespersons are chosen and another round is played as time allows. Award bookmarks to the team with the most points. The bookmarks can feature famous Americans, inventors, or others according to the theme selected for the game. Or, you can give the winning team candy and give all a bookmark.

Sample Biography Questions

These are questions we used with the books listed on page 41. Display books so children can see the covers for additional help as they play the game.

1. This inventor created 300 products from peanuts, including shoe polish, perfume, and butter. (George Washington Carver)
2. This inventor created the first fire department and lending library, and invented bifocal glasses and the stove that bears his name. (Benjamin Franklin)
3. Our nation's third President was also the author of the Declaration of Independence. (Thomas Jefferson)
4. These brothers invented and flew the first airplane in 1903 at Kitty Hawk, North Carolina. (Orville and Wilbur Wright)
5. This artist's twin brother died when they were two years old. The artist paints murals today in Mexico. (Diego Rivera)

6. This playwright's father was a glove maker. He has become the best-known playwright in the world, and wrote *Romeo and Juliet* and *Julius Caesar*. (William Shakespeare)

7. This writer was born on the night Haley's comet was seen and died the night it was next seen, 74 years later. He is famous for his books about Tom Sawyer and Huckleberry Finn. (Samuel Clemens/Mark Twain)

8. This "railroad conductor" helped 300 slaves escape to freedom before the Civil War. (Harriet Tubman)

9. This writer had wealthy parents but few playmates. Her friends were the rabbits and other pets about which she wrote. (Beatrix Potter)

10. This scientist created vaccines to prevent rabies and smallpox, and a way to kill germs in fresh milk. (Louis Pasteur)

11. Although she came from a wealthy family, she preferred to nurse injured and dying soldiers on the bloody and dangerous fields of the Crimean War. (Florence Nightingale)

12. Some Native Americans called him "The Raven." He helped Texas gain its freedom from Mexico at the battle of San Jacinto. (Sam Houston)

13. This young flyer came close to being the first to fly around the world at the equator, but she died in the attempt. (Amelia Earhart)

14. He became a sailor on an English ship at the age of 10. He was the first English sea captain to sail around the world. (Sir Francis Drake)

15. He was born and raised in Tennessee, but died at the Alamo fighting for Texas and its freedom from Mexico. (Davy Crockett)

16. This scientist proved that some sharks can remain motionless and not drown, as previously thought. (Eugenie Clark)

17. She was the wife of a President and was the first First Lady to have a public life of her own. She became a United Nations diplomat and human rights leader. (Eleanor Roosevelt)

18. One of twelve children, he spent his later years planting apple trees across the country so no one would go hungry. (Johnny Appleseed/John Chapman)

19. She became Queen of Egypt and later married one of the rulers of Rome. (Cleopatra)

20. This man was involved in the war for America's freedom and became its second President. (Samuel Adams)

Suggested Bibliography

Adler, David A. *A Picture Book of Davy Crockett.*
_____. *A Picture Book of Eleanor Roosevelt.*
_____. *A Picture Book of Florence Nightingale.*
Ferris, Jeri. *Go Free or Die: A Story About Harriet Tubman.*
Fritz, Jean. *What's the Big Idea, Ben Franklin?*
_____. *Why Don't You Get a Horse, Sam Adams?*
Gerrard, Roy. *Sir Francis Drake: His Daring Deeds.*
Giblin, James Cross. *Thomas Jefferson: A Picture Book Biography.*
Greene, Carol. *George Washington Carver: Scientist and Teacher.*
Holland, Gini. *Diego Rivera.*
Kellogg, Steven. *Johnny Appleseed: A Tall Tale Retold.*
Lasky, Kathryn. *A Brilliant Streak: The Making of Mark Twain.*
McGovern, Ann. *Shark Lady: True Adventures of Eugenie Clark.*
Parker, Steven. *Louis Pasteur and Germs.*
_____. *The Wright Brothers and Aviation.*
Sanford, William R. *Sam Houston: Texas Hero.*
Stanley, Diane. *Bard of Avon: The Story of William Shakespeare.*
_____. *Cleopatra.*
Wade, Mary Dodson. *Amelia Earhart: Flying for Adventure.*
Wallner, Alexander. *Beatrix Potter.*

Silent Game

This is a bingo-type game I developed originally to play with kindergartners who have difficulty reading a printed game board. You can adapt it for any objective for which you can locate at least 20 pictures (use a 4 x 4 inch grid). See page 218 for blank board.

I used Christmas seasonal stickers to make the game boards. To do this, you will need these pictures: cup (to represent hot cocoa), gingerbread man, tree light bulb, Christmas tree, candy cane, poinsettia, ornament, mistletoe, reindeer, snowflake, stocking, cookies, candle, angel, holly, Santa, wreath, sleigh, dove, gift, star, bell, bow, elf, and free space. If you cannot find stickers, use clip art or simple outline drawings.

Vary the order in which you attach the stickers to the class set of cards. You should have more picture choices than cards so they will be different. Make a master card that contains all the stickers and make a transparency of it. Enlarge these pictures and cut them apart so you have 20 transparent pictures.

Play the game like regular bingo. Instead of calling out the name of the picture, show it on the overhead projector. Students look at the picture, match it, and cover it. If desired, give children candies or marshmallows for markers, which they are not to eat until the game is over. Calling out "bingo" when it is achieved is the only sound students are to make in this silent game. I play Christmas music in the background as we play. This is a relaxing game in the midst of the holiday hyperactivity! You can vary the game by including Hanukkah and Kwanzaa symbols as well. Be sure to vary your music if adding symbols from other holidays.

Action Games

Games involving movement or handling objects involve the kinesthetic intelligence. One example is to play *Follow the Bouncing Ball.* After teaching the Dewey decimal system, you can review the categories with this game. You will need one or two vinyl beach balls.

With a permanent marker, divide the ball into sections that are about 3 x 3 inches. Inside each section, write a general Dewey number, such as 300-399. Label other sections with letters such as E, B, F, REF, and others you use in your library. If you use other spine stickers, such as genre stickers, holiday stickers, or State Award Winners, you can add them as well.

Play the game in a large circle. If you have a teacher or volunteer who can assist a second group, divide the class and use two balls. This is a better arrangement because children have more chances to play and stay interested longer. Throw the ball to a student in the circle, who catches it with two hands opened on the sides of the ball. The child has two choices. She can choose either category on which her thumbs are resting. She must then name the type of books that would be found in this section. If correct, she earns a point for the circle team. If incorrect, Mr. Dewey gets a point. She then throws the ball to a person across from her. Play continues until all have a first turn, then continues until all have a second turn or time

runs out.

Because students are touching, talking, and having fun, they remember the Dewey categories better. When they become "expert" at remembering the categories, have students play with the same balls, but have them name a particular title that would be found in that section.

◀

If you are doing a kinesthetic or visual center in the classroom or library, you may find yourself needing recipes for papier-mâché, play dough materials for a salt map. Find all of this and more in *Recipes for Art and Craft Materials* by Helen Roney Sattler (Lothrop, Lee & Shepard, 1987).

Class-Sized Game Board

We use shower curtains to make floor games that students can walk on. Buy sew-on hook and closure tape. Glue lengths of the grabby half to the side edges of the shower curtain to help it grab the carpet. If you have a tile floor, tape the edges down to prevent slipping. You can make a game board by gluing large felt lily pads in a path on the curtain. Students roll a large die, made from a large foam cube or covered box, to move.

Make several different sets of game cards that students draw when they land on a pad and must answer to get to stay. Diecut frog shapes make good game cards, or you can buy a frog-shaped notepad at the teacher supply store. Some suggestions are to have questions about Caldecott books, library rules, parts of a book, or any curricular objective you have been studying.

You need two shower curtains (buy liners instead of curtains as they are much cheaper) to make a large game board for the wall. You also can buy vinyl by the yard (45 inches wide) in different thicknesses at fabric stores. I used a dark liner for the background and a clear one to make pockets. Cut pockets from the clear liner and tape them on with colored vinyl tape. Use your wall-sized board to play games in which the students choose the category and answer a question for play money.

My curtain game has six columns and six rows, with a pocket row for category titles and five more rows of pockets below. When I made it, I laid it out on my kitchen floor, which has large ceramic tiles. I carefully taped the opaque liner to the floor and used the tile grid lines to get the pockets lined up straight. I taped them on with alternating colors of vinyl tape, available at school supply stores and hardware stores.

Slip in large pieces of construction paper or tagboard for the category titles and the questions. You can reuse them for years without laminating. Here are some categories to include in your game:

Name That Author	Parts of a Book
What's My Title?	Reference Section
Which Genre?	Using the (Card or PAC)
Medal Winners	Catalog
Library Manners	Library Rules

The sixth column allows you to use the game board as a grid. Use your giant pocket chart for pictures of book characters that you have cut from posters, catalogs, or damaged books. Behind the picture, put the name of the character. Use the top row to include the numbers 1-5 and the first column for the letters A-E. Students then ask to guess the picture. A game might go like this:

> **Game announcer:** Which picture would you like to guess, Team A? Cheryl?
>
> **Cheryl:** I would like to guess the picture at A-5. I think the big red dog is named Clifford.

Your student helper acts like a studio assistant and removes the picture with a flourish. Behind it is the paper square with the name "Clifford" revealed. Team A scores a point, and play moves to Team B.

You can use this same approach to display paper copies of books in the pockets. Students in teams use the grid numbers to identify the book, then have to state the genre. For this game, use books that are commonly read or are obviously a certain genre based on the title and cover picture.

Use nine of the squares to make a large tic-tac-toe board. Cut out and laminate a set of five tagboard X's and five O's. Give one set to each team. When they answer a question, they can step up to place their piece in a pocket. I like using this format because games are over quickly, winners are declared frequently, and chances to start over are many.

Scavenger Hunt

In addition to building skills, games can break the ice, build rapport, and encourage laughter and camaraderie. This past year, I realized that some

of our fifth graders had heard my library orientation speech every fall since they were five years old. To review library procedures for our "experts" and for the new students, I created a game.

I made a list of questions I would expect the library-literate student to know. Each child selected a question slip and prepared to answer it for the class. I paired the new students with the ones who had been at our school longest. I gave them time to locate their answers and plan their method of delivery. Next I read a question, and the appropriate students demonstrated the answers. There was lots of movement and conversation as the students went about this fun way to review the rules.

These are the slips we used. Students were required to go to the shelves and find noted books. Then they showed the class where they went. Some questions required acting out the answers.

Help! I need a true book about snakes! Where do I look?
I loved the fiction book about Shiloh. Now I want the sequel by Phyllis Reynolds Naylor. Where do I find it?
I love Dr. Seuss books because of their funny pictures and words. Can you find one of his books for me?
I'm returning my book before my class library day. Where do I turn it in?
Before I can leave my class to come to the library on my own, I must have a pass. What does it look like, and how do I display it?
I'm checking out a book without my class. What do I take to the check-out counter besides the book I want?
Find as many places as you can where students may read quietly.
What do we use to mark a book's place on the shelf when deciding to choose it? Where do you get one of these?
I need facts about Benjamin Franklin. Where can I find a book about him?
I need to know if the book I want is checked out already. How can I find out?
I want to get *Wait Until Helen Comes* by Mary Downing Hahn. This is a Bluebonnet Medal winner. Where is it?
I want to find a magazine to read during BEAR time. Where should I look?

I like to read on my back, and hardcovers are too heavy to hold up for long. Where can I find paperback versions of my favorite fiction books?

What is the one section from which I cannot check out books?

I'm reading to a kindergarten buddy. Where can I find some books for him?

Oh no! My water bottle leaked, and I've ruined my library book. What do I do next?

I want to donate a book to the library for my birthday. How do I do this?

Bingo Games

Before doing a lesson on sounds and the words we use to represent them (onomatopoeias), we match sounds to their sources. You can use a tape recorder and your imagination to tape sounds around your home, school, and neighborhood. Some suggestions are:

bacon sizzling	pencil sharpening
raking leaves	car starting
washing machine	school bell ringing
phone ringing	shower running
closing a car door	newspaper rustling
uncorking a bottle	garage door opening

▶

Don't have time to make 25 different bingo cards? Pass out blank cards with 25 squares to students. Have them put FREE SPACE in the center square. Then call out about 28 words. Tell students to write the word in any square, but to ignore 3 of the words. After you call out all the words, students will have different cards, and you can begin play. For younger students, make a 4 x 4 inch card and write words to be used on an overhead projector. See the templates on pages 47 and 48.

Make a bingo card with the names of the things you have recorded. Play as usual, except when students hear the sound, they should cover the words. After students have covered the word for that sound, tell them what it is. They can correct their guess if needed.

Bingo games are quickly made and quickly played. For additional ideas, read *Ready-to-Use Reading Bingos, Puzzles and Research Activities for the Elementary School Year* by Barbara Farley Bannister (The Center for Applied Research in Education). Each game pertains to a topic, such as *Share a Scare Reading Bingo* and *Favorite Authors Bingo*. Each square has a genre, title, or author. Used as an individual log, students read five books, black their squares on the front of the sheet, and record their bibliographic information on the back.

I adapted these bingo games to make a blackout bingo for entire classes. Reproduce a different bingo for each class in a large format suitable for posting on the library wall. Each time a student from the class reads a book, draw a line in the related square from corner to corner or side to side. Someone from each class should read a book for each of the 25 squares. Put the book titles read by the class on a list below the bingo card. Award a small prize to the class that first completes a bingo card or to all classes that complete the bingo by a certain date. We usually let winners have an extra book at check-out time that week.

Stars of the Show

Many learners enjoy performing before an audience. Supply slips with book titles written on them and teach your students to play Book Charades. They also can act out a commercial for a favorite book. Or, they can be assigned parts, given puppets, and asked to improvise a story. Students might want to perform their own adaptations of a fairy tale scene, which they must plan in five minutes and perform in three minutes. Students must work as a team to plan the story. Be sure to set a time limit for planning. The game is based on quick thinking and improvisation.

Here are some scenarios you might try with students. If desired, students can use puppets or make paper plate masks that can be glued to tongue depressors and held before their faces as they perform. Use the following as examples and ask your students to think of others.

Goldilocks begins to feel bad about messing up the bears' house and their things. What could she do? How will she explain to the three bears when they return? (three bears, one girl)

What if the frog prince was really a dog instead of a prince? This dog has really bad breath. How will he get someone to kiss him? (dog, number of people decided by group)

How would the story change if the King had been satisfied when the miller's daughter spun straw into gold the first time? (girl, king, Rumplestiltskin)

What if Snow White was mean to the seven dwarves? How would the story change? (girl, seven dwarves, wicked stepmother, prince)

Suppose Little Red Riding Hood's grandmother was not home when the wolf came. What if the tough grandfather was? (wolf, grandfather, girl)

Software For Every Interest

Chances are that if you are in my age group, the thought of learning games may first bring a picture to your mind of board or folder games keyed to objectives. To our students, learning games may first suggest a computer game. CD-ROM programs are plentiful and fit well with many areas of the elementary curriculum. They also can provide enrichment in the classroom or in the library media center for those students who enjoy problem solving, besting the computer, and working independently or with a partner. To find the best CD-ROMs, use professional magazine reviews, such as those in *School Library Journal*, *Booklist*, or *The Book Report*. Also refer to the professional review resources on the Internet for recommendations.

Software publishers today have come a long way from the early electronic flash card programs. Modern programs use color, sound, animation, clever design, and solid educational practices to help students learn. While teaching curricular topics such as math concepts or spelling words, many programs will suit the various abilities of your students.

Provide the following programs for your teachers to check out or establish designated computers in your library media center that are identified by type of program. By attempting programs that cater to a variety of learning preferences, students will stimulate their different intelligences.

Looking for good software to buy for your library or classroom? Try these two sites for help. At *SuperKids Educational Software Review* <www.superkids.com>, you can read reviews and ratings [of h]undreds of educational software programs, and see the [best]seller list and the top choices. If you want to "test drive" [th]e software before buying, go to *The Kids Domain* at <www.kidsdomain.com/down/index.html>. You can [dow]nload recommended software in dozens of categories, including art, math, computer toolbox, thinking games, and many others. Programs include shareware, freeware, and commercial demonstrations.

Creativity Software

Making Music (Grolier, grades preK-6) lets students see and hear the components of music and how it is composed.

Children's Songbook (Grolier, grades preK-6) contains 15 instrumental versions of traditional musical favorites from around the world. Each song has animated lyrics, notations, illustrations, background information, and a challenging game.

HyperStudio (Knowledge Adventure, grades K-6) allows students to make a written computer production that combines text, graphics, animation, sounds, video, and Internet links.

Music Loops for Multimedia (FTC, grades 3-6) contains 330 half-minute music loops to import into classroom productions made on multimedia programs, such as *HyperStudio*.

Writing and Reading Poetry (Visions, grades 2-5) includes 45 activities that allow students to explore poetry and to expand their creativity in producing their own poetry.

Fun with Architecture (Grolier, grades 3-6) provides students with the Metropolitan Museum of Art's 45 building shapes, 20 building textures, and historical templates to build the Empire State Building or their own creation.

MovieWorks (Interactive Solutions, grades 4-6) provides all tools needed to make a QuickTime movie, video, or multimedia presentation.

Mask World (Visions, grades 3-6) includes 24 worldwide myths and 300 pages of masks that go with them. Plays are for three to seven characters.

MiDisaurus (Musicware, grades preK-5) uses an on-screen keyboard or an optional MIDI keyboard to build musical skills with animation, games, and tunes.

Community Construction Kit (Tom Snyder, grades K-4) allows students to design, print, cut out, and construct their own three-dimensional communities from four building styles that provide models of the real thing.

Problem Solving Software

Carmen Sandiego Think Quick Challenge (The Learning Company, grades 4-6) permits one to four students to try to retrieve stolen loot by answering content questions in eight different curricular areas.

Fizz and Martina's Math Adventure (Tom Snyder, grades 1-6) presents an animated math adventure. Teams of students must solve the math problems, explain their strategy in pictures or writing, and then answer questions about their work.

That's a Fact Jack! Read (Tom Snyder, grades 3-6) is an interactive game show in which contestants have to answer questions about the book they have all read.

Memory Challenge (Critical Thinking, grades K-6) provides a variety of randomly generated patterns to strengthen memory in several skill levels.

Slam Dunk Typing (The Learning Company, grades 3-12) combines a simulated basketball environment with typing exercises.

Strategy Challenges I and II (Edmark, grades 3-6) provides problem solving games from around the world, including Mancala, Nine Men's Morris, Go-Moku, Chess, Tablut, and Surakarta.

Thinkin' Things (Edmark, grades K-6) comes in a variety of packages suitable for each grade.

I Spy (Scholastic, grades K-4) offers a collection of puzzles and riddles that includes more than 1,300 objects and word searches.

Simulation and Strategy Games

The computer is a great tool for simulations. Tom Snyder has made a name for himself with his CD-ROM products that involve students in simulations, notably *Decisions, Decisions*. In these simulations, students role-play people involved in making a decision drawn from history or from contemporary issues. They follow a five-step model for decision-making taught within the program. Each member of the team has part of the information needed to make the critical decision.

For example, in one situation, the team has just been sworn in as lord of the family fief. The problem is to set priorities. They hear the advice of a merchant, a landowner, a steward, and the village priest. Then the group discusses choices, using additional information they each have. They make the decision, and the computer tells them of the consequences of their actions. The students then reassess their goals and take further action. Simulations involve the Constitution, the Revolutionary War, Immigration, Violence in the Media, and Prejudice, among others. These are suitable for grades 5 and up. Lower grades can participate in a similar but simplified series called *Choices, Choices*.

A variety of Tom Snyder math simulations involve topics of high interest, such as a search and rescue for a missing boater, and helping Fizz and Martina solve math mysteries. Along the way, players use basic operations, fractions, geometry, and measurement. For more information and free 45-day trials, visit the Tom Snyder Web site at <www.tomsnyder.com>.

Online simulations are available at no extra cost. The Association for Promotion and Advancement of Science Education has a sleuthing simulation at its Web site, <www.discoverlearning.com/forensic/docs/index.html>. Students try to solve the international heist of an endangered species. They have to look for clues, take notes, do research, and other activities to help track down the thief.

Students on a Think Quest team have developed a simulation called *The Hex Agency*. Students use math skills to work through the various parts of this site to track down international criminals. Look for it at <library.thinkquest.org/17932>.

Following are some of the many print sources for problem solving games and games involving strategy:

Hewavisenti, Lakshmi. *Problem Solving.* Gloucester Press, 1991. These are puzzles and games that involve higher level thinking skills.

Kidder, Harvey. *The Kids' Book of Chess.* Workman Publishing, 1990. Provides some inexpensive chess sets for checkout by students as they learn.

Lipman, Doug. *Storytelling Games.* Oryx Press, 1995. Includes games that practice math, science, verbal, speaking, and thinking skills.

Internet Games

The following Internet games are educational, involve no violence, and are free. Try the following sites with your students:

Wacky Web Tales <www.eduplace.com/tales/index.html>

These tales are made in the same way as Mad Libs. This site has the advantage of quick tips about the parts of speech. Students can create a Wacky Tale about subjects such as *Track of Bigfoot* or *Lessons Aesop Never Taught.*

Hangman <www.superkids.com/aweb/tools/words/hangman>

This variation of the popular school game involves topics such as U.S. Presidents, Sports, Astronomy and even the Periodic Table.

Creative Kids <creativekids.ca>

Two educators from Canada have assembled activities for online and offline, brainteasers, adventures, drawings, stories, games, and jokes. Be sure to mark the box that turns off the e-mail and snail-mail offers.

Kids' Place <www.eduplace.com/kids/index.html>

Houghton Mifflin Publishing Company has set up some excellent games at this site. *Fake Out* teaches new words, *GeoNet* develops geography skills, and *Wacky Web Tales* encourages creative word choices. There are also pages of brainteasers, word finds, and a reading discussion group called Reading Dimension. Students can discuss recommended books and access related Web sites.

Mancala <imagiware.com/mancala>

In correlation with a third-grade unit on Africa, I helped students make the traditional African game called Mancala (see page 139). The rules, history, and a diagram of the game are available at this site. We used modified egg cartons and pinto beans. Students made the game in the classroom, then played in the library. I taught them the rules, and we played a demonstration game on the overhead projector. As students played, they began to discover some strategies that have made this such a deceptively challenging game.

I gave students the Mancala Web address on a bookmark so they can play the game on the computer without any supplies. They enjoyed playing with their families at home. This game appeals both to the logical/mathematical and kinesthetic intelligences, because much movement of beans is required for winning.

Numerous children's games have been adapted to the computer. John Rickey has set up a Web site called *Room 108* <www.netrover.com/~kingskid/>. Here, students can play electronic versions of jigsaw puzzles, *Hangman, Tetris, Connect Four, Rubik's Cube, Mastermind, Dominoes*, and *Chinese Checkers*. The realism of these virtual games is a tribute to Rickey's programming skills, and students will gain many of the same advantages of the traditional games.

◄ Find hundreds of interesting and educational game sites by "drilling down" at the *Yahooligans* Web site. This site is monitored for children and is a directory rather than a search engine. Begin at <www.yahooligans.com>. Under the heading "Computers and Games," click on games. Then select another topic or scroll down to the more than 45 game sites listed on the screen. By drilling down to other layers, you will find math games, interactive stories, traditional and board games, and hundreds of others. Educators have screened all for quality and appropriateness for children.

(see page 218 for reproducible full page)

Lotto Board

Bingo Board

Songs and Chants

Librarians have long used Mother Goose rhymes, and often begin and end storytimes with a chant or a song. Give us a topic, and many of us can whip up a song about it to the words of a familiar tune. These songs are fun to use, provide a change of pace, and facilitate memory skills by tying material to music.

Think about the songs you learned in camp, Scouts, or at school. Many of them can be used as the tunes for curricular adaptations. Here is a list of ones I remember, many of which you will find used in this book.

Michael Row the Boat Ashore
She'll Be Comin' Round the Mountain
This Old Man
Pop Goes the Weasel
Clementine
Oh, Susannah
Wheels on the Bus
London Bridge
Jimmy Crack Corn
This Land Is Your Land
Twinkle, Twinkle Little Star
Yankee Doodle
When Johnny Comes Marching Home
Alouette
Camptown Races
I've Been Working on the Railroad
When the Saints Come Marching In
B-I-N-G-O
Skip to My Lou

Have You Ever Seen a Lassie?
Rock-A-Bye Baby
How Much Is That Doggie in the Window?

Students can use these melodies or others that they know, to write their own songs about library skills, curriculum, and books.

Sing Along with the Tooth Fairy

February is Dental Health Month. One of the things we do with our younger students is learn about correct tooth brushing. We use this song with a dental mouth model and a large toothbrush.

Tooth Care
(to the tune of "Row, Row, Row Your Boat")
Brush, brush, brush your teeth!
Scrub them side to side.
Brush them up from gum to crown,
And decay won't make you frown!
Repeat demonstration and song for top row of teeth, substituting "down" in the third line.

We finish the lesson by sharing lost tooth traditions. Although our students are from many ethnic backgrounds, all have a version of the tooth fairy and a tradition for what to do with the baby teeth they shed. If you have less variety of tradition, you may want to share Selby Beeker's *Throw Your Tooth on the Roof: Tooth Traditions from Around the World* (Houghton Mifflin, 1998) or Birdseye's *Air Mail to the Moon* (Holiday House, 1988).

For instructions for the tooth fairy pocket, check your collection for origami books. Use the instructions for making a cup. In the last step, however, fold both flaps forward. Instructions also can be found at the *Fascinating Folds* site at <www.fascinating-folds.com/diagrams/beginners/cup/cup.htm>. Make the same adjustment with the last step to make a pocket.

Finally, make origami tooth fairy pockets. Insert a piece of candy corn as a substitute tooth and seal with a sticker. Tell students they can make one of these any time they lose a tooth and need a handy place to keep it until they get home.

Shelf Marker Sing-along

You can keep the library more organized if students faithfully and carefully use shelf markers. These are paint stirrers, strips of heavy cardboard, or commercial plastic strips made to be inserted in place of a book while a student considers whether the book "fits." We use a shoe store analogy (see page 75) to explain the importance of choosing a book that fits. Our rule is to never check out a book unless we try it on first. We try them on not with our feet, but with our eyes. While trying on the book, we hold its place with a marker.

The first few weeks that we use the markers, we ask students to march to the shelves to the rhythm of the "Shelf Marker Song." They can use their marker to keep time by raising it up and down.

"Shelf Marker Song"
(to the tune of "Peanut Butter and Jelly")
First you put the marker in,
Then you take the book out.
Check the fit,
Open it,
See if it's for you!
MARKER! MY SHELF MARKER!

If you find a book that fits,
Take your marker out.
Doesn't fit?
Put it back!
Your marker tells you where!
MARKER! MY SHELF MARKER!

Songs with Students

We act out Maria Polushkin's *Mother, Mother, I Want Another* (Crown, 1978) when we do our friendship unit. I tell the story while students use puppets to act out the mother mouse, baby mouse, duck, frog, pig, and donkey. The book has a refrain for each animal that we sing to the tune of "Twinkle, Twinkle Little Star." Because only six students get a puppet part, the audience can be included in singing the refrains. Have them sing each animal's part in a different kind of voice (squeaky, harsh, whiny) for more fun.

For students learning French and Spanish, I made a glove puppet (page 31) to sing "Bingo" in each language. I made pompom puppies on the end of each finger of a gardening glove and attached a felt letter below each pup to spell out "Bingo."

Students can make finger puppets using paper figures with side tabs that wrap around their fingers. In this repetitive song, a letter is replaced with a clap on each successive round until by the sixth round, you are clapping all five letters without speaking. As we sing, we "pop up" the sung letter from its hiding place in our palm. This is a great dexterity exercise for young fingers. We sang first in the traditional way, then learned it in French and Spanish.

English "Bingo"
There was a farmer
Had a dog,
And Bingo was his name, OH!
B-I-N-G-O *Repeat these letters twice more, unfolding puppet pups as you say each letter.*
And Bingo was his name, OH!
Repeat rhyme five more times. Each round, leave off an additional letter, beginning with B. Clap in its place, until with the last round, you are rhythmically clapping all five letters.

Spanish "Bingo"
Hay un ranchero
Que tiene un perro,
Y se llama Bingo, OH!
B (beh), I (ee), N (en-ay), G (hay), O (oh)
Repeat these letters twice more.
Y se llama Bingo, OH!
Repeat five more times, as done traditionally, leaving off letters and substituting claps.

French "Bingo"

Il y a un fermier
Qui a un chien,
Et il s'appelle Bingo, OH!
B (beh), I (ee), N (en), G (jay), O (oh) *Repeat these letters twice more.*
Et il s'appelle Bingo, OH!
Repeat five more times, as done traditionally, leaving off letters and substituting claps.

Singing in the Spring

It seems as if every school in America, and possibly the world, may celebrate spring by planting bean seeds. Lessons are learned about plant structure and the plant cycle. We use Ruth Kraus' *The Carrot Seed* (Harper & Row, 1945), to encourage patience on the part of the young planters. My friend Aileen Kirkham and I collaborated on this song, which we use to act out the process of planting a garden.

"Planting Our Garden"
(*to the tune of* "If You're Happy and You Know It")

1. We dig a hole that's small and round, diggity dig—DIG, DIG! *Repeat twice.*
    We dig a hole that's small and round. *Repeat twice.*
    We dig a hole that's small and round, diggity dig—DIG, DIG!

Use this same pattern for the following verses:

2. We drop the seeds into the hole, plippity plop—PLOP, PLOP!
3. Cover them up with good brown dirt, rakity rake—RAKE, RAKE!
4. We spray them each with cool water, squirty squirt—SQUIRT, SQUIRT!
5. Gotta pull those pesky weeds up, yankity, yank—YANK, YANK!
6. We have to chase away the birds, zippity, git—GIT, GIT!
7. And last we pick fresh food to eat—yummy, yum—IN MY TUMMY!

You have probably noticed that all the songs in the previous lessons also incorporated other intelligences and involved movement, puppetry, and action. These lessons are some that students remember longest and think are the most fun because they involve several ways to process information.

Rhythm Reward

It's not a daily occurrence that classes return all their books on time. When we have only one or two students who forget their books, we celebrate with the book chant "Who Brought Their Books Back?" We sit in a circle and clap our hands on our knees as we say the chant. I begin it and call on the name of a child, who then calls on another, and so on until everyone has had a turn.

"Who Brought Their Books Back?"
(*to the rhythm of* "Who Stole the Cookie from the Cookie Jar?")

All sing.	Who brought their books back right on time?
I sing.	_____ (Marty) brought his books back right on time!
Marty sings.	Who me?
All sing.	Yes, you!
Marty sings.	You're right!
All sing.	Who else?
Marty sings.	_____ (Chris) !
All sing.	Chris brought his books back right on time!

Internet Resources for Books

Musical abilities can be engaged by having the student write a song about a curricular area to a well-known children's melody or add background music to a presentation or story. To allow access to a variety of music for these tasks, try searching the Internet. Following are some sites that will provide resources for your students.

Some of these sites require plug-ins, an added program that enhances your computer's ability to play or record movies, sounds, and other graphic files. Your computer will prompt you to load them if you do not have the proper ones. They are free and can be loaded from the Internet. It will take from 5 to 25 minutes to load the plug-ins, so be sure that you preview these sites and load plug-ins if needed before assigning them to students.

Children's Music Web's Radio Refrigerator <www.childrensmusic.org/fridge.html> At the click of the appropriate button, children can access MIDI files (sound files) for popular music for younger students, older students, and in Spanish. Also at this site are lullabies, active exercise music, and music from around the world.

Monty Harper, children's songwriter, performer, and recording artist, maintains the site. Some of the files are 20 minutes in length, so downloading time will be longer at this site. Ask students to be patient and give them offline activities to do while they wait.

Classical Midi Archives < www.prs.net/index.html>
Pierre Schwab has mounted an ambitious and busy site that includes more than 8,800 classical MIDI files from 657 composers. Some adult help will be needed to navigate this cluttered site. It has a search engine, so you can locate music by title or composer. This is an excellent site for students who know which classical songs or people they want to hear. It is not useful to surf files trying to find the appropriate one for a certain emotion or scene; the site is large, and downloading of MIDI files is time-consuming.

Judy and David's Online Songbook <JudyandDavid.com/Songbook/Songbookcover.html>
Judy and David are popular children's performing musicians from Canada. This married couple has videos, CD-ROMs, and cassettes from their various performances that you can order online at this site. They also have the words to hundreds of children's songs. Though the music is not available for each song online (you have to buy the specified tape), it is useful to have the original words. If you ever find you can't remember the words after the third line or so of a song, this site will help. Many of the songs have lesson plans that include dance, movement, and other curricular connections that appeal to a variety of intelligences.

The Portrait Gallery of Classical Composers <www.geocities.com/Vienna/Choir/4004/>
R. Christian Anderson works with the Houston Symphony Orchestra. He thought children and adults might want to put a face to various composers' names and musical compositions. He has carefully selected a portrait or photograph for each of hundreds of classical composers from around the world and from a variety of musical backgrounds.

▶

Music Adventureland at <www.netrover.com/~kingskid/cards/adventure.html> lists a variety of nouns, feelings, and other words, each accompanied by a musical interpretation. Have students listen to the music and try to match the music with a word on the list. Some of the words are island, blue, and bad day. The site also has songs that you can use as melodies for curricular adaptations.

Books to Sing

Many children's books can be sung. You can learn the song from the musical score printed in the back of the book. Some books come with a cassette that sings the song. Use the tapes in the following ways. First, listen to the tape in advance of presenting the story. Then you can sing as you read the book. Of course, you will want the students to sing with you. I have an average voice, but no student has ever complained. Instead, they willingly join in the song, especially if it has a bouncy refrain or silly words. Second, play the tape as you share the book so students can hear the music as well as the words. Last, share the tapes with students who want to rewrite the words but need to hear the melody. This is useful for songs that have a traditional melody, such as "Peanut Butter and Jelly" or "The Wheels on the Bus."

You can buy books on tape from a variety of bookstores, commercial book orders offered to students, or online bookstores. Here are selections I have used with great success with my students:
Cat Goes Fiddle-I-Fee retold by Paul Galdone
Little Rabbit Foo Foo retold by Michael Rosen
Miss Mary Mack adapted by Mary Ann Hoberman
Peanut Butter and Jelly retold by Nadine Westcott
There Ain't No Bugs on Me by Jerry Garcia and David Grisman
The Wheels on the Bus adapted by Maryann Kovalski
28 Folk and Fairy Tale Poems and Songs by Meish Goldish

A cassette tape accompanies the last book. Favorite stories and songs have been rewritten to go with songs children may know. "The City Mouse and the Country Mouse" is sung to the tune "The Bear Went over the Mountain," for example. Suggestions for sharing, a curricular activity, and a short book list of related books accompany all selections. Activities are simple enough for young grades, for example, having students tap wooden blocks together to make the sound of the three billy goats trip-trapping across the bridge. Activities also can be used in independent centers with students who are strong readers.

Music is a part of every culture, every major holiday or celebration, and a companion as we travel, shop, or worship. Tap into its enormous potential and that of the musical intelligence, as you provide instruction and assignments for your students or share curricular ideas with your teachers.

Dramatics and Tours

Allow movement while learning and capitalize on your learners' kinesthetic abilities. Include movement, action, and manipulating props, puppets, game pieces, and computer keyboards in your lessons to encourage active learning.

Hands-on Activities

In my library lessons, I try to incorporate hands-on activities as often as I can. For example, we learned about the parts of plants that we eat for *Tops & Bottoms*, a story by Janet Stevens (Harcourt Brace, 1995). I gathered as many vegetables as I could for students to see and touch. We had papier mâché vegetables, some flannel board ones, and a few fresh ones from the grocery, such as a parsnip, a turnip, and garlic cloves.

After I read the story, I passed around the vegetables. We used a line of yarn on the floor to represent the soil line, and students told me whether each vegetable was a top, a bottom, or a middle grower. If we usually eat just the tops (lettuce, cabbage, asparagus), the student placed the vegetable above the line. Root crops such as carrots, potatoes, and onions went below the line. "Middles" straddled the line. These included tomatoes, peppers, squash, corn, and other things that grow on inedible plants.

For a follow-up activity, each pair of students received a strand of yarn and pictures of various labeled vegetables for them to place on the line.

Follow-up stories included Ann McGovern's retelling of *Stone Soup* (Scholastic, 1968), Judi Barret's *Cloudy With a Chance of Meatballs* (Atheneum, 1978), and Ruth Kraus' *The Carrot Seed* (Harper & Row, 1945).

The Story of Joe

Do you know the story of Joe? He works in a button factory, and you can tell his action story at the beginning of any lesson to get students involved and active. As you tell the repetitive story, you end up stamping a foot, rubbing your stomach, patting your head, and other actions until all are giggling and moving.

Hi! My name is Joe. I've got a wife and three kids. I work in a button factory.

One day my boss said to me, "Are you busy Joe?"

I said, "No."

"Then push this button with your right hand," he says. *Push button with right hand. Repeat the lines in the first paragraph, substituting the following for the last line.*

"Then push this button with your left hand," he said. *Push button with left hand while continuing to push first button with your right hand. Repeat this process until your students are pushing with their right hand, left hand, right foot, left foot, head, and tongue. Then recite the last verse:*

Hi! My name is Joe. *Say this while pushing a button with your tongue and continuing all the other actions.* **I work in a button factory.**

One day my boss said to me, "Are you busy, Joe?"

And I said, "YEEEEESSSSSSSS!!" *Stop all other motions and grab your head with both hands.*

Another rhyme we do to get students moving goes well with our nutrition unit. It is a song by Scott Beasley called "Pizza Hut" (Bridge Records, 1991), and students must use their bodies to make the signs for McDonalds, Kentucky Fried Chicken, and other fast-food havens. After singing and acting, students are ready to settle down and hear about the food pyramid and how "you are what you eat."

Dewey Aerobics

The Dewey categories are difficult for most children to remember. We have signs on all our bookcases explaining the categories. We have played games with the Dewey categories and even had a scavenger hunt. But the most effective method I have found for helping children remember their way around the library is an action-packed story.

I tell the following story to teach the Dewey categories by associating them with body parts. Then I point out the part and have students name the section. You also can play Simon Says by saying things such as "Simon says to reach for the 500s, Animals and Natural Science." All should touch their neck. The students themselves become Dewey guides.

Begin with the area above the top of the head as you start with the 000's. This is what we remember about each.

000—Generalities—above the head
This section includes so many different things that one body can't hold them all, so it is "over our head."

100—Philosophy—point to the brain
This section contains things we wonder about, such as Big Foot, UFOs, and optical illusions.

200—Religion and Mythology—eyes
These topics are taken on faith, not on what we can see.

300—Social Sciences, Holidays, Folktales—smile
Celebrations make us smile, and sometimes folktales do as well.

400—Languages—mouth
Around the world we all speak, though the words may sound different.

500—Animals and Natural Science—neck (giraffe)
We make sure students know what else is in this section besides animals, but the 500s are best known for animals.

600—Applied Science—shoulders (shoulder to the grindstone)
In this section are the books that explain how people take what they know and apply it to make something.

700—Arts and Crafts, Music—hands (clap)
We use hands to draw and to do magic, origami, and calligraphy. We also use them to applaud the performances of others and to make music.

800—Poetry, Plays, Jokes, and Riddles—heart
We talk about how these kinds of books often come from the heart as well as the mind.

900—History and Geography—feet (stomp)
Our feet and the books in this section can take us to other places or back in time.

Biography—Books About Real People—whole body from head to toe
The people in this section were human just like us. But they accomplished things that made them famous.

Creative Dramatics

Whenever you act out a story without memorizing a script, you are doing creative dramatics. We do it from simple dramatics to complicated ones.

Make a simple origami frog to accompany Robert Kalan's *Jump, Frog, Jump* (Greenwillow, 1981). Find the directions and patterns for the frog in Robert Lang's *Origami Animals* (Crescent Books, 1992) or at the Web site called *Jumping Frog* <www.users.waitrose.com/~pureland/frog.gif>. Each time you read the question on the page, "How did the frog get away?" students act out the refrain with their frogs. Or, if you have enough room, allow students to be the frogs, jumping in place at the refrain. Before doing this, be sure to model the frog behavior and discuss the consequences of poor frog actions!

Use actions to help students remember the sequence of a plot. Assign an action, such as snapping fingers for the hero and hissing for the villain, to accompany each character's name. Students perform each action as you say the person's name throughout the story.

Pantomime is a good physical activity. Students can act out the parts as you read. They can use only their bodies and faces, not their voices. Assign parts of the group to each character or allow each student to act out the entire story. We found that good stories for this are *Cook-a-Doodle-Doo!* by Janet Stevens (Harcourt Brace, 1999), William Steig's *Pete's a Pizza* (HarperCollins, 1998), or a scene selected by the students. Our older students have chosen scenes from Christopher Paul Curtis' Newbery winner *Bud, Not Buddy* (Delacorte, 1999) and from the various Harry Potter books by J. K. Rowling.

Full dramatics are appropriate for Jan Brett's *The Mitten* (Putnam, 1989) and *Gingerbread Baby* (Putnam, 1999), or Kathy Parkinson's *The Enormous Turnip* (Whitman, 1986). Whether students improvise the actions or wear character masks and perform directed actions, they will enjoy the change of pace and will more easily remember the plots of the stories.

Performance Without Practice

There's a bit of a show-off in all of us, and I've discovered there's a lot of show-off in children. Many of them enjoy being the center of attention, especially if it is fun and makes them look good. Such a way of spotlighting children in a positive light is Readers' Theater.

RT, as it is nicknamed, is exactly like real theater minus the sets, costumes, makeup, rehearsals, and memorization. All you need is a set of scripts and a group of students. Scripts are readily available. Simply make the appropriate copies, highlight the character's part on each script, and select the readers.

One way to assign parts is to tape numbers on the backs of student chairs. Assign arbitrary numbers to characters. When a student sits in a particular chair, he or she will have that part. If a student does not wish to participate, he or she can choose a replacement.

We begin our RT event with a humorous script from Caroline Feller Bauer's book *Presenting Readers' Theater: Plays and Poems to Read Aloud* (Wilson, 1996). "The Emperor's Prized Possession" is short, funny, and involves the audience with their own participatory sounds. Students are highly motivated and clamor for their turn. We have done more serious plays, but the best introduction to RT is a humorous one.

RT is a great reading motivator, particularly for older students. It can be done impromptu by simply assigning parts and reading the scripts. Providing students with a hat or other bit of costume often puts them more readily into character. Students can add actions or adopt a special voice.

◄

The story of the *Titanic* and its tragic sinking is a powerful one to share with your older students, particularly reluctant readers. Aileen Kirkham has written an RT script for grades 2-5 about the people on the *Titanic*. It is a 15-minute play told by 13 characters. The script is available for $10. The characters include family members from first-class, members of the crew, and immigrants from steerage. Order from Aileen Kirkham, 13611 Lost Creek Road, Tomball, TX 77375.

Sources for Scripts

Suzanne Barchers has written short scripts grouped by reading levels in *Fifty Fabulous Fables: Beginning Readers Theatre* (Teacher Ideas Press, 1997). Her previous book, *Readers Theatre for Beginning Readers* (Teacher Ideas Press, 1993), has 20 scripts based on fables and folktales for grades 1-3.

Anthony D. Fredericks has published two books for Teacher Ideas Press. *Frantic Frogs and Other Frankly Fractured Folktales for Readers Theater* (1993) and *Tadpole Tales and Other Totally Terrific Treats for Readers* (1997) provide scripts for readers of all abilities. *Frantic Frogs* has fractured adaptations of fairy tales for grades 4-8. Your younger readers will enjoy the 25 scripts, based on Mother Goose and fairy tales, found in *Tadpole Tales*.

You can even tap your students' dramatic streak in the curricular areas. Your students who enjoy writing can adapt science and history to RT scripts. Use Kendall Haven's *Great Moments in Science: Experiments and Readers Theater* (Teacher Ideas Press, 1996) as examples.

If you need guidelines for performing RT, count on author Aaron Shepard. You can use his online tips (see sidebar) or use the information and scripts in his book *Stories on Stage: Scripts for Readers' Theater* (H.W. Wilson, 1993).

▶

Aaron Shepard's RT at <www.aaronshep.com/rt/index.html> includes over two dozen ready-to-print RT scripts for folktales as well as articles on storytelling and other topics. Students may prefer to use ready-made scripts, possibly as a follow-up to writing their own.

Judy Sierra provides activities and scripts for cultural awareness that will meet the needs of your visual and interpersonal learners. *Multicultural Folktales for the Feltboard and Readers' Theater* (Oryx, 1996) can be used as scripts for readers, to perform for visual learners, or to perform by kinesthetic learners on the flannel board. Nancy Polette has written 19 cultural folktales into scripts and included multicultural activities in *Reading the World with Folktales* (Book Lures, 1993).

Scripts Created by Students

Students can write their own scripts based on books they have read. Picture books can be summarized in a script. Students can dramatize a single episode from a chapter book. Nancy Polette has written scripts based on scenes from children's books that can serve as examples to your young writers. Look for Polette's book *Readers Theatre Booktalks* (Book Lures, 1994).

Aaron Shepard provides guidelines for rewriting in his Web site (see sidebar). He explains what to leave out, what to add, and how to stage the story so it stays faithful to the author's intent, but is enjoyable for a viewing audience. To make it easier for beginners to practice, he also provides one-page summaries of his own stories. Students can mark on the sheets, deleting tag lines and excessive description, highlighting parts for each speaker, and putting actions into parentheses to be included in the script as stage directions.

We used Aesop's fables as practice because they are short and complete in a single page. Here is my adaptation of "The Lion and the Mouse." Remember that copyright laws protect a modern author's story. If adults adapt an authored story, they must get the author's permission first. Students have more leeway, but if they perform it for money, they must get permission from the

author as well. In all cases, give credit for the original work in the program or as a narrator's speech at the beginning of the performance.

"The Lion and the Mouse"
(an adaptation by Pat Miller from the fable by Aesop)

Narrator 1: Long ago, when the earth began, animals could speak to one another.

Narrator 2: In the cool shade of an African jungle, a young mouse was playing near a large, sleeping lion.

Narrator 3: He was having fun running up the lion's tail and jumping from his hip to his soft, floppy paws.

Mouse: Wheeee!

Lion: (roaring loudly) Who is it that has no respect for the king of the jungle?

Narrator 1: The lion placed his large paw on the young mouse, pinning him to the ground.

Mouse: Goodness, it's just me, a little mouse.

Lion: How dare you disturb my rest, you little pip-squeak. I should make a naptime snack of you!

Mouse: Forgive me, King, for I am young and inexperienced. If you will free me and give me a second chance, perhaps some day I can do a kindness for you.

Lion: How can a miserable miniature mouse be of help to the royal lion of the jungle?

Mouse: You never know, Your Highness, but I will not forget your kindness.

Narrator 2: The lion was so amused at the courage of the little mouse beneath his huge paw that he let him go.

Narrator 3: The mouse wasted no time rushing to the edge of the clearing, but before he ducked from sight, he waved to the lion.

Mouse: I won't forget!

Narrator 1: Some time later, the lion was caught in a hunter's trap.

Narrator 2: He was completely snared in a heavy net that had swept him up and was now hanging from a tree.

Narrator 3: The lion's roars of anger were fearful to hear, and no animal dared get close to the furious king.

Narrator 1: No one, that is, except the mouse.

Mouse: Here I am, King. I've come to help you and return a favor for your sparing my life.

Lion: I don't see how such a tiny creature can save me, but please try.

Narrator 2: The mouse jumped to the bottom of the mesh and began chewing on the rope with his sharp teeth.

Narrator 3: It took several hours, but the mouse did not give up. Finally, he gnawed a hole big enough for the lion to slip through.

Lion: You were right, little mouse. I should not judge my friends by their size, but by their actions.

Action Rhymes

Some action rhymes are done with just the fingers and are called fingerplays. Others involve hand movements and body actions. Think of the rhymes we loved as children and find ways to incorporate them into your lessons. We began a study of infectious diseases (just before cold and flu season) with the performance of "Ring a Round of Rosies." This rhyme refers to the wearing of medicinal herbs around the neck during the bubonic plague of the Middle Ages. We then talked about more helpful precautions for avoiding illness, such as vaccinations, washing hands often, covering sneezes and coughs, and other healthful practices. We followed the discussion with a reading of Susan Perry's book *A Cold Is Nothing to Sneeze At* (Child's World, 1993).

We all know the actions for "The Itsy Bitsy Spider" and "This Old Man." Use fingerplays to introduce your story or subject. Explore the ones your students already know and share the following resources:

I Saw Esau: The Schoolchild's Pocket Book. Edited by Iona and Peter Opie. Candlewick Press, 1992. This book contains 170 childhood rhymes, including jump rope rhymes, tongue twisters, riddles, and jeers.

1001 Rhymes & Fingerplays. Warren Publishing House, 1994. Rhymes are grouped in categories, such as "Me and My Community," "Nature," and "Celebrations and Special People."

Brown, Marc. *Play Rhymes.* Puffin, 1993. Small illustrations beside each line show the hand motions for 12 finger plays.

Cole, Joanna. *Anna Banana: 101 Jump-Rope Rhymes.* Morrow Junior Books, 1989. The 101 rhymes include childhood favorites, such as the rope starter rhyme, "Bluebells, cockle shells, Eevy, Ivy, over."

Virtual Tours

Field trips can be excellent learning experiences for all students, particularly the more active learners. Nothing compares with firsthand experience, especially if it involves hands-on activities and exposure to artifacts. In our district, students are allowed one field trip per year, and the trip is limited to places the buses can reach between the times of the scheduled school pickup and delivery routes. Needless to say, we are severely limited in our "on-the-spot" learning activities.

It's not comparable in activity, but well-planned field trips via computer can be instructive and fun. Gail and Garry Cooper have written a helpful book called *Virtual Field Trips* (Libraries Unlimited, 1997). The trips are arranged by topics, including "Historic Time Travel" (Olympics, *Titanic*), "Worldwide Travel" (33 countries, Mt. Everest), and museums and libraries of all kinds. Field trips for primary grades include an anthill, Mr. Rogers' Neighborhood, and Professor Bubbles' Bubblesphere. All sites are annotated.

The Internet lets you take virtual field trips to places that fit all areas of the curriculum. Suggest some of these to teachers who wish to venture outside the walls of their classrooms.

Trips for Writers

Welcome to Shakey's Place!
<library.advanced.org/10502>
Visit the Globe Theatre to find out about the life of Shakespeare. Read summaries of plays, production notes, and the full text of his plays and sonnets. There are pictures, other Shakespeare resources, a bulletin board, and a chat room. Don't leave without trying the games and puzzles.

Pilkey's Web Site O' Fun <www.pilkey.com>
Fans of the Dumb Bunnies and Captain Underpants will enjoy visiting Dav's site. He has posted his autobiography in cartoon form. He has included puzzles, trivia games, and printable coloring pages of some of Dav's most popular characters.

The United Nations Cyber School Bus <www.un.org/Pubs/CyberSchoolBus>
Visit the United Nations and get involved in world social concerns. This site contains resources for teachers and students, such as games, puzzles, activities, and lesson plans. Students may enjoy reading this site in French or Spanish.

Trips for Artists

The Tokugawa Art Museum <www.cjn.or.jp/tokugawa/index.html>
Visit this art museum through pictures and sounds. You also can view the site in Japanese.

The Louvre
In this virtual museum of the 350 rooms of the Paris museum, you can see over 1,500 pieces of art and their descriptions. You also can take the Paris virtual tour at this site.

The Metropolitan Museum of Art <www.metmuseum.org/home.asp>
This is the largest art museum in the United States. On this virtual tour, you can view 3,500 works of art. The site includes educational resources and a search engine.

Cartoon Corner <www.cartooncorner.com>
In our library, the *Calvin and Hobbes* books by Bill Watterson (Andrews, McMeel and Parker) are some of our most popular books. At this site, students can learn to draw cartoons, discover what a cartoonist does, and read the comic strips of Emmett Scott.

At Home in the Heartland Online <www.museum.state.il.us/exhibits/athome>
Students can travel through time to experience family life during five time periods, beginning in 1700. Resources include primary documents, maps, and lesson plans. This site is sponsored by the Illinois State Museum.

Mind Trips

Gallery of Interactive Geometry <www.geom.umn.edu/apps/gallery.html>
Play with geometry with this virtual exhibit of 10 geometric puzzle-type situations.

The Money Game: World School Investment Challenge <www.moneygame.com>
Students can become virtual investment managers through this simulation game.

Lemonade Stand <www.littlejason.com/lemonade>
This is another simulation to give children real-world math experiences. Players are given $5 to start their lemonade stand, and have to pay rent, advertising costs, and the cost of the lemonade. Based on daily weather reports, players must decide how much lemonade to make and how much to spend on advertising.

Smithsonian Institution <www.si.edu>
Museums at this site appeal to each of the intelligences. Students can visit 17 museums, including the Space Museum, The Museum of African Art, and the Zoo. Older students might want to tour the 11 research centers online at this site.

Time and Place Travel

Virtual Boston: Freedom Trail <www.vboston.com/VBoston/Content/FreedomTrail/Index.cfm>
This virtual tour of Boston's Freedom Trail takes you to 18 of Boston's most famous points of historic interest, including the Bunker Hill Monument and the *U.S.S. Constitution*.

Old Sturbridge Village <www.osv.org/pages/descrip.htm>
Learners can take an online tour of Old Sturbridge Village in Massachusetts. Through text, graphics, maps, and audio downloads, students can see and hear village life in the 1830s.

A Day in the Life of Thomas Jefferson <www.monticello.org/Day/jefferson/sunrise/home.html>
You can spend a day at Monticello with Thomas Jefferson. Visit Jefferson's office, tour his farm, stroll in the gardens, and even have breakfast and dinner with him in the dining room.

Lower East Side Tenement Museum <www.wnet.
org/tenement>
This totally interactive site depicts life in a New
York City tenement from 1870-1915. By clicking
on the windows of the tenement, vignettes of
day-to-day life are presented graphically with
accompanying text.

The Virtual Field Trips Site <www.field-guides.com>
This site is useful for scientific virtual field
trips. You can visit deserts, oceans, salt marsh-
es, volcanoes, and natural wonders of the
world. You also can virtually investigate fierce
creatures, tornadoes, and sharks.

Classroom Connect <classroom.com>
The Quests are live and available by subscription ($109.95 for one classroom license) at this
site. In the past, students have accompanied
Quest teams as they investigated why the
ancient Anasazi people abandoned their
dwellings. Students could follow in the footsteps
of Marco Polo to see if he really traveled all the
way across the great Silk Road.
You can take CyberTrips to Egypt, Paris, Kenya,
Mount Everest, or Washington DC with the 64-
page curricular guides and related resource
Web sites, also from Classroom Connect. Each
CyperTrip costs only $54.95 and makes 18 tour
stops that emphasize the geography, history,
and culture of the place visited.

Musical Trips

Cyberkids <www.cyberkids.com>
The *Cyberkids* site contains original works of
fine and performing art by young artists from all
over the world.

Fit Trips

Ancient Olympic Games Virtual Museum <devlab.
dartmouth.edu/olympic>
What were the ancient Olympics really like? You
will find lots of information here about these
forerunners of our modern Olympic games.
Visitors can go from room to room at this virtual
museum and learn about the history, contests,
and anecdotes of the ancients. This site also
includes a slide show of modern Greece.

As you prepare lessons for the library or with
the teacher for the classroom, don't forget active
learning. Just as smells can bring back memories
that often have been forgotten, movement—
whether real or virtual—can make learning more
permanent.

Tender Loving Care

Odds are that you are the only person at your school who teaches every child and assists every teacher. No matter where you are in the continuum, from totally traditional to completely computerized, you provide a key element that never becomes outdated: your personal touch.

Do you integrate technology into lessons you plan with teachers? Do you provide resources, suggest Web sites, and co-teach lessons? All these are powerful ways to become useful to your overworked colleagues. However, nothing seems to build support and goodwill more than old-fashioned tender loving care.

Try a few of the ideas in this chapter to spoil your faculty and notice how teacher involvement with library programs increases. Whether they are word smart, logic smart, or body smart, all teachers appreciate your being heart smart and doing considerate things for them and their students.

Render Personalized Service

Many of your teachers, particularly the new ones, may not know what an asset you are. At the beginning of the school year, make business cards for each teacher, using a word processing program and sheets of perforated cards from an office supply store. Use a template from *Microsoft Publisher* or an inexpensive business card program. Once the school address, phone, and fax are put into the template, it's a simple matter of changing teacher names. Provide a blank for teachers to write in their individual e-mail addresses. Print two or three sheets for each teacher.

Attach a note to the sheets of business cards saying, "Let us personalize your library service!" Follow that with a list of many of the things you can do for teachers to help them with lesson planning and instruction. After we printed this list on colorful computer paper and distributed it, we had many teachers visit the library to say thanks for the business cards and to take advantage of the services we had promoted.

FREE BOOK!

*We received
your list of Reading Favorites!
In appreciation of your
timely participation, please
redeem this coupon at our next
Book Fair.*

(value $_____)

Teacher: _____

Signed: _____

Book Fair Coupon

Personalized Service List

Share Teacher Favorites

You can increase student interest in your
library collection by publishing lists of their teachers' favorites. For Children's Book Week or
National Library Week, ask teachers to provide a
list of 20 of their favorite children's books.
Request that they name titles that are available in
your library. Type each list in a bookmark form.
Under a treasure chest filled with books or a similar picture, add the title "Mrs. _____'s Favorite
Books." Make copies for each class of their
teacher's list and give them to the teachers to dis-

tribute during a national reading week. They may
want to do an impromptu booktalk before giving
bookmarks to students.

As an incentive for teachers to participate
promptly, give them a free book coupon for your
next book fair. If you don't have a book fair coming
up, allow them to choose from a box of paperbacks you maintain for prizes. We had high
teacher participation, numerous student requests
for books, and positive parent comments.

Seek To Relieve Stress

Special attention is most appreciated during
times of stress. To boost teacher morale and to
attract attention to the library during the hectic
weeks before the Christmas holiday, invite your
staff to the library for spiced cider and cookies. I
bought a large tin of fancy European cookies,
made the cider in a Crock-Pot, and set out plates,
cups, and napkins on a festive cloth. I provided
several comfortable chairs and quiet seasonal
music in the background. Holiday books were featured as a backdrop for the refreshments. This
inexpensive treat provided a needed break as well
as some handy quick reads for busy days.
Something similar could be done for Valentine's
Day or before spring break.

Offer Coupons

A handmade coupon book given to me by one
of my own preschoolers inspired me to design one
for each teacher for the New Year. Here is a sample of ideas:

▲ I will teach a lesson in your classroom.

▲ Good for one guest read-aloud by me

▲ Exchange for chocolate from the library

▲ Good for $1 off at the book fair

▲ Redeem for an extra 30-minute library class.

The cover of the coupon book is a bookmark,
and all coupons expire by the middle of May. This
approach initiates communication, gets you into
the classrooms, and brings teachers to you to
claim your services.

Spoil Your Support Staff

Some of your best allies are your school secretary and the custodians. Don't forget to be kind to them. Send cards on their birthdays. You can do this electronically if they use a computer, but I prefer to mail them to their homes. In this day of e-mail, voice mail, and faxes, people are pleased to see something personal in their stack of bills in the mailbox. Include a coupon redeemable at your upcoming book fair or a gift certificate to a local bookstore.

Every now and then, leave a treat on your desk for the custodian who cleans up your library. Bring a cake for the whole custodial staff on major holidays. Publicly thank them and the secretary for their help by including them in your newsletter. Give them a discount at your book fair just as you do with your teachers. Make a bulletin board to thank the "elves" who mysteriously appear and clean your library, cart away your book boxes, and keep you looking good!

Find Reasons to Celebrate

When you receive a large delivery of new books, celebrate with your teachers. Send them an invitation to see your new arrivals. Make the invitation like one for a baby shower. Set the new books on counter tops as well as in baby seats, bathtubs, and strollers borrowed from some of your young mothers. Add refreshments and perhaps a door prize or two. Be prepared to point out relevant books for each grade level.

You can show teachers some personal attention by remembering their birthdays. For that special day, place a bookplate in the book of their choice from your collection. For summer or holiday birthdays, ask teachers to select an "unbirthday." Then visit the class on the birthday to read it aloud. This is a hit with students as well as teachers. Teachers will enjoy your thoughtfulness and the quiet read-aloud time, and the only cost is the bookplates. Make a public announcement the morning of the birthday so everyone can wish the teacher well throughout the day.

You
are
invited
to see
our
newest
arrivals

Outside of Invitation

Our new books
Are here,
And we'd like you
To meet them!

Date: _____

Time: _____

Place: Library

Refreshments will be served

Inside of Book Shower Invitation

Teacher Birthday Book Certificate

Buying cards for staff members'
birthdays may be a bit much for your
budget. You can use desktop publishing programs
to make them a personalized card. Or, try sending
them a digital card that will sing and dance on their
computer desktop! You can select cards at this address:
Blue Mountain Arts <www.bluemountain.com>. This
site also provides cards for Jewish, Muslim, Hindu,
Buddhist, Native American, Baha'i, and
Christian major religious holidays.

Library Medicine

Tension is highest for most teachers during the week of state achievement tests, but you can provide a stress remedy. About two weeks prior to the tests, put a plastic medicine bottle filled with candy in each teacher's mailbox. Buy the bottles from a nearby pharmacy and add a label. Under the name of your library, spell RELIEF vertically in capital letters. For each letter, name resources or services in the library that are suitable for the test week. Library relief also can be used to introduce the library at the beginning of the year or to relieve the doldrums of late winter.

On each label, add an Rx for two refills. If teachers bring their bottles back to the library, refill them with candies. Your "patients" may appreciate any resources or services you mention as you supply them with more sweets. Each refill gives you an opportunity to become invaluable to your colleagues and to lift their spirits by your kindness.

Give More Than They Request

Teachers are often unaware of the multitude of resources available in your media center. One tool that will help them is a library brochure listing a variety of services (page 65-66).

Walker Station
School Library

We are eager to serve you!

Library Staff:

Pat Miller
Librarian

Sandy Henson
Assistant

281-634-4406

Teachers and Librarians
Working Together

How can we help?

- Pull resources for your units

- Teach you and your students to use our magazine database, our online catalog, and the Internet.

- Give booktalks by genre, subject, curriculum topic, or author

- Co-plan lessons that can be taught in your room or ours.

- Work with your research projects to teach students the Big Six problem-solving model

- Do read-alouds, puppet shows, Readers' Theater, creative dramatics, or other reading promotions with your students.

- Borrow materials for you from Region IV ESC and interlibrary loan.

How you can help:

- Let us know what units you are studying, and assignments students will be researching.

- Contact us when you need to order videotapes, instructional materials, or books. We can help!

- Sign up for flexible classes for instruction or research.

- Let us help you plan for multi-media productions with the digital or video cameras, *HyperStudio*, or *KidPix*

- When your overhead bulb burns out, send down the entire cart and machines. We'll clean it and put in a fresh bulb.

- We can tape programs for you from *Cable in the Classroom* participants. Plan with us.

- Schedule changes? Let us know how we can accommodate you.

- We can provide Internet sites, CD-ROMs and computer training if you plan with us in advance.

Special Events

November
Fall Book Fair
Grandparents' Day

March:
Spring Book Fair

May:
Book Swap
Discovery Fair

June-July:
Tuesday/Thursday afternoons
Summer Library

Each grade level will be visited by at least one author.

We will have special activities for Children's Book Week (Nov) and National Library Week (April).

Celebrating a birthday? Contact us to arrange for a visit from the Birthday Bear by donating a book to the library

Additional Information

Region IV ESC Film Library delivers videotapes every Monday and Thursday evening.

Videotapes can be ordered from the catalog or online at <www.media.esc4.net>. Films can be kept for one week. See us for ordering assistance.

Laminating is done in the VIPS room on Tuesdays and Thursdays.

We have still cameras, a digital camera and a camcorder for check out. You supply your own film, videotape, and developing costs.

We use Reading Counts (Electronic Bookshelf), a reading incentive program. We will train you or your class in its use as needed.

We also partner with Pizza Hut for Book It! and with Six Flags over Texas to do 600 Minutes.

Resources A-Z

Alphabet books
Big books
Computers on wheels
Dictionary sets
Encyclopedias
Friendly assistance
Great book collection
Happy to get books for you on interlibrary loan
Internet access and instruction
Just ask us!
Kid-friendly programs
Laser discs
Magazine database
Newspapers
Online catalog
Presentations to order
Quick online video orders from Region IV
Recorders for audio tapes
Slide projectors
Transparencies
Unlimited patience
Videotapes
Welcoming facility
Xtra hands when needed
Yes, we can help
Zest for lifelong learning!

Learn to use your automated system to provide bibliographies for teachers. Make them on requested topics and keep a copy in a large binder. Run bibliographies for summer or holiday reading lists for students. Teachers value media lists, especially listed in Dewey order. My teachers have lists of our big books, videos, and software arranged by subject. These are kept with their plan books, and I always bring a set to our collaborative planning meetings.

Develop a materials request form for uniformity and make the forms readily available to teachers. If you have a networked computer system, make sure your form is available from the network, e-mail, or your library web page.

Along with bibliographies, keep lists of topical film orders if you order them from a centralized education service center. Next year, when teachers want that great video on African-American history that they used, simply pull out the order form, change the dates, and resubmit. Be sure to investigate whether your service center has a Web site. It may have the resource inventory online, allowing you to search by keyword, read summaries on screen, and order.

◄

To keep your bibliographies and other lists organized, use preprinted alphabetical tabs available from your local office supply store. They also are found in some library supply catalogs.

Teacher _____**Date** _____

MATERIALS REQUEST FORM

Subject _____

Topic _____

Length of Unit _____ Start Date _____

I need the following:

☐ co-planned lessons (Best time to plan _____)

☐ books

    approximate number _____

    reading level(s) _____

    fiction? _____   nonfiction? _____   picture books? _____

☐ reference materials

☐ videotapes

☐ display space in library

☐ research time in the library (Suggested times: _____)

☐ Web sites

☐ computer time

☐ other requests or needs:

_____

_____

_____

Materials Request Form

Provide at least one Web site for each topic requested by teachers. Keep a copy of these in your bibliography folder as well. Make it a habit to pull resources not only from your shelves, but also from the Internet, periodicals, professional books, and even interlibrary loan.

our procedures, such as overnight circulation of magazines and subject labels on every library shelf, came from our students' suggestions.

Teacher _____ Date _____

Unit Topic: _____

Have you seen this?

I thought this site might be helpful for you and/or your students:

Title: _____

URL: _____

Notes: _____

_____

_____

_____

Internet Site Suggestion Form

Write notes, making a suggestion or two, and attach them to a book or other resource. Give teachers at least one more item than they requested. They will appreciate your keeping them in mind, and you will be building a rapport that may lead to increased collaboration.

Solicit Input

Students and teachers feel more ownership in the library when they help to select the books and other materials. Provide students and teachers a way to suggest books they would like for you to buy or borrow from other libraries. If you do use interlibrary loan, keep a list of books borrowed and plan to buy those that are in print if you think they will be needed again.

Have a suggestion book in the library with suggestion forms and pencils. Inform students, possibly through your library newsletter or web page, of how you act on their suggestions. Some of

Fill Requests

Occasionally, spoil your patrons by going to the bookstore to get an item that is in demand. If your budget supports such an idea, you'll find that timeliness often makes up for less desirable bindings. When Marc Brown's *Arthur* books were read aloud to our kindergartners, we ran out of copies. It was worth the trip to our local bookstore for more paperback copies to see how happy every child was to get one. When I bought Brown's *Arthur's Underwear* (Little Brown, 1999) the day it was released, my students were thrilled.

If you choose to buy the book suggested by a patron, alert him or her when the requested material arrives. We use the same form, printed on card stock, for book requests, interlibrary loans, and notification that a book on hold is available. Attach the form directly to the book. Unless the student has an overdue book, we check out the book and leave it in the homeroom teacher's box. It is a real treat for them to receive a book they specially requested.

Your Book Is Here!

Here is the book you requested:

☐ to be held   ☐ from interlibrary loan   ☐ for purchase

Student Name _____

Homeroom Teacher _____

Please return by _____

Remember that others may be waiting for this book, so return promptly. Thanks!

Book Request Form

Assist Parents

Is your library open to your school community? Our parents can check out five books per child. Borrowers at our school library include live-in grandparents, nannies, sitters, and work-at-home parents. Our public library is not close, and we serve the needs of home schooling families, older families whose grandchildren come to visit, and families with children not yet in school. We loan books to anyone in our attendance zone on the strength of a completed information form. We have lost only a handful of books over the last nine years, but have circulated thousands of books that would have remained on the shelves. The goodwill in the neighborhood is well worth the books lost.

Provide helpful Internet addresses to families in your library newsletter. Families without computers can access those in your library or in the public library, though computers are becoming as popular as televisions in many homes. Addresses to begin with are the *Homework Central* family of sites <www.bigchalk.com>, divided by grade levels. These sites provide more than 14,000 lesson plans, a site for parents only, and helpful links for hundreds of curricular areas needed by students for assignments.

Another useful parent site is *Education Central* (K-12) at <www.parentsoup.com/edcentral>. It includes Chats, Boards, Experts, Resources, and Fun and Games. Topics include raising gifted children, ADD/ADHD, home schooling, college costs, and developmental milestones. This large site can be searched by subject and by age group.

If you have school e-mail, be sure to give your address to parents. It's one more way to communicate with your students' first teachers. Mounting a library Web page is an even more effective way to keep parents informed.

If you are not yet ready to develop a Web page, be sure you have a library newsletter that goes home to parents. Use it to recognize book donors, include student reviews, feature new books, and publicize library lessons, programs, and author visits. Perhaps you have a technically gifted parent volunteer who would do this for you. I e-mail my articles to a work-at-home mother, and she converts them into a beautifully illustrated newsletter that comes out each grading period.

Support Technology Efforts

Teachers are at various stages in their technology development, particularly about computers. You can support them in their efforts by providing means for training. For the word smart, provide the following books:

Benson, Allen C. *Connecting Kids and the Internet: A Handbook for Librarians, Teachers and Parents.* From Internet safety to curricular integration, this book covers all the basics.

Classroom Connect: The K-12 Educator's Practical Guide to Using the Internet Commercial Online Services <www.classroom.com>. (magazine) This newsletter, issued nine times annually,

◄

Two excellent sites for learning to develop a Web page are *Writing HTML for Teachers* <www.mcli.dist. maricopa.edu/tut> and *How To Create a Home Page* <shianet.org/info/ create.html>. Both are nontechnical sites that will have you designing a respectable, basic Web page.

contains short articles that are easily understood and applied, and many useful Web sites.

Fleck, Tim. *HyperStudio for Terrified Teachers: Grades 3-5*. This book has two main sections: a tutorial that teaches *HyperStudio* to yourself and your students, and a student project section that gives you ideas and examples for integrating this powerful tool into instruction.

Handler, Marianne G., Ann S. Dana & Jane Peters Moore. *Hypermedia as a Student Tool: A Guide for Teachers*. This edition includes lessons involving hypermedia across the content areas, and how to use the World Wide Web as a research tool and source for visuals in hypermedia programs.

Holden, Greg. *Creating Web Pages for Kids and Parents*. I figured that a guide to creating Web pages for kids ages 7-15 would be just what I need to do my own! Included is a disk with copyright-free graphics and lots of hints and explanations. You will have a Web page when you use this book.

MultiMedia Schools: A Practical Journal of Multimedia, CD-ROM Online & Internet in K-12. This journal is published five times annually by Information Today, Inc. The subtitle says it all.

Schrock, Kathleen and Midge Frazel. *Microsoft Publisher for Every Day of the School Year*. In this slim book, Schrock covers the basics of *Microsoft Publisher* in 69 pages, followed by 65 pages of ideas. Included is a CD-ROM that contains 180 templates of school-related items to adapt or to stimulate ideas for other uses of the program.

▶ *HyperStudio* users may want to subscribe to *HyperStudio Forum, The Newsletter of the HyperStudio Network*, published by Roger Wagner Publishing. For an annual fee of $29, you receive four issues of the magazine and a "Best of HyperStudio" disk. You also can subscribe to their e-zine (e-magazine) entitled *eForum*. The e-mail address is *DavidC99@aol.com*. Write in the subject box: eForum; in the body box: your name and e-mail address. You will hear back from them within a few days.

▶ Share experiences and questions with thousands of your colleagues worldwide through the listserv, LM_NET, for school librarians. To subscribe, send an e-mail message to listserv@listserv.syr.edu. In the first line of the message, type: SUBSCRIBE LM_NET First Name Last Name. Send the message, and within the hour, you will receive confirmation and directions for posting and using the archives.

Williams, Robin and John Tollett. *The Non-Designer's Web Book*. Sixteen chapters take you from reasons for a Web page and sound Web design to registering your site. Each chapter concludes with a quiz (answers in the back), and jargon is minimal.

If teachers want their own copies to highlight, supply them with ordering information. Make a bookmark that lists the names, phone numbers, and Web addresses (if available) of local bookstores. Include the number or Web address of an out-of-print book resource as well. End with a paragraph about how to order, including using the ISBN number.

Those with strong logical/mathematical and intrapersonal intelligences may enjoy learning technology over the Internet. Free classes are available, and many of them are brief and developed for novices. More formal classes are offered for a price. These can last several weeks. In some cases, they even can be counted towards a college degree. At Connected University by Classroom Connect, you can enroll and choose six-week classes from a list of 40. Go to their site at <www.classroom.com> for price listings and other learning opportunities for your staff. A 30-day free trial is available.

Those who have a well-developed interpersonal strength may learn better in a group with a teacher with whom to interact. Our local computer store offers one-day classes in a variety of programs and at three skill levels. I took all three levels of *Microsoft Word* to prepare for writing this book, and their trainers and workbook were invaluable. Check with your local leisure learning provider, community center, or YMCA. Even public libraries are offering computer classes. Take a friend and try one.

◀ At Online Class, <www.online class.com/General/strategies.html>, you can register for a two-week workshop called *Strategies for a Successful Online Adventure*. The course includes extensive reading material, guideli for integrating the Internet into the classroom, hel links on the World Wide Web, and an e-mail discus group of workshop participants. Cost is $95 and c size is limited to 30. You can take the class in your pajamas at midnight while munching on snacks and listening to your favorite CD.

► Help will even come to you! By e-mail subscription, you can receive the latest educational Web sites and discussions related to use of the Internet in K-12 education. Simply subscribe to *Classroom Connect Mailing List.* It is a free service, and also can ask questions, sign up for Internet Projects, and read archived postings. Send an e-mail to *crc-request@listserv.classroom.com.* In the body of the message, type "subscribe digest crc" without quotation marks. Friendly experts will be as close as your e-mail. Check out their *Connected Teacher* site for lesson plans, curricular ideas, and other time-savers.

Though we all are harried and overwhelmed by our tasks, the time and effort invested in these perks are definitely worth the return in goodwill and appreciation. They might be just the things that take you from invisible to invaluable. They will definitely make you a personal asset as well as a professional one.

Centers

More often in professional literature and at conferences, we are hearing more about learning styles and multiple intelligences. Our school, for example, was a Texas Mentor School for learning styles for several years. Now, we are making a greater effort to teach to the multiple intelligences (MI), the brainchild of Dr. Howard Gardner and other brain-based research.

Learning Styles

Learning styles are the preferred ways in which a student learns. The style includes the way information is processed and the types of environmental factors that are most conducive to learning for that person. There are numerous theories and models about the styles or modalities through which learners process and remember information. No longer do learning styles simply mean auditory, visual, or kinesthetic.

Rita and Kenneth Dunn developed a model, based on differing conditions, that includes the preferences students have for learning. The preferences are in the following areas:

▲ immediate environment (sound, heat, light, and design)

▲ emotionality (motivation, responsibility, persistence, and structure)

▲ sociological needs (self oriented, peer oriented, adult oriented, or combined ways)

▲ physical needs (perceptual preferences, time of day, food intake, and mobility)

► Today, some educators have determined six learning styles based on a combination of the basic three. Read more about these six learning styles, how to recognize them, and how to use them to deliver more effective instruction at *A Symphony of Learning Styles* <www.weac.org/kids/june96/styles.htm>.

Most often, we teach to our own learning strengths. Do you know which yours are? You can take a learning style inventory online. Answer them and submit your questionnaire to discover your learning style(s). It is most useful to identify your weaker styles so you can develop them. Go to this address to answer *Evaluating Your Learning Style* <webster.commnet.edu/faculty/~simonds/styles/intro2.htm>.

Multiple Intelligences

In 1983, Howard Gardner, Professor of Education at Harvard Graduate School of Education, presented his theory of multiple intelligences. Dr. Gardner was investigating the cognitive potentials in normal and gifted children as director of Harvard University's Project Zero. He also was interested in which parts of the brain controlled certain mental functions and their disturbance due to brain damage.

From this research, Dr. Gardner developed his theory of the criteria of an "intelligence." He also studied the abilities needed for a person to be successful in various careers and activities. In his book *Frames of Mind: The Theory of Multiple Intelligences* (Basic Books, 1993), he explained seven intelligences that he had discovered. His theory is that all people have several intelligences, one or two of which are very strong. This is due to the construction of the brain, the value placed on that intelligence by the culture, or the ways in which the person was taught. Teachers and librarians can help students use their minds better if they know and value the variety of ways in which each child learns.

Dr. Gardner believes that intelligences are developmental and will change as we mature. Capitalizing on the various intelligences of each student greatly increases the child's understanding of what he or she is learning. The child also can demonstrate that new knowledge in a variety of ways.

Verbal: *Crossword Puzzles* can be completed on your computer screen if you go to <www.mindfun.com/cross2.htm>.

Logic: *Mastermind* is played on screen the same way as the commercial game. Get it free at <www.javaonthebrain.com/java/mastermind>.

Musical: Everything you could possibly want to know about the piano, how to play it, its history, and many other things can be found at *Music Magic: A Piano Exploration* <library.thinkquest.org/15060/index.html>.

Kinesthetic: *The Fruit Game* <www.2020tech. com/fruit> is a deceptively tricky online game that has a simple goal: Be the last to pick a piece of fruit. Be warned—this game is addictive.

Intelligence	Skilled at:	Like to learn with:
Picture Smart	drawing, art, building, designing, daydreaming, visualizing, using color	illustrations, puzzles, costumes, displays, movies, pictures, visuals, charts, art of all kinds
Word Smart	decoding, memorizing facts, debating, vocabulary and word games, writing	reading, writing, speaking, telling stories
Logic Smart	doing experiments, solving problems working with numbers, asking questions, exploring patterns	categorizing and classifying, problems, sequences, reasoning
Body Smart	body language, sports, dancing, acting, crafts	manipulatives, movement, sensory exercises, hands-on tasks
Music Smart	playing an instrument, singing, musical expression, keeping time, responding to music	rhythm, melody, songs, music
Self Smart	being original, being aware of others and their feelings, intuitive, following instincts, setting goals, pursuing interests	working alone, individualized projects, self-paced instruction
Others Smart	understanding people, leading, organizing, communicating, mediating conflicts	working in groups, cooperating, interviewing, sharing project work

MI Resources

Walter McKenzie, Jr., educational consultant and instructor at Connected University <www.classroom.com>, has developed an extensive site called *I Think… Therefore… MI!* at <surfaquarium. com/im.htm>. Bookmark this site if you would like to set up a computer in your library media center as an MI interest center. McKenzie lists 10 sites for each intelligence. Here are some examples:

Visual: *Etch-A-Sketch* <www.www.etch-a-sketch.com>, based on the Ohio Art product, can be drawn on, using the mouse and buttons on the virtual game.

Here is a list of numerous works on the multiple intelligences, notably Howard Gardner's own works:

How Are Kids Smart? Multiple Intelligences in the Classroom. (videocassette) National Professional Resources, Inc., 1995.

Multiple Intelligences: The Theory in Practice. Basic Books, 1993.

Multiple Intelligences: Developing Intelligences for Greater Achievement. (two videocassettes and guidebook) Produced with David Lazear. The Journal, 1995.

David Lazear wrote a book in collaboration with Howard Gardner called *Teaching for Multiple Intelligences* (Phi Delta Kappa, 1992). Practical ideas are available in Anna O'Connor's book *Seven Windows to a Child's World: 100 Ideas for the Multiple Intelligences Classroom* (IRI/Skylight, 1994), Bruce Campbell is a practicing elementary teacher who has written *The Multiple Intelligences Handbook: Lesson Plans and More* (Campbell & Associates 1994). If you can afford only one book, invest in *Multiple Intelligences: The Complete MI Book*. This book, by Dr. Spencer Kagan and Miguel Kagan, contains thousands of ideas and reproducibles for using MI in your library or classroom.

Everyday Uses of MI

Once you become familiar with the different intelligences, you may find ways to make the simplest activities more accessible to all your readers. When you need silence, for example, you can ask for it in a variety of ways to connect with the strengths of all your students. One effective way is to say, "If you can hear my voice, please say, 'Shhhhhhh.'" You'll be amazed how quickly children will settle. Blinking the lights or holding up a quiet sign that uses a hand signal engages the visual learner.

When you need attention, teach students to watch for the *Follow the Librarian* game. Silently begin to touch your shoulders, then your nose. Then wiggle your hands while looking intently at each child. As soon as they catch on, they will imitate what you are doing. Soon you will have the attention of all your students, even your active kinesthetic learners.

Selecting a Book

In the busy life of the library, classes come and go, independent students need service, teachers request materials, the phone rings, and the computer goes down. There is not always time in a tight, fixed schedule to do full-fledged lessons that appeal to all the ways of learning. Even a flexible schedule does not always lend itself to a lengthy teaching time.

It will be helpful to your students, however, if you keep the different intelligences in mind any time you do a lesson. For example, we all talk to children about how to select a book their size. The five-finger method may work for those with a visu-

al strength. Those children are often aware that they have miscalled a word and can correlate that error to holding up a finger. If the child has five fingers up by the end of a page of text, the book is too difficult.

This method is not as successful with children who have not developed their visual and verbal strengths. When you plan this lesson, as any lesson, keep in mind that students will learn what is taught to their learning strengths, and if emotions can be raised during the lesson, learning will "stick" longer.

When I introduce the lesson on book choice to younger students, I rely on humor to make the point memorable, as well as to reach as many of the multiple strengths as I can. We compare book choice to trying on shoes. I bring in a variety of attractive shoes in different sizes and styles, from house slippers to fancy dress shoes for both male and female students. Some are baby shoes, and some are obviously adult shoes. I tell students that we are pretending that they have money to buy a pair of shoes and ask which they would like to have. I call on a student, ask which pair he likes, and lend that pair to the student. I tell the child that I expect to see him wearing the shoes at all times during school. Then I ask him to put on the shoes. He may discover the shoes do not fit, or they might be inappropriate for school.

Because this experience appeals to the kinesthetic and visual intelligences, students understand the comparison between fitting shoes and finding a book that fits. Logical students also appreciate the comparison, and when we talk about trying on a book with their eyes, they know what I mean.

We make a list of factors that influence our choice of shoes. My students have come up with fit, appearance, price, how well they will last, and color. Then we list the factors that influence our choice of books. They list interesting cover, right amount of pages, size of print, difficulty of words, and amount of illustrations.

We enact how they try on a pair of shoes and make observations. Then a student acts out choosing the right book, thinking aloud for the benefit of the group. This way of making the point appeals to students with an interpersonal intelligence. Seeing their classmates in action makes a stronger impression on students than my explanation.

For a few weeks, allow different students to

show the group how they would choose a book. Let them act out and explain why they would or would not choose from a variety of books you have set out for them. Make sure some are too hard, some too easy, some unappealing, and so on. Children enjoy watching their friends "teach," and there are always many volunteers willing to demonstrate this technique.

This is an example of an informal plan that appeals to many of the intelligences. The more you are aware of the characteristics of each intelligence and what appeals to each, the better you can make even the simplest of lessons reach more readers.

Teaching Students To Use Their Intelligences

Learning centers in the library meet the same needs they do in the classroom. Use them to reinforce skills, to provide interesting practice, and to convene a group to solve a problem together. Consider setting up seven areas in your library for the various intelligences. Centers can all revolve around a theme or can function independently. Here is a list of suggestions:

Visual: crafts, filmstrip in viewer, video

Verbal: books on tape, books

Math: games, problem solving situations, computer applications

Musical: cassettes and tape player, musical instruments, repetitive books, poetry

Interpersonal: puppets, scripts, games, computer simulations

Intrapersonal: books written in diary form

Kinesthetic: pop-up book, Eric Carle's novelty books, books with odd shapes

▶

Neuroscience for Kids <faculty.washington.edu/chudler/ neurok.html> shows, through text and graphics, the workings of the human brain and spinal cord. There are many follow-up activities and experiments, from making a "brain" to various games and puzzles.

Centers may incorporate numerous intelligences and can include manipulatives, task cards, a computer, or comfortable pillows with a selection of books. Include instructions, examples as appropriate, and needed materials at each center.

Reaching Every Reader

Each intelligence can be developed and is exhibited in the types of products students make as well as the types of assignments that interest them. Dr. Gardner, in his videotape *How Are Children Smart?* (National Professional Resources, 1995), explains that there is no one way to teach to the intelligences. Cooperative learning, thematic units, project-based instruction, inclusion, performances, and presentations all are sound methods.

Reading is a linear, visual/spatial skill. If we are going to turn on all students to reading, we will have to excite the nonvisual children through their other intelligences. Beginning on page 82, activities are presented that cover each of the intelligences; some cross several intelligences. Include activities that appeal to two or three intelligences when you design your lesson plans. You are the one who knows the wealth of resources in your library. Suggest varied activities that take advantage of your resources and all parts of the brain. When you are aware of the best ways to reach every reader, you can be a great asset to teachers as you plan cooperatively.

Planning Sheets

The next pages can be used when planning your own lessons. Take several with you when you are planning with teachers. Such a form will help you focus on at least three intelligences per lesson. Make a conscious effort to widen your teaching repertoire beyond your own intelligences—beyond the usual verbal or logical lessons that dominate today's classrooms. In that way, you will tap into the multiple intelligences of your students, and all of you will learn more than you thought possible.

Center Activity Planning Sheet (page 1)

Center Name:	Date(s) of use:	Grade(s):

Objectives

Multiple Intelligences

visual/spatial
verbal/linguistic
mathematical/logical
musical/rhythmic
interpersonal
intrapersonal
bodily/kinesthetic

Materials

Preparation

Evaluation

Center Activity Planning Sheet (page 2)

Center Name:	Date(s) of use:	Grade(s):

Activities	Bibliography

Sample Center Activity Planning Sheet

Center Name: Harvest Time	**Date(s) of use:** October 15-31 **Grade(s):** 2-3

Objectives

1. Know how corn and apples grow (plant cycle).
2. Compare/contrast types of apples.
3. Learn about the different uses of corn.
4. Role-play a scarecrow and learn its importance.
5. View modern farms and how food is produced and harvested.
6. Create a song about apple or corn harvesting.
7. Use an almanac to locate answers.
8. Observe and name a variety of apples.
9. Write a how-to sheet for scaring crows.
10. Research and list apple products.

Multiple Intelligences

<u>visual/spatial</u>
<u>verbal/linguistic</u>
<u>mathematical/logical</u>
<u>musical/rhythmic</u>
interpersonal
intrapersonal
bodily/kinesthetic

Materials

scarecrow, crow puppet, Indian corn, numerous (at least six) varieties of fresh apples, books and videos or film strips or TV/VCR, two FS viewers, sequence pictures, corn products, two slates, colored chalk, graph paper, pie graph paper, xylophone, drum, tape recorder, familiar song tapes, paper, pencils, colored pencils, markers or crayons

Prepare

answer sheet for the eight corn products, bags of corn products, copies of center worksheets (one per child or group)

Evaluation

Check against answer sheets or present to group to be scored with rubrics designed by the teacher, with class input if appropriate.

Sample Center Activity Planning Sheet (page 2)

Center Name: Harvest Time	**Date(s) of use:** October 15-31 **Grade(s):** 2-3

Activities

1. Set up two filmstrips or videos in two viewers. Students view while completing a list of two categories: same, different.
2. After reading *The Apple Tree* or listening to it on tape, students should arrange pictures in order.
3. Students should handle the following in zipped plastic bags. They can make guesses about which are which and record their guesses on a record page.
   corn oil, corn syrup, corn starch, corn meal, corn tortilla, corn flakes, corn pops, popcorn
4. Read the story *The Little Scarecrow Boy* or *Jeb Scarecrow's Pumpkin Patch*. Plan a play about a father scarecrow teaching his scarecrow children how to scare birds. Or, act out the book. Students may use crow puppets and scarecrow.
5. Create a work song to sing while picking apples or corn with at least three verses and a chorus.
6. Which states produce the most corn? The most apples? Make a bar graph of the top three states.
7. Arrange apples from smallest to largest. Sketch each apple, color it, and research its name.

Bibliography

Brown, Margaret Wise. *The Little Scarecrow Boy.* HarperCollins, 1998.

Dillon, Jana. *Jeb Scarecrow's Pumpkin Patch.* Houghton Mifflin, 1992.

Flanagan, Alice. *The Zieglers and Their Apple Orchard.* Childrens' Press, 1999.

Fowler, Allan. *Apples of Your Eye.* Children's Press, 1994.

Hall, Zoe. *The Apple Pie Tree.* Blue Sky Press, 1996.

Landau, Elaine. *Apples.* Children's Press, 1999.

Maestro, Betty. *How Do Apples Grow?* HarperCollins, 1992.

Saunders-Smith, Gail. *Apple Trees.* Pebble Books, 1998.

__. *Eating Apples.* Pebble Books, 1999.

On the next pages are center and lesson ideas for 12 topics addressed in the elementary curriculum. The first 10 are correlated to the months of school, beginning with *Teeth Tales* in August. This is a good get-acquainted topic for the first month of school. Pick a lesson or center, or implement all activities for each topic to appeal to all of the multiple intelligences and learning styles.

Teeth Tales

Subject: Science, Health

Grades: K-5

Hardware: computer with Internet connections, tape player

Software: music tapes or CD player and discs, handmade puppets

Pre-lesson Class Preparation: Gather supplies and books, and copy patterns and worksheets for selected activities. Make puppets for Activity Eight.

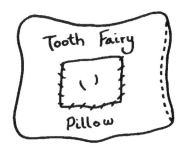

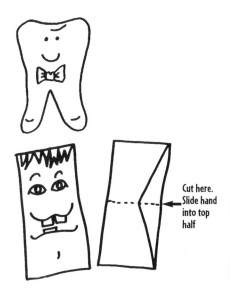

Cut here. Slide hand into top half

VISUAL CENTER

Activity One: Making a Tooth Fairy Pillow

Supplies:
(Per child) two 3-inch squares of felt, one 1-inch square of felt, batting or cotton balls, glue, and markers or paint

Evaluation:
None

Procedure:
1. Make a tooth fairy pillow. Paint or write the words "Tooth Fairy Pillow" on one 3-inch square. Attach the 1-inch square in the center of the other larger felt square, gluing or stitching three sides to form a pocket that opens at the top.

2. When both squares are dry, glue three sides of the 3-inch squares together, checking that the tooth pocket and words are on the outside.

3. Let glue dry, then stuff loosely with batting and glue the open end shut. Use a few clothespins to hold the glued edge tightly while it dries. Students can use their Tooth Fairy Pillow to put a lost tooth under their bed pillow, and the Tooth Fairy can use it to leave money.

Activity Two: Making Envelope Puppets

Supplies:
Legal sized envelope per child, drawing materials

Evaluation:
Child will make a puppet that will fit his or her hand.

Procedure:
1. In follow-up lessons, you may want to have a talking tooth puppet discuss teeth care or losing teeth. You can make one from an envelope or make one from slightly stuffed felt and attach it to a stick.

2. Envelope puppets are so inexpensive that students could each create their own. Good books with which to follow are Lucy Bate's *Little Rabbit's Loose Tooth* (Crown, 1975), Marc Brown's favorite, *Arthur's Tooth* (Little, Brown, 1985), or William Steig's *Doctor DeSoto* (Farrar, Straus, Giroux, 1982) for older readers. Paul Shower's *How Many Teeth?* (Harper Collins, 1991) is an easy science book that explains the basics of teeth and their growth and loss.

VERBAL CENTER

Activity Three: Writing Questions

Supplies:
Computer with Internet connection, paper strips and pencils

Evaluation:
Students correctly write a question and answer about dental health after viewing an Internet movie.

Procedure:
1. Go to the Internet site called *ADA Kids Corner* <www.ada.org/consumer/kids/index.html>. This site features Dudley the Dinosaur at the Under 13 site. Students can view three movies: *Dudley and Gramps Brush and Floss, Dudley's Dental Quiz,* or *Healthy Snacks with Dudley.* Each movie takes about six minutes to load, so have dental word games printed from this site, available to play while waiting.

2. Several games and coloring sheets can be printed from this site. When the movie is loaded, a picture will be displayed without instructions. Click on the picture to run the movie. At the end, you can click on it again to review. Have students prepare several questions for the next student, who views the video to answer. Answers should be on the back of the question strips.

Activity Four: Tooth Customs

Supplies:
Books mentioned in Activity One

Evaluation:
Base assessment on a rubric or give credit for participation.

Procedure:
1. Ask students what they do with their teeth when they lose them. Record each child's response.

2. Read *Throw Your Tooth on the Roof: Tooth Traditions from Around the World* by Selby Beeker (Houghton Mifflin, 1998) or Marlene Brill's *Tooth Tales from Around the World* (Charlesbridge, 1998) to the class. Depending on the age of your audience, students contribute a sentence to a class story chart or write a paragraph about a custom with which they are unfamiliar.

Teeth Tales

LOGIC CENTER

Activity Five: Chart Dental Care

Supplies:
Computer with Internet connection and printer

Evaluation:
Students bring in completed tooth-brushing chart for extra credit.

Procedure:
1. Go to the Web site *Dr. Rabbit's No Cavities Clubhouse* <www.colgate.com/Kids-world/index.html>. The site includes games about tooth care and healthy snacks, which can be played alone or with a partner.

2. Visit the Tooth Fairy page to get a special message after a child loses a tooth.

3. Print out a tooth-brushing chart for students to complete at home for one week (especially Dental Health Week).

Activity Six: Dental Pictograph

Supplies:
Ten large tooth patterns (use tooth pattern on p. 82), chart on chart tablet

Evaluation:
Use tooth pictograph to compose math problems through the months. Students should explain how they arrived at their answers.

Procedure:
1. With younger children, make a large tooth for each month of the school year. Each time a child loses a tooth, write her initials inside a square for that month.

2. After the first month, find the total of lost teeth and have students predict how many will be lost in the next month. Have a list of students on a chart tablet and record their monthly predictions. Record the actual count at the end of each month and have students predict for the following month. As you repeat monthly, students should become better at refining their estimates.

Student names	Aug. estimate	Aug. actual	Sept. estimate	Sept. actual

MUSICAL CENTER

Activity Seven: Sing a Song of Healthy Teeth

Supplies:
Envelope puppets, tape player and music cassettes or CD-player and discs (optional), writing materials

Evaluation:
Children can teach their song to the class or contribute to a group song.

Procedure:
1. Students may want to write songs about tooth care, good eating, getting enough sleep, or other healthful habits. They can write them to the tunes of traditional childhood songs or current popular songs.

2. They can sing these with their handmade puppets or perform the songs themselves.

Activity Eight: Learn a Hygiene Song

Supplies:
Brush and comb puppets, sponge puppet

Evaluation:
None

Procedure:
1. Teach students the hygiene songs by moving the appropriate handmade puppets as if they are dancing and singing. Sing several times so students can join in. Strive for a fun and boisterous rendition to relieve any embarrassment. Use a sponge puppet (p.86) for this first song.

"Soap and Water"

by Aileen Kirkham
(*to the tune of the* "Hallelujah Chorus")

Soap and water, soap and water,

With a washcloth,

Or a sponge,

Will really get you clean.

Soap and water, soap and water,

Scrub yourself clean

Every day,

Or else you will stink!

Topic #1 Teeth Tales

Comb and Brush Puppets

Sponge Puppet

"Brush Your Hair"

(*to the tune of* "Row, Row, Row Your Boat")

Use with comb and brush puppets (below)

Brush, brush, brush your hair.

Then it will look so fine!

Braid it, curl it, cut it, dye it.

"I'm proud that it is mine!"

2. Read *Harry the Dirty Dog* by Gene Zion (Harper & Row, 1956) for primary grades and *Mrs. Piggle-Wiggle's Won't-Take-a-Bath Cure* by Betty Bard MacDonald (HarperCollins, 1975, c1947) for older grades. Discuss reasons for bathing. With fifth graders, body odor is more obvious, and some students may be unaware of what they can do to minimize it. This is a good time to discuss showering, deodorants, and shampooing. To keep the tone light, you may want to have a display of shampoos, deodorants, and soaps with facial features attached.

KINESTHETIC CENTER

Activity Nine: Brushing Their Teeth

Supplies:
A large, clean floor brush (the kind with soft bristles) attached to a broom handle to simulate a large toothbrush

Evaluation:
Students demonstrate correct tooth-brushing technique.

Procedure:
1. After watching a tooth-brushing demonstration by the school nurse, or on a filmstrip or a video, children act out the procedure.

2. Line up a group of children to be the teeth. They should face away from the audience. Select a child to be the brusher. Have her brush the teeth, pretending that the belt lines are the gum lines and the shoulders are the crowns of the teeth. Show how to brush from the gums up. This can be a giggly exercise that makes dental health a lot of fun.

INTERPERSONAL CENTER

Activity Ten: Invite a Veterinarian

Supplies:
Stuffed dogs and cats, pet toothbrushes, computer with Internet connection, *Doctor DeSoto* by William Steig (Farrar, Straus, Giroux, 1982)

Evaluation:
Students compose a class list of questions to ask the veterinarian and review the answers after the vet leaves.

Procedure:
1. Share the story about the mouse dentist, Dr. DeSoto, who helps a fox with a toothache. Then visit the site *Pets Need Dental Care, Too* <www.petcental.com/index.htm> to inform students how they can help their dogs and cats avoid a trip to Dr. DeSoto.

2. Use stuffed animals to practice tooth-brushing technique.

3. Invite a veterinarian to talk about pet dental care.

4. Conclude the vet's visit by reading Dav Pilkey's book *Dog Breath: The Horrible Trouble with Halley Tosis* (Blue Sky Press, 1994).

Teeth Tales

INTRAPERSONAL CENTER

Activity Eleven: Polling Worldwide

Supplies:
Computer with Internet connection, e-mail capability, writing materials

Evaluation:
Students share survey results with their class or grade level.

Procedure:
1. Go to the *CyberKids* site at <www.cyberkids.com>. This is a chat room, monitored by adults, for children to the age of 13. If you are wondering about lost tooth customs, for example, you can post your question and wait for responses.

2. Conduct a survey with the class to find what customs they use with their teeth and how many students subscribe to each.

3. When you write to another class, especially in another country, ask them to do the same survey. Compare results.

4. There also is a monthly e-zine and place to publish children's work at this site. For February, consider submitting the best writings on the subjects of dental health, a visit from the Tooth Fairy, or other toothy topic. A privacy section provides sensible considerations, such as cautioning children about using their real names.

Fall Harvest Topic #2

VISUAL CENTER

Activity One: Comparing Apples and Corn

Supplies:
TV and VCR, videotapes, pencils, compare/contrast sheet in the form of a large apple and large ear of corn that intersect, answer sheet.

Evaluation:
Score on worksheet based on answer sheet

Procedure:
1. Watch videotape about apples.
2. Write facts about apples in the apple shape. Pause the VCR if you need to write.
3. Watch videotape about corn.
4. Write facts about corn in the corn shape.
5. Write three facts that are the same for both corn and apples. Write them on the chart where the apple and corn cross each other.

Activity Two: Observing Apples

Supplies:
At least five kinds of apples numbered to match the answer key, magnifying glasses, crayons, colored pencils, art paper cut into 6-inch squares, books mentioned, answer key

Evaluation:
Check number on apples with answer key. Partner or teacher evaluates apple drawings compared with real apple. If picture resembles apple in size, color, and pattern, score three. Score two if only two variables show in picture, one for each variable.

Procedure:
1. Arrange the apples from smallest to largest.
2. Draw two of them as accurately as possible for size, shape and color. Write the name of the apple at the bottom of the card.
3. Use Laundau's *Apples* (Children's Press, 1999), Fowler's *Apples of Your Eye* (Children's Press, 1994), or Maestro's *How Do Apples Grow?* (HarperCollins, 1992) to find the names of each. Write the name of each under your drawings.
4. Check the names with the answer key.

Subject: Science
Grades: 2-3
Hardware: VCR and TV, tape recorder and player, video camera
Software: videos about corn and about apples
Pre-lesson Class Preparation: Students need to know how to pause the videotape to take notes. They should know how to record on a tape and how to speak to a video camera. Read all assignments to students before starting and make sure they know what to do. Stock all centers. Explain task sheets and record keeping pages, and where to keep their centers folder. Develop a rubric for performances and teach students how to complete it. Purchase and prepare products, p. 93.

Fall Harvest

WRITING CENTER

Activity Three: Scarecrow School

Supplies:
Books, lined paper, pencils, rubric

Evaluation:
Develop a rubric.

Procedure:
1. Read *The Little Scarecrow Boy* by Margaret Wise Brown (HarperCollins, 1998) or *Jeb Scarecrow's Pumpkin Patch* by Jana Dillon (Houghton Mifflin, 1992).

2. Write a how-to instruction sheet for new scarecrows. Explain how to scare crows. Have at least three ways to scare birds.

Activity Four: Cooking Up Apples

Supplies:
Slates or lined paper, colored chalk, colored pencils, cookbooks with apple desserts

Evaluation:
Six items = C, nine items = B, twelve items = A

Procedure:
1. Use *Eating Apples* by Saunders-Smith (Pebble Books, 1998) or other cookbooks to list as many kinds of apple recipes and products as possible (for example, apple butter, apple fritters, apple juice).

2. Write your list in color, using chalk or colored pencils.

3. Show your list to your teacher before leaving the center.

MATH CENTER

Activity Five: Top Crops

Supplies:
World Almanac for Kids, U.S. map to color, crayons or colored pencils, graph paper, or graphing mat and objects

Evaluation:
Answer key for state list and map. Teacher evaluates graphs after allowing child to explain.

Procedure:
1. Use the *World Almanac for Kids*.

2. Look up the states that grow apples. Write the names of the three states that grow the most apples and how much they grow. Make a graph to show how the three states compare.

3. Look up the states that grow corn. Write the names of the top three states that grow corn and how much they grow. Make a graph to show how the three states compare.

4. On the map of the United States, color the top corn-producing states yellow. Color the top apple-producing states red. Write three sentences about what you discover.

Activity Six: Round and Round

Supplies:
Books, multiple sets of pictures from bud to pie, answer key

Evaluation:
Score on answer sheet

Procedure:
1. Read Zoe Hall's *The Apple Pie Tree* (Blue Sky Press, 1996) or listen to it on tape. Or, you can read Gail Saunders-Smith's book *Apple Trees* (Pebble Books, 1998).

2. After reading the story, arrange the pictures (page 233) in sequential order.

3. Check your answers.

Leaves grow

Tiny flower buds appear

Petals blow off

Small green apples appear

Apples get bigger

Apples are ready to pick

MUSICAL CENTER

Activity Seven: Whistle While You Work

Supplies:
Paper, pencils, xylophone, drum, tapes of traditional children's songs, books about apples or corn, performance rubric

Evaluation:
Develop a rubric or have students develop one.

Procedure:
1. Create a work song to sing while picking apples or corn. It should have at least two four-line verses and a chorus.

2. Include facts in your song about the way apples or corn grows.

3. Write your song.

Activity Eight: State Songs

Supplies:
Books about Johnny Appleseed (John Chapman), U.S. map, books about state songs, *The World Almanac* for Internet addresses for each state, answer key, song rubric

Evaluation:
Score on answer key for state list, rubric score by teacher for song

Procedure:
1. List the names of the states in which John Chapman lived and traveled.

2. Research the state song of one of the states. Use the *World Almanac* to find the Internet address for state information for each state.

3. Learn the state song. Explain what it means to the class. If you want, teach the class to sing it.

ACTION CENTER

Activity Nine: Corn Capers

Supplies:
Answer key, zipped bags—zipped, stapled, and numbered—of corn oil, corn starch, corn syrup, corn meal, corn tortilla, corn flakes, corn pops, unpopped corn, popped corn; stand-up tents with names of corn items

Evaluation:
Score on answer sheet

Procedure:
1. Handle the zipped bags of corn materials in this box. Do not open them.

2. Can you match them with their names? Put a name tent next to each bag.

3. Check your answers. Correct if needed.

Activity Ten: Living Life Cycle

Supplies:
Books, bookmarked Internet sites, performance rubric

Evaluation:
Answer sheet for life cycle and rubric for action pantomime

Procedure:
1. Learn the steps in the life cycle of an ear of corn or an apple. Use books or Internet if needed.

2. Create an action pantomime of all the steps. Act out planting, growing, weeding, and other steps. Teach it to at least one other student.

GROUP CENTER

Activity Eleven: Scarecrow Play

Supplies:
Books, paper, pencils, word processing program, performance rubric

Evaluation:
Performance rubric completed by five students

Procedure:
1. Read *The Little Scarecrow Boy* or *Jeb Scarecrow's Pumpkin Patch*.

2. Plan a play to act out the book or write one about a father scarecrow teaching his scarecrow children how to scare birds.

3. Be ready to act out your play for the class.

4. Check the rubric before your performance. Choose three students to rate your play.

Activity Twelve: Interviewing John Chapman

Supplies:
Books about John Chapman (Johnny Appleseed), toy microphone, lined paper and pencil, videotape and video camera, performance rubric

Evaluation:
Performance rubric completed by three students

Procedure:
1. Work with a partner. One of you will be John Chapman, and one will be one a reporter from Channel Two News.

2. Write the questions and answers that might be asked if you could go back in time to interview Johnny Appleseed.

3. Write at least seven questions. Have Johnny answer them in a personal way. One answer should be funny.

4. After practicing your interview, ask your teacher to tape your interview.

5. Show the videotape to the class. Ask three of your classmates to complete the video rubric.

The Skeleton

VISUAL CENTER

Activity One: Draw a Human

Supplies:
Skeleton pattern for each child (see page 213), brads for connecting joints, art paper, drawing and coloring media

Evaluation:
Pictures that are humanly proportioned will be hung in a display of "People at Work and Play."

Procedure:
1. Cut apart and assemble the human skeletons, using brads for the joints.

2. As a group, brainstorm all the things a person can do at work and at play that are assisted by their skeleton (for example, dig a hole, type on a computer, jump rope, climb trees, dance).

3. Select a person and an activity.

4. Place the skeleton on a sheet of wax paper and tape the bones into a position that looks like it is doing the activity you have chosen.

5. Tape wax paper with skeleton to a window. Lay a sheet of drawing paper over the skeleton and draw the person, adding the outline of clothes and hair.

6. Take papers from window. Complete drawing by adding color. You may wish to make a collage and add glitter or fabric.

7. Mount on display board.

Subject: Science

Grades: 3-4

Hardware: tape recorder, computer with CD-ROM drive

Software: *A.D.A.M., The Graph Club* (Tom Snyder Productions), and blank audiocassettes

Pre-lesson Class Preparation:
Gather books and supplies listed below, copy a skeleton pattern for each student, and copy worksheets for each student.

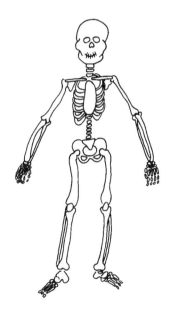

VERBAL CENTER

Activity Two: Record a Story

Supplies:
Tape player, blank cassette tapes, copies of the following books:

DeFelice, Cynthia C. *The Dancing Skeleton.* Aladdin Paperbacks, 1996.

Steig, William. *The Amazing Bone.* Farrar, 1987.

Johnston, Toni. *The Soup Bone.* Harcourt, Brace and Jovanovich, 1990.

Other picture books from your library that relate to bones or the human skeleton.

Evaluation:
Play tape for another group that will evaluate it according to a rubric developed by the teacher or class.

Procedure:
1. The group reads the books and selects one to read aloud. The group selects a narrator for the story or sections of the story, and a reader for each character's voice. The group decides if they will do sound effects and if they will use different voices for each character.

2. After planning, students practice reading aloud.

3. When they feel the story is ready, they record their voices.

LOGIC CENTER

Activity Three: Skeleton Comparisons

Supplies:
Reference sites and books about animal skeletons, graph paper or a graphing program, such as Tom Snyder Production's *Graph Club*, pencils, crayons or markers, Skeletal Comparisons worksheet (page 230)

Evaluation:
Teacher will evaluate graphs for accuracy.

Procedure:
1. The adult human body has 206 bones. Research to find the number of bones in at least two other vertebrate animals.

2. Record the animal's name and number of bones on the Skeletal Comparisons worksheet.

3. Graph the number of bones in each animal and compare with a human.

4. Add a title and your name to the graph.

5. Display it on the Skeletal Comparisons display board.

Activity Four: Analyze the Data

reproduce full page at 230

Name _____

Skeletal Comparisons Worksheet
Complete the chart by examining the graphs of our class.

Animal	Number of Bones	Rank by number of bones

Supplies:
Class book of blank pages, copies of completed Skeletal Comparisons worksheet, pencils, 3 x 5 inch note cards on which to record original math problems

Evaluation:
Teacher will judge the correctness of each list.

Procedure:
1. Use this worksheet and the Skeletal Comparison graphs (from Activity Three) to collect the data found by the class.

2. Make a list of animals from the one with the fewest bones to the one with the most.

3. Write a question that uses some of the facts from the graphs, for example, "Why does a python have more bones than a goldfish?" or "How many bones are found in three owls?"

4. Add your questions to the class book called "Skeleton Problems."

MUSICAL CENTER

Activity Five: The Bone Connection

Supplies:
Various simple musical instruments if desired, tape recording of "The Bone Connection," tape player

Evaluation:
Students will be able to identify all the major bones.

Procedure:
1   Students sing the song, pointing to the appropriate part of the body. This may be best introduced to the large group, then practiced in the center.

2.   Students test one another by pointing to a bone and having the other name it.

"The Bone Connection"

by Charlotte Wilson
(*to the tune of* "Mulberry Bush")

Cranium, clavicle, patella, phalanges

Cranium, clavicle, patella, phalanges

Cranium, clavicle, patella, phalanges

All clap phalanges together!

Humerus, ulna, radius, metacarpals

Humerus, ulna, radius, metacarpals

Humerus, ulna, radius, metacarpals

All clap phalanges together!

Ribs, sternum, pelvis, vertebrae

Ribs, sternum, pelvis, vertebrae

Ribs, sternum, pelvis, vertebrae

All clap phalanges together!

Femur, tibia, fibula, metatarsals

Femur, tibia, fibula, metatarsals

Femur, tibia, fibula, metatarsals

All clap phalanges together!

KINESTHETIC CENTER

Activity Six: Connect the Virtual Skeleton

Supplies:
Computer with Internet connection

Evaluation:
Program evaluates correctness when the on-screen skeleton claps for the student.

Procedure:
1. Go to *The Human Skeleton* site <www.medtropolis.com/vbody/bones/index.html>.

2. Listen to the narrated movie to learn facts about your skeleton.

3. Zoom in on any bone about which you are curious to find more facts.

4. When you have studied the skeleton, try to assemble it on screen. Click the "Build a Skeleton" button. If you choose incorrectly, the bone will not "stick."

Activity Seven: Skeleton Assembly Game

Supplies:
Two sets of individual skeleton bones, diagram of a human skeleton for checking answers, question/answer cards. At Halloween, you can get large plastic skeletons that pop apart. You also can buy skeleton fabric that builds a skeleton. Reinforce the fabric with iron-on felt before cutting it out. School supply stores sell cardboard skeletons that can be disassembled. **Note:** If your disassembled skeleton has more than 15 parts, you will need to add an appropriate number of questions (two per additional bone).

Evaluation:
Students check partners' answers for accuracy against an answer key.

Procedure:
1. This activity is to be done after students have learned about the skeleton. It is an informal test of their knowledge. Divide the class into two groups. Each group has a pile of cardboard, fabric, or plastic human bones. Use a bowl or box to contain the questions that students draw on their turn.

2. Game proceeds in this manner: Team One selects a question and asks Team Two. All team members can help with the answer. A correct answer allows the team to select a bone to lay on the floor to assemble their skeleton. Begin with the skull. The questioning team corrects an incorrect answer, but the bone is not placed.

3. Game continues until one team has completely assembled its skeleton.

The Skeleton

Skeleton Game Questions

1. True or false. A baby's skull is not solid.

2. What is the name of the last bone of your spine?

3. What do your bones produce for your body?

4. What is the name for the soft material inside a bone?

5. How many bones are in the human adult skeleton-152 or 206 or 274?

6. True or false. A baby has more bones than an adult.

7. True or false. Your nose does not have a bone inside it.

8. What do you call the stiff material that shapes your nose and ears?

9. Name a joint of your body.

10. What does your skull protect?

11. What do your ribs protect?

12. How many bones protect your abdomen?

13. What is a job of the skeleton?

14. What mineral makes your bones strong?

15. What is a good drink to build up your bones?

16. Which is the longest bone in your body?

17. What is the scientific name for your kneecap?

18. What is the scientific name for your skull?

19. What is the scientific name for your finger and toe bones?

20. What is the scientific name for your backbones?

21. What is the scientific name for your hipbones?

22. Why is your backbone made of many separate bones?

23. Which part of your skeleton is a hinge joint?

24. Which part of your skeleton is a swivel joint?

25. Which part of your skeleton is a ball and socket joint?

26. True or false. A bone can repair itself.

27. What is the scientific name for your breastbone?

28. True or false. Your fingernails are made of the same material as your bones.

29. True or false. Animal skeletons have the same jobs as a human skeleton.

30. Where are the smallest bones of your body?

31. True or false. Bones are alive.

32. True or false. Giraffes and humans have the same number of neck bones.

Skeleton Game Answers

1.	True or false. A baby's skull is not solid.	**TRUE**
2.	What is the name of the last bone of your spine?	**TAILBONE**
3.	What do your bones produce for your body?	**BLOOD**
4.	What is the name for the soft material inside a bone?	**MARROW**
5.	How many bones are in the human adult skeleton-152 or 206 or 274?	**206**
6.	True or false. A baby has more bones than an adult.	**TRUE**
7.	True or false. Your nose does not have a bone inside it.	**TRUE**
8.	What do you call the stiff material that shapes your nose and ears?	**CARTILAGE**
9.	Name a joint of your body.	**ELBOW, KNEE, WRIST, ANKLE, or HIP**
10.	What does your skull protect?	**BRAIN**
11.	What do your ribs protect?	**HEART or LUNGS**
12.	How many bones protect your abdomen?	**ZERO**
13.	What is a job of the skeleton?	**SUPPORT BODY, PROTECT BODY, or HELP YOU MOVE**
14.	What mineral makes your bones strong?	**CALCIUM**
15.	What is a good drink to build up your bones?	**MILK**
16.	Which is the longest bone in your body?	**THIGH BONE OR FEMUR**
17.	What is the scientific name for your kneecap?	**PATELLA**
18.	What is the scientific name for your skull?	**CRANIUM**
19.	What is the scientific name for your finger and toe bones?	**PHALANGES**
20.	What is the scientific name for your backbones?	**VERTEBRAE**
21.	What is the scientific name for your hipbones?	**PELVIS**
22.	Why is your backbone made of many separate bones?	**SO YOU CAN BEND**
23.	Which part of your skeleton is a hinge joint?	**KNEE or ELBOW**
24.	Which part of your skeleton is a swivel joint?	**WRIST, ANKLE, OR NECK**
25.	Which part of your skeleton is a ball and socket joint?	**HIP or SHOULDER**
26.	True or false. A bone can repair itself.	**TRUE**
27.	What is the scientific name for your breastbone?	**STERNUM**
28.	True or false. Your fingernails are made of the same material as your bones.	**FALSE**
29.	True or false. Animal skeletons have the same jobs as a human skeleton.	**TRUE**
30.	Where are the smallest bones of your body?	**INSIDE THE EAR**
31.	True or false. Bones are alive.	**TRUE**

The Skeleton

INTERPERSONAL CENTER

Activity Eight: Measuring One Another

Supplies:
Cloth tape measure for each pair, skeleton on which to record measurements, compare/contrast worksheet, a growth chart or two tape measures stapled to the wall

Evaluation:
Participation and completion of the charts are marks of success in this group interaction.

Procedure:
1. Partners measure one another to record five measurements on a skeleton picture on their compare/contrast sheet (page 231).

2. After measurements are completed, students compare with five other students. They record the measurements of the other group and the comparisons.

3. Students might want to line up in order of one of these measurements, then another, as a check on the accuracy of their measurements.

reproduce full page at 231

Name _____ **Date** _____

SKELETON COMPARE/CONTRAST

Have a partner measure you for each of these measurements: Record the inches next to the part of the skeleton.

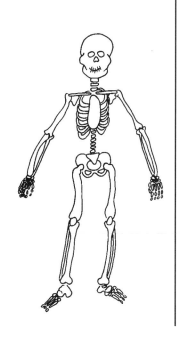

Measurement	Bone Name	Comparison (circle one)	Student Name
	Skull (Cranium)	less same more	
	Thigh bone (Femur)	less same more	
	Thumb	less same more	
	Hand (from wrinkle at wrist to tip of longest finger)	less same more	
	Height	less same more	

The Jacket I Wear in the Snow

VISUAL CENTER

Activity One: Dress Up Drawings

Supplies:
Drawing materials, photograph of each student

Evaluation:
Give credit if students draw themselves dressed for the occasion.

Procedure:

1. In *The Jacket I Wear in the Snow*, students learn about all the items needed to go out in the snow. In this activity, they think about what they wear for other occasions. Write these on the board to let students brainstorm clothing:

   flower girl or ring bearer

   baseball (or other sport) game

   going to church or temple

   a day at the beach or pool

   Halloween

   a sleep-over party

2. Students brainstorm clothes for each. Be sure to include feet, head, and hands for any special clothing. You may want to include accessories, such as a beach towel or a candy bag.

3. Students draw a picture of themselves dressed for an occasion. Glue their school picture (head only) to the paper before they draw it so the proportions will be better. After drawing is complete, label the drawing *The Clothes I Wear for _____ (occasion)"*

Subject: Reading, Science

Grades: K-1 without the synonyms lessons, 2-3 with thesaurus lesson

Hardware: computer with CD-ROM drive and Internet connection

Software: *Microsoft Bookshelf,* word processing program

Pre-lesson Class Preparation:
Find pictures of winter clothing or bring in the real things. Two sets of winter clothing are needed for the winter clothes relay. Gather books and run copies of worksheets.

The Jacket I Wear in the Snow

VERBAL ACTIVITIES

Activity Two: Snow Clothing

Supplies:
Thesaurus for each pair of students or *Microsoft Bookshelf*, "What Do We Wear in the Snow?" worksheet for each pair (page 232), writing paper and materials, word processing program if desired

Evaluation:
Check answers against the key.

Procedure:
1. For older students, point to the jacket and ask students to name other words for a jacket (coat, windbreaker, overcoat). Do the same for one or two other items on the line.

2. Show students the thesaurus or a CD-ROM version such as *Microsoft Bookshelf*, and teach them how to find synonyms for "coat."

3. Have students complete worksheet, possibly with partners taking a different word. Check together when completed.

4. As an extension, make a clothing dictionary in which students define or draw each item to explain the differences among gloves, mittens, and a muff, for example.

reproduce full page at 232

Name_____

"What Do We Wear in the Snow?"

Use a thesaurus to find synonyms for different types of winter wear:

Winter Clothing Type	Synonym	Synonym
gloves		
boots		
coat		
scarf		
cap		
sweater		
pants		
shirt		
underwear		

The Jacket I Wear in the Snow

Name_____

"What Do We Wear in the Snow?" Answer Key

Use a thesaurus to find synonyms for different types of winter wear:

Winter Clothing Type	Synonym	Synonym
gloves	mittens	muff
boots	Wellingtons, galoshes, rubbers	overshoes, gumboots, ski boots
coat	jacket, windbreaker, overcoat	parka, anorak, cape
scarf	muffler, neckerchief	babushka, stole
cap	hat, hood	stocking cap, earmuffs
sweater	cardigan	pullover, sweatshirt
pants	trousers, slacks, corduroys	jeans, leggings, ski bib
shirt	blouse	turtleneck
underwear	long johns, thermals	camisole

The Jacket I Wear in the Snow

Activity Three: Writing an Adaptation

Supplies:

Writing materials or word processing program, Ketteman's *Bubba the Cowboy Prince* (Scholastic, 1997), Internet connection, synonym worksheets from Activity Two

Evaluation:

Students may want to read their adaptations to the class. If necessary, compose a rubric to evaluate each story.

Procedure:

1. Our second graders write adaptations of fairy tales. As a follow-up to this lesson, read aloud Helen Ketteman's book *Bubba the Cowboy Prince*. In this adaptation of the Cinderella story, the hero is a cowboy with a wicked stepdaddy and two lazy, wicked stepbrothers. The richest rancher is Miz Lurleen. The Western setting and details are hilarious.

2. After the reading, tell students that an adaptation must change at least three major things about the original story. Students list the major changes in the story.

3. For younger students, use the clothing synonym worksheet (Activity Two) to rewrite *This Is the Jacket I Wear in the Snow*.

4. Older students might want to brainstorm summer wear and write a different adaptation called *These Are the Glasses I Wear in the Sun*. They could begin it with a smudge on sunglasses, then build a repetitive story based on their brainstorm list.

5. An alternative adaptation of *The Jacket I Wear in the Snow* could be *The Hat I Wear in the Rodeo*. Use *Sarah's Rodeo Page* <mama.indstate.edu/prentice/sarah> to research the life and clothing of cowboys. This site, winner of six awards for excellence, covers four areas. You can click on "Rodeos and Associations," "Cowfolk," "Horse and Agriculture Information," and "The General Store."

LOGIC ACTIVITIES

Activity Four: Temperature Chart

Supplies:
Student almanacs, world and U.S. maps, writing materials

Evaluation:
Present information to the group for verification.

Procedure:
1. Students use an almanac to locate temperatures around the world. Have them list five countries, other than the United States, in which they would need the clothing listed in *The Jacket I Wear in the Snow* and five in which that kind of winter clothing would be unnecessary.

2. Locate those countries on the world map. Hypothesize why people in those countries do or don't need winter clothing (for example, proximity to the equator).

3. Students could do the same with the states of the United States.

MUSICAL ACTIVITIES

Activity Five: This Is the Way We Wash Our Clothes

Supplies:
Book *The Jacket I Wear in the Snow*

Evaluation:
None

Procedure:
1. The book on which these activities are based is a repetitive book that helps young students to learn about winter clothes. Students can practice that vocabulary by singing the old song "This Is the Way We Wash Our Clothes." Verses are:

> This is the way we wash our clothes,
>
> Wash our clothes, wash our clothes.
>
> This is the way we wash our clothes,

So early on a _____ morning. *Use the day on which you are singing.*

> This is the way we wash our jackets,

Repeat as above. Repeat verses, substituting the names of various items of clothing and pantomiming the actions. Act as though you are washing the clothes in a large, sudsy tub of water, then rinsing them, then hanging them on the line.

2. Sing the song again, using summer clothing.

KINESTHETIC ACTIVITIES

Activity Six: Old Clothes Relay Race

Supplies:
Two sets of oversized clothing, such as a pair of pants, a shirt, a jacket, a neck scarf, and a pair of gloves or mittens. Cups, hot chocolate, and marshmallows (optional)

Evaluation:
None

Procedure:
1. Play winter clothes relay race. Have two piles of selected clothes at one end of the relay course. Divide the class into two rows and have the same item for each team.

2. At a signal, the first student on each team runs down the row, dons the clothing, then runs back and takes them off at the feet of her relay partner. That partner must put them on, run to the end of the relay, take them off, then run back and tag the hand of the next relay partner. Game is over when an entire team has worn the clothes.

3. Have hot chocolate for all participants—marshmallows optional!

Activity Seven: Clothesline Sequence

Supplies:
Pictures or actual clothing that is mentioned in Neitzel's book, clothesline, clothespins

Evaluation:
Students will match the clothesline pictures to the story.

Procedure:
1. Distribute articles of clothing or pictures of them from the story.

2. As you read or tell the cumulative, repetitive tale, the student hangs the added item of clothing to the clothesline. This visual will help with the repetitive group retelling of the story.

3. After the story, discuss the purpose of each item on the clothesline.

Craft or discount stores sell tiny clothespins. They are useful for clipping sequence pictures to a clothesline, as we do in this lesson.

The Jacket I Wear in the Snow

INTRAPERSONAL ACTIVITIES

Activity Eight: Preparing for Weather

Supplies:
Book and site mentioned below, books about weather disasters

Evaluation:
Students report to the class about ways they can be prepared in cases of tornado, flood, hurricanes and other disasters. (Select disasters likely in your area.)

Procedure:
1. In *The Jacket I Wear in the Snow*, a child prepares for the weather by dressing warmly. Students are to answer these questions:

   What are other ways to prepare for weather besides choosing the proper clothing?

   How do meteorologists predict the weather?

   How do you prepare for a tornado or a drought?

2. Research the answers, using library materials or *Dan's Wild, Wild Weather Page* <www.whnt19.com/kidwx>. There is an A-Z weather index at this site that gives explanations, tips, and even lesson plans for a variety of weather conditions.

3. Logic smart students will be able to develop a plan to defend against a weather disaster that might be experienced in your area. Have them include a plan for indoor preparedness and what to do if they should be caught outdoors, such as on a field trip. Help the class be prepared by having students share their plans.

4. Read *Cloudy with a Chance of Meatballs* by Judi Barrett. Students might want to write their own tall tale based on another weather problem that they researched in this activity.

Book List

Our classes use these books to research winter for their own works. See the bibliography at the end of the book for publishing information.

Alderson, Sue Ann. *Pond Seasons.*

Bancroft, Henrietta. *Animals in Winter.*

Baxter, Nicola. *Winter.*

Berger, Melvin. *What Do Animals Do in Winter? How Animals Survive the Cold.*

Chapman, Gillian. *Winter.*

Fowler, Allan. *How Do You Know It's Winter?*

Saunders-Smith, Gail. *Warm Clothes.*

_____. *Winter.*

Topic #5 Something from Nothing

Subject: English Language Arts, Social Studies

Grades: 2-4

Hardware: tape or CD player, computer with word processing software

Software: *Storybook Weaver*, recording of "If I Were a Rich Man" from the musical *Fiddler on the Roof*

Pre-lesson Class Preparation:
Duplicate figures (see p. 113) and laminate, or trace on felt or fabric. Attach a Velcro button to each to adhere to a flannel board or add magnetic tape for a metal board. You may want to duplicate for each pair of students and distribute them in envelopes for sequencing or retelling.

If You Give a Mouse a Cookie Sequence Pictures

VISUAL CENTER

Activity One: Design a Vest

Supplies:
Large paper sack per child, drawing and coloring materials

Evaluation:
Give credit if students can explain why their vest design is suitable for the character selected.

Procedure:
1. Trace a child-sized vest on a paper sack. Have students design a vest for themselves, based on a theme, or a vest they think a certain storybook character or famous person would wear.

2. Students can write a paragraph or two explaining their design and the character for which they designed it.

3. Have a fashion parade for another class so students can model their vests and explain the characters for which they were designed.

Activity Two: Sequencing Stories

Supplies:
Small sequence pictures for a children's book, storage envelope

Evaluation:
Pictures are numbered on the back for self-checking.

Procedure:
1. Provide other sequential books, such as *If You Give a Mouse a Cookie* (Harper & Row, 1985) and Laura Numeroff's other two cautionary books, *If You Give a Moose a Muffin* (HarperCollins, 1991) and *If You Give a Pig a Pancake* (Geringer, 1998).

2. Copy sequence pictures (page 234), laminate them, and put them in a small manila envelope. Put the story name on the front and the sequence numbers on the back of each piece.

3. Students can use the pictures as a game, on a flannel board, or with a story pocket apron.

WRITING CENTER

Activity Three: Writing a Script

Supplies:
Aaron Shepard's *Tips for Scripting*, computer with Internet and CD-ROM capabilities, *Storybook Weaver* or other word processing program, or pencil and paper

Evaluation:
Students perform their version of *Something from Nothing*.

Procedure:
1. Use Aaron Shepard's page *From Story to Stage: Tips on Scripting* <www.aaronshep.com/rt/Tips.html> for guidelines on writing and performing scripts. At his home page, click in search box and type "Readers on Stage." Select the document called "Tips on Scripting."

2. Use a word processing program such as Storybook Weaver to have students rewrite *Something from Nothing* as a Readers' Theater script. Groups could write the dialogue for the tailor, the child, and the mother.

3. Students can add other minor characters without detracting from the plot. One group writes the narrator's part.

4. Put parts together, polish, and perform!

Something from Nothing

Activity Four: Where Did I Come From?

Supplies:
Patricia Polacco's book *The Keeping Quilt* (Simon & Schuster, 1988), books for researching heritage, database (optional)

Evaluation:
Each student should supply at least one country name to the chart after talking with his family.

Procedure:
1. The illustrations in *Something from Nothing* portray a country and time unlike our own. Discuss illustrations.

2. Follow up with Polacco's book *The Keeping Quilt.*

3. Students may wish to find out more about their heritage. Chart their findings about the countries of their ancestors.

4. For older students, you may want to extend the assignment. Challenge students to find a book that has something to do with their heritage and share it with the class. They should prepare to tell what in the book relates to their heritage and explain it if it is a picture, unusual word, or a custom with which fellow students may be unfamiliar. You may have to review use of the automated or card catalog to search for subject.

5. Keep a database of countries and related fiction books for use by future researchers.

MATH CENTER

Activity Five: Greater Than and Less Than

Supplies:
Several 3-inch paper circles marked with the greater than/less than symbols, flannel board sequence pictures in pairs, flannel board

Evaluation:
Students should work in pairs to check one another. An answer key can be supplied if students are still new to the concept of greater than/less than.

Procedure:
1. Use the flannel board sequence pictures (pages 214 and 215) in pairs with greater than/less than symbols. Draw the symbols on several 3-inch paper circles. Students are comparing the size of the items.

2. Put up the jacket on one side of the board and the button on the other. Ask for a volunteer to correctly place the greater than/less than sign between the two items.

3. Continue with a variety of pairings.

reproduce from page 214 and 215

Blanket

Button

Jacket

Vest

Written Story

Tie

Handkerchief

Something from Nothing

Activity Six: Countries of Origin

Supplies:

World map, push pins, computer with Internet connection, worksheet with a flag outline at the top and lines below

Evaluation:

Student can locate their countries on a map and can identify the flags of those countries.

Procedure:

1. Students ask their parents about their countries of ancestry.

2. Have them locate information on their countries through the Yahooligans Internet search index at <yahooligans.com>.

3. Complete a sheet that includes the outline of a country's flag at the top.

4. If it is age-appropriate, add several interesting facts about their mother countries to the flag sheet.

5. On a world map, put pushpins in their countries of origin.

6. Graph the results by country.

Activity Seven: Retelling a Story

Supplies:

Sequence pictures of clothing (p. 214 and 215), copy of *Something from Nothing*

Evaluation:

Students can self-check with an answer key provided with the pictures.

Procedure:

1. Begin by discussing the meaning of recycling.

2. Say, "We're going to hear a story about a tailor who was very good at recycling. Listen carefully to the things he is able to make from recycling a blanket." Tell *Something from Nothing*, using flannel board figures to reiterate the sequence. Using the figures also will remind you of the story order as you tell it.

3. Ask students to use the clothing pictures to retell the sequence of the story. Give them the set in an envelope and give all a few minutes to arrange them in sequential order. Check together out loud or have students check against an answer key in the envelope.

MUSIC CENTER

Activity Eight: Making Wishes

Supplies:
Song "If I Were a Rich Man" from the musical *Fiddler on the Roof*, player for the song, writing materials

Evaluation:
Student sings song or teaches the class to sing it.

Procedure:
1. Explain that in *Fiddler on the Roof*, one of the daughters marries a tailor. Her parents worry that they will always be poor. In "If I Were a Rich Man," the father sings about what his life would be like if he were rich.

2. Students use the tune to write a song about what they would do if they were a rich boy or girl.

ACTION CENTER

Activity Nine: Stitching the Tailor's Blanket

Supplies:
6-inch squares of plastic canvas, several large blunt needles (available in plastic or metal at craft stores), yarn of various colors

Evaluation:
Students complete the "blanket" and take it home to be recycled as a drink coaster.

Procedure:
1. Cut a 12-inch length of yarn and thread it through the needle. If you prefer, use masking tape to wind tightly around the end of the yarn to make it stiff and needle-like.

2. Using the plastic canvas, do a simple needlepoint stitch to create a small woven blanket. Each time the needle is threaded, the student can change color, if desired.

3. The student takes the coaster home or displays it in a side-by-side pattern that makes the class coasters appear to be a large quilt.

GROUP CENTER

Activity Ten: What If?

Supplies:
None

Evaluation:
Student playing the part of the tailor can tell which arguments he or she thinks are convincing and why.

Procedure:
1. Ask the following questions:

   What if the tailor had not been so poor that he had to reuse every scrap?

   What if he had met a persuasive friend who could talk him into buying a new coat instead of cutting it down?

   What would be some good reasons for buying a new coat instead of recycling it?

   How else could the tailor get a new coat besides buying it?

2. Students form groups of four. One is the poor tailor, and the other three think of convincing reasons why the tailor should get a new coat from one of them and how he will afford it.

The Mitten Topic #6

VISUAL CENTER

Activity One: Puppet Making

Supplies:
Computer with Internet connection and supplies particular to each puppet

Evaluation:
Students use directions from this site to successfully construct a puppet.

Procedure:
1. Students can make puppets from directions at the *Puppetry Traditions Around the World* site. Go to <www.sagecraft.com/puppetry/traditions/index.html> to find puppets from 12 countries and instructions for making them.

2. Have students make the puppets to feature in a worldwide puppet museum or to accompany a folktale from that country.

Activity Two: Gingerbread Baby in Disguise

Supplies:
The Gingerbread Baby by Jan Brett (Putnam, 1999), coloring page of *The Gingerbread Baby* from <www.janbrett.com>, display space for gingerbread babies, and materials for writing, drawing, and coloring

Evaluation:
Develop a rubric for successful completion of this activity.

Procedure:
1. After reading Brett's *The Mitten,* share another of her books called *The Gingerbread Baby.* Print the coloring page for the gingerbread baby and use it as a tracing shape. Have students trace out a gingerbread baby and disguise it as something the fox and the villagers wouldn't want to eat.

2. Have students write a paragraph to accompany their gingerbread baby and display both in the hall with a caption, "Stop, Stop, as Quick as You Can! Don't Eat Me Because…"

Subject: English Language Arts, Science

Grades: 2-4

Hardware: computer with Internet connection

Software: *The Graphing Club* (Tom Snyder Productions)

Pre-lesson Class Preparation: Gather art materials, writing materials, and books for selected activities. For Activity Eight, you need masks for each animal in *The Mitten* and a large tagboard mitten. Make copies of coloring page(s) from Jan Brett's site and copies of worksheets as needed.

Activity Three: Making Mittens

Supplies:
Scissors, construction paper of various colors, paints, markers, crayons and assorted decorations (sequins, beads, flower appliqué, and other common ideas), atlases, encyclopedias, almanacs

Evaluation:
Students complete a pair of mittens for the display board.

Procedure:
1. Have students trace a mitten shape around their hand and cut out four of them, adding an inch all around. Use construction paper or have students bring fabric or felt from home. Stitch or staple together. Decorate the mittens with paints, markers, or decorations.

2. For older students, have them locate countries or states where it is cold enough to wear mittens. Use almanacs, atlases, and encyclopedias. You might want to introduce an atlas computer program, such as *Cartopedia*.

Activity Four: Animal Venn Diagram

Supplies:
Animal chart worksheet (page 217), Jan Brett books, nonfiction books about the mammals in Brett's *The Mitten*, writing supplies

Evaluation:
Check answers against answer key.

Procedure:
1. Complete the animal chart worksheet with students to identify what they know about each animal. Read or tell the folktale by Jan Brett. Have them listen for words that describe each animal.

2. After reading, look back over the story to find words that describe the animal and add any of them to the chart. Use the nonfiction books to complete the data chart. Point out to children the difference in the amount of factual information in a fiction book vs. a nonfiction book.

3. Use the chart information to make a Venn diagram, pairing two of Brett's animals.

   reproduce full page at 217

Name _____ **Date** _____

ANIMALS FROM JAN BRETT'S *THE MITTEN*

Research to complete the chart. For type of eater, write one of these:

C = carnivore, a meat-eating animal

H = herbivore, a plant-eating animal

O = omnivore, an animal that eats plants and meat

Animal	Descriptive Words	Habitat	State(s) in Which Found	Type of Eater
Snowshoe Hare				
Red Fox				
Brown Bear				
Great Horned Owl				
Hedgehog				
Badger				
Mole				
Field Mouse				

Name _____ **Date** _____

ANIMALS FROM JAN BRETT'S *THE MITTEN* Answer Key

Research to complete the chart. For type of eater, write one of these:

C = carnivore, a meat-eating animal

H = herbivore, a plant-eating animal

O = omnivore, an animal that eats plants and meat

Animal	Descriptive Words	Habitat	State(s) in Which Found	Type of Eater
Snowshoe Hare	Big kickers	Wooded areas, fields	Some kinds of hare in all states	H-herbivore
Red Fox	Shiny teeth	Wooded areas, fields, deserts	All 50	O-omnivore
Brown Bear	Lumbering	Forests, mountains	AK, OR, WA, CA	O-omnivore
Great Horned Owl	Glinty talons	Heavy forests, marshes, cliffs	All 50 states	C-carnivore
Hedgehog	Prickly, looking under wet leaves for things to eat	Woods, fields, meadows	Not native to U.S.	C-carnivore
Badger	Has diggers	Grasslands, woods, mountains	CA, AZ, TX, NM, CO, OR, ID, MN, IN, IL, KY, OH, MI	C-carnivore
Mole	Tunneling along	Underground	All states except Rocky Mt. states	C-carnivore
Field Mouse	No bigger than an acorn	Fields, houses, barns, underground	All states except Northeastern seaboard	O-omnivore

WRITING CENTER

Activity Five: Describing Woodland Animals

Supplies:
Copies of completed chart from Activity Four, nonfiction books about animals, particularly those in Brett's book

Evaluation:
Rubric

Procedure:
1. Use the completed data chart or facts from the following list of Web sites to write a descriptive paragraph about one of the animals in *The Mitten*.

2. Print their reports in a book, make multimedia pages using *HyperStudio*, or mount the information on your school's Web page.

   Badger: <www.qni.com/~badger/>

   Snowshoe hare:
   <www.museum.state.il.us/exhibits/larson/lepus_americanus.html>

   Red Fox: <janus.state.me.us/ifw/wildlife/mamtable.htm>

   Great Horned Owl: <oz.uc.edu/~verriljr>

   Hedgehog: <www.abdn.ac.uk/mammal/hedgehog.htm>

   Wood Mouse: <www.abdn.ac.uk/mammal/woodmous.htm>

   Brown Bear: <www.nature-net.com/bears>

MATH CENTER

Activity Six: Comparing Two Mittens

Supplies:
Two versions of *The Mitten*, one by Jan Brett and the other by Alvin Tresselt

Evaluation:
Class makes their own evaluation.

Procedure:
1. Read, discuss, and compare the illustrations of Brett's version of *The Mitten* with Tresselt's version (Lothrop, 1964).

2. Have students evaluate the stories based on criteria drawn up by the class (illustrations, number of animals, humor). Have them list what they like and dislike about both.

Activity Seven: Story Animal Sizes

Supplies:
Graph paper, *The Graph Club* (Tom Snyder Productions) or graphing mat and counters, beginning encyclopedia or easy books about animals, copies of Animal Sizes worksheet for each child (page 216)

Evaluation:
Students note page number for their answers on their size chart.

Procedure:
1. Use research materials to complete "Animal Sizes" chart on size and weight of animals. If a range is given, take the largest size and weight for each animal.

2. Use graph paper, graphing mat, or software program to represent the comparative weights of each animal.

reproduce full page at 216

Name _____

ANIMAL SIZES

Animal	Size	Weight	Page of information source

Name _____

ANIMAL SIZES Suggested Answer Key

Animal	Size	Weight	Page of information source
Snowshoe Hare	28 inches	12 pounds	Varies
Red Fox	39 inches	29 pounds	
Brown Bear	96 inches (8 feet)	1,500 pounds	
Great Horned Owl	20 inches	6 pounds	
Hedgehog	12 inches	39 ounces	
Badger	31 inches	37 ounces	
Mole	9 inches	6 pounds	
Field Mouse	6 inches	2 ounces	

ACTION CENTER

Activity Eight: Re-enacting the Story

Supplies:
The Mitten by Jan Brett, cardboard animal masks (available at bookstores or printed from Jan Brett's Web site <www.janbrett.com>), large tagboard mitten shape

Evaluation:
Applause by the audience

Procedure:
1. To use masks from Jan Brett's Web site, print, cut out and glue them to tongue depressors. This allows children to hold them in front of their faces and is more hygienic if you plan to reuse the masks with multiple classes. You also could pin them to the students' shirts.

2. Assign the animal parts and pass out the masks. You might want to have an animal puppet make the selections of students. As the animal is named, have the student act out appropriate movements and then get into the mitten by standing behind it. When the bear sneezes, everyone flies out of the glove!

3. Two students hold up the giant tagboard mitten. Retell the story and allow students to act it out.

VISUAL CENTER

Activity One: Punxsutawney Phil Performs

Supplies:
Plastic 9- to 12-inch flowerpot, groundhog puppet, groundhog books (see book list at the end of this lesson), photograph of groundhog or woodchuck if available, groundhog fact sheet (page 126)

Evaluation:
Students can retell details about groundhogs to check for comprehension.

Procedure:
1. Cut a hole in the back of a large plastic flowerpot that is large enough to insert arm and puppet (below).

2. Use a store-bought puppet or make one from a brown sock. This will be your Punxsutawney Phil, searching for his shadow.

3. Share a nonfiction book about groundhogs. I like Emilie Lepthien's book *Woodchucks* (Children's Press, 1992). If time is limited, just tell students something about groundhogs. (See fact sheet.)

4. Tell students you would like to introduce them to Punxsutawney Phil. Act as if he is shyly coming out of his hole and looking around. According to German or British custom, February 2 is the day when the woodchuck awakens from hibernation and peeks out from his burrow to check environmental conditions. Legend has it that if it is a sunny day, and the groundhog sees its shadow, it will be frightened back into its den, and there will be six more weeks of winter. If it is a cloudy day, and the groundhog cannot see its shadow, it will stay out of its hole, and that means spring will soon arrive. Explain to students that legends were first told to answer "Why?" questions. In this case, perhaps, the question was "Why isn't spring coming yet?"

Subject: English Language Arts, Social Studies

Grades: 2-5

Hardware: computer with Internet connection, simple musical instruments

Pre-lesson Class Preparation: Gather books and supplies mentioned in each activity, make puppet for Activity One, and bookmark sites.

◄

You can order a 5-inch finger puppet ($11.95) or a 9-inch hand puppet ($21.95) of the official Punxsutawney Phil. Order them from *The Underground World of Punxsutawney Phil*, 1-800-203-READ. You also can order them online at <www.groundhogs.com/index.htm>. This also is the site to order books and cassettes about *The Fearless Forecaster*. View the souvenir catalog of the Punxsutawney Chamber of Commerce, which includes five different puppets and five stuffed versions. That address is <www.penn.com/punxsycc/souv.html>.

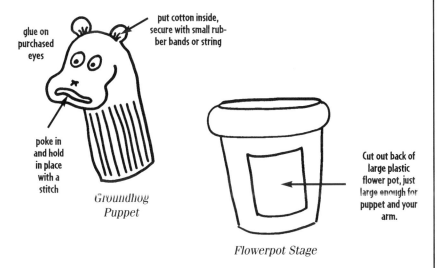

glue on purchased eyes

put cotton inside, secure with small rubber bands or string

poke in and hold in place with a stitch

Groundhog Puppet

Cut out back of large plastic flower pot, just large enough for puppet and your arm.

Flowerpot Stage

Groundhog Fact Sheet

Also can be spelled "ground hog"

▲ A groundhog is the same animal as a woodchuck.

▲ It is in the same family as squirrels, but is larger.

▲ Foxes, coyotes, wolves, bears and eagles are enemies of groundhogs.

▲ Woodchucks dig burrows that contain several compartments and have many entrances.

▲ Groundhogs sit up at the entrance to their burrow to check for danger.

▲ They eat dandelion greens, clover, plantain, grasses, and garden vegetables and fruits.

▲ Woodchucks do not "chuck," or eat, wood.

▲ They live in Canada, and in the Eastern and Midwestern United States.

▲ Woodchucks hibernate all winter in special underground dens.

▲ A woodchuck, or groundhog, is two feet long, including its bushy tail.

▲ It has grayish-brown fur on the upper side of its body and yellowish-orange fur on its belly.

▲ Groundhogs are excellent diggers and dig extensive burrows.

Activity Two: Weather Folklore

Supplies:
Farmer's almanacs, books of quotations, other books on weather lore, writing materials

Evaluation:
Student will accurately find, cite, and illustrate a weather lore.

Procedure:
1. Students, in groups or individually, locate other legends, traditions, and folklore about weather. A Web site that will help is *North Carolina Traditional Weather Lore* <ncnatural.com/wildflwr/fall/folklore.html>.

2. Write the folklore on paper that is lined at the bottom and has space for a picture at the top. Write weather lore and illustrate it for a "What Will the Weather Be?" bulletin board. Be sure to cite sources.

WRITING CENTER

Activity Three: Groundhog Story

Supplies:
(Per child) paragraph sheet, groundhog figure, craft stick

Evaluation:
Students receive credit for a paragraph that uses at least two of the vocabulary words and includes a picture.

Procedure:
1. Give each student a paragraph sheet and a groundhog figure. If you send a completed model back with students, this activity can be completed in the classroom.

2. Students color and cut out a groundhog, then glue it to a tongue depressor or craft stick. Cut a hole where indicated in the paragraph sheet. If you fold the sheet in half lengthwise, it is easier to cut the hole.

3. Students use words from the word bank to tell about groundhogs and Groundhog Day. They also can learn the woodchuck tongue twister, "How much wood could a woodchuck chuck if a woodchuck could chuck wood?"

   WORD BANK: groundhog, shadow, legend, Punxsutawney Phil, winter, hibernation, spring, six weeks, hole, woodchuck

Groundhog Figure

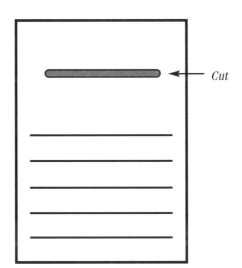

Cut

Paragraph Sheet

Activity Four: Canadian Groundhog Day

Supplies:
Computer with Internet access, writing materials

Evaluation:
Prepare an answer key based on Web information.

Procedure:
1. Explain that the United States celebrates Groundhog Day by watching the shadow of Punxsutawney Phil, a groundhog on Gobbler's Knob in Pennsylvania. Canadians predict the weather by watching Wiarton Willie, an albino groundhog, come out of his hole near the 45th parallel by Lake Huron. This location is exactly halfway between the North Pole and the equator. Both locations (and numerous others in the U.S.), claim their groundhog can tell folks whether they can count on putting their winter clothing away soon.

2. Students research both celebrations and their traditions. For more information on the Canadian celebration, look at *Welcome to Wiarton Willie* <www.wiarton-willie.org/index.cfm>.

3. Students construct a Venn Diagram that compares and contrasts the two traditions.

MATH CENTER

Activity Five: Weather Forecasting

Supplies:
Computer with Internet connection, almanacs, writing materials

Evaluation:
Check prediction in March for accuracy.

Procedure:
1. Look up the *Official Groundhog Site* <www.groundhogs.com/index.htm>. Dr. Julia Moutran has recorded the official sighting of Punxsutawney Phil for the years since 1898. In which years was spring supposed to come six weeks earlier, according to the groundhog predictions? Record your answers.

2. Use an almanac to check the temperatures for the Pennsylvania winters in those years and see if Punxsutawney Phil was accurate for those years. What was his forecast for this year? Was it accurate?

3. After this year's Groundhog Day, students record the groundhog's "prediction." Check in March to see if the weather in Pennsylvania bore out the prediction.

MUSIC CENTER

Activity Six: Shadow Song

Supplies:
Simple musical instruments

Evaluation:
Students will perform with instruments while singing. You might ask your music teacher to give students instructions in writing rhythm patterns for simple instruments. Another evaluative option would be to have students write rhythm patterns to play for a specific instrument, perhaps as backup to another student's song.

Procedure:
1. To most people, it makes little sense that a sunny February 2 will portend six more weeks of winter. To help children remember the folklore, have them act out this chant.

"There's a Furry Groundhog"

(*to the tune of* "I'm a Little Teapot")

Look! A furry groundhog

Small and brown.

He pops his head out

To peek around.

If he sees his shadow,

Back he'll go.

Then six more weeks

Of winter's cold!

2. Using simple musical instruments, some students can be the band.

3. If desired, students can use a different tune to make up other songs about the groundhog.

ACTION CENTER

Activity Seven: Being the Groundhog

Supplies:
Book *What Happened Today, Freddy Groundhog?* By Marvin Glass (Crown, 1989)

Evaluation:
None

Procedure:
1. Read the book, which tells the story of the days before Freddy pops up before the TV cameras on Groundhog Day.

2. Students act out being Groundhog Day groundhogs. They crouch down in their individual, imaginary burrows. Sing "The Groundhog Song" (from Activity Six) with the boys using male pronouns and the girls female pronouns. Act out the song with popping and peeking around, then with an "eek!" quickly drop back down into the burrow for an extended hibernation.

3. After numerous repeats, students (and teachers) will no longer be confused about what it means when a groundhog sees its shadow. My kindergartners loved doing this one so much that we did it repeatedly. The enthusiastic student groundhogs paused when my knee gave a loud and dramatic snap, and we decided that some "old" groundhogs couldn't do a lot of popping out of the ground. We did a few more repeats, but this time I acted the part of the Channel Two news camera person while they popped up to give the weather forecast!

Activity Eight: Making a Weather Station

Supplies:
Listed at Web site, depending on instrument made

Evaluation:
Display instruments in the library. Students can explain to their class how they work and (if possible) test them at school.

Procedure:
If you don't want to rely on a groundhog for weather information, make a weather station of your own. *Making a Weather Station* is a site available from the Miami Museum of Science at <www.miamisci.org/hurricane/weathertools.html>. It includes detailed instructions to make simple weather instruments from household materials, including a barometer, rain gauge, anemometer, wind scale tool, and a wind streamer for wind direction.

INTRAPERSONAL ACTIVITIES

Activity Nine: Celebrate Groundhog Day

Supplies:
Check site for supplies.

Evaluation:
Have a "Hogtivity Day" in your library and enjoy the fun.

Procedure:
Use the events planned by the faculty and staff of West End Elementary School in Punxsutawney, Pennsylvania. Some of these "Hogtivities" include "Toss the Hog," "Hot Hog," and "Groundhog Bingo." You can get some of these ideas online by writing to the Punxsutawney Chamber of Commerce or by looking at the *Hogtivities* site at <www.groundhog.org/hogtivities>. Find the address of the Chamber of Commerce when you scroll down to the "Just for Fun" section.

Activity Ten: Will You See the Groundhog?

Supplies:
A computer with Internet connection. If you have no connection, you can modify this scavenger hunt to be used with reference and nonfiction books.

Evaluation:
Check answers against the answer sheet.

Procedure:
Either in partners, trios, or independently, students use their scavenger hunt sheets and the Web sites or reference books to locate information about Groundhog Day and its furry little namesake.

Groundhog Day

Name _____ **Date** _____

GROUNDHOG SCAVENGER HUNT

1. What are three names for the groundhog?_____
   _____

2. How long is its tail? _____
   _____

3. How much does a groundhog weigh? _____
   _____

4. How long does a mother groundhog raise her 4-5 babies? _____
   _____

5. What are the enemies of the groundhog? _____
   _____

6. How many species are there? _____
   _____

7. Play the groundhog's sound. What does it sound like to you?_____
   _____

8. Are they found wild in our state?   _____
   _____

9. What animal was first used to predict an early spring? _____
   _____

10. What was the first name of Groundhog Day?_____
    _____

11. Who is Punxsutawney Phil? _____
    _____

12. What does a woodchuck eat?   _____
    _____

13. How much wood could a woodchuck chuck if a woodchuck could chuck wood? _____
    _____

BONUS: The scientific Latin name for a groundhog is *Marmota monax*. What does it mean?

Name _____ **Date** _____

GROUNDHOG SCAVENGER HUNT Answer Key

1. What are three names for the groundhog? **marmot, woodchuck, whistle-pig**

2. How long is its tail? **4 to 6 inches**

3. How much does a groundhog weigh? **4-14 pounds**

4. How long does a mother groundhog raise her 4-5 babies? **2 months to less than 1 year**

5. What are the enemies of the groundhog? **Foxes, coyotes, wolves, bears, snow leopards, and eagles**

6. How many species are there? **14 species of marmots**

7. Play the groundhog's sound. What does it sound like to you? **Birds chirping, mice squeaking**

8. Are they found wild in our state? **Found in Canada, and in eastern and central U.S.**

9. What animal was first used to predict an early spring? **Hedgehog**

10. What was the first name of Groundhog Day? **Candlemas Day**

11. Who is Punxsutawney Phil? **The groundhog who lives on Gobbler's Knob in Pennsylvania that looks for its shadow every February 2 and predicts the weather**

12. What does a woodchuck eat? **Dandelion greens, clover, grasses, and garden vegetables and fruits**

13. How much wood could a woodchuck chuck if a woodchuck could chuck wood? **700 pounds**

BONUS: The scientific Latin name for a groundhog is *Marmota monax*. What does it mean? **solitary mountain mouse**

Anansi and the Moss-Covered Rock

VISUAL LESSON

Activity One: Making a Dashiki

Supplies:
An old sheet, a tablecloth, or a length of fabric that is 2 2/3 feet long by 36 or 45 inches, paint supplies or markers, needle and thread per student, scissors, books with African designs

Evaluation:
Have a style show or wear them to lunch.

Procedure:
1. Cut fabric to size. Preserve as many selvages (finished edges) as possible. Fabric should come below the child's knees, front and back.

2. Decorate fabric in African designs, using tempera paint, markers, or crayons. Let dry.

3. Cut a head hole by folding the fabric in half width-wise and cutting a 6-inch cut in line with the center of the fold, and a 6-inch cut in a T-shape through only the front half of the fabric.

4. Stitch a seam on both sides of the length about 8 inches from each outside edge. Stop the seam 12 inches from the top. Hem bottom and stitch down the edges of the collar to keep from fraying.

5. Model your new dashiki.

Subject: Social Studies, English, Language Arts

Grades: 3-5

Hardware: computer with Internet access and CD-ROM drive

Software: Classroom Connect's *Cybertrip: Egypt* or *Cybertrip: Kenya* (Order at <store.classroom.com>.)

Pre-lesson Class Preparation:
Make two large tagboard cards, one that says FOLKS TELL and one that says FOLKTALE. Prepare transparent mancala board (see directions in Activity Five). Bring in a dashiki (or make one) and mancala board as models. Gather books and supplies noted in activities. If making dashikis (Activity One), prepare a letter to parents requesting materials.

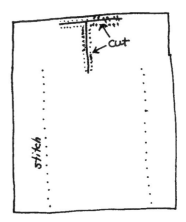

Dashiki pattern

Anansi and the Moss-Covered Rock

VERBAL LESSON

Activity Two: Anansi and the Moss-Covered Rock

Supplies:

World map, small potted plant, puppets (can be paper plate, hand, mask, or sock) to represent: a spider, a lion, a zebra, a bush deer, and a hippo. They can even be plastic animals if they are large enough to be seen. You must have the spider and the bush deer, but you can use any three African animals you have on hand (remember, a tiger is not found in Africa!). You also need Eric Kimmel's *Anansi and the Moss-Covered Rock* (Holiday House, 1988), other Anansi books (see end of lesson for list), a coconut, bananas (I buy plastic ones from the craft store), and a yam or sweet potato. Substitute a cantaloupe if you can't find one of the above. Get a moss-covered rock or any large rock with "green stuff" on it. I use peel-and-stick felt from the craft store, but you could add green paint or glue tissue paper for moss. Have a basket in which to hide props.

Evaluation:

Students can retell story if desired.

Procedure:

1. On a world map, have students locate your state and locate Africa. On which continent is our state? Is Africa a country?

2. Say, "Today I will be acting out a folktale from Africa that uses some African foods. Let's see how many of these you recognize. I'll read you several clues. Think about them carefully. Give me your guess when I say, "What am I?" Read facts (page 141) and have students guess. When they guess correctly, show them the food item.

3. Explain what a folktale is. Tell students that this story has come to us all the way from the continent of Africa, across the Atlantic. Folks have been telling this story possibly for hundreds of years, even before America was a country! We could call this a *Folks-Tell*, but the word has changed over the years to *Folktale*. Show the two cards to impress that fact on visual learners.

4. Show students the book *Anansi and the Moss-Covered Rock*, emphasizing that it says "retold" by Eric Kimmel because it is a folktale.

5. Have the bush deer hidden in sight behind a nearby fake or real plant before beginning the story. Focus student interest by explaining that Anansi is what is called a "trickster character." He is clever, greedy, and lazy. Can they think of any other trickster characters? They may mention Wiley E. Coyote from the roadrunner cartoons, Bugs Bunny, the coyote from Native American tales, or the fox from *Little Red Riding Hood.*

6. Read or tell the story, beginning with a spider puppet, a lion puppet, and a sweet potato. (I keep a small table near my storytelling chair to act as a "stage.") Stop after the part where the lion falls unconscious. Then ask for students to help. Appoint one to be the lion and two others to wait on the side. Read or tell the story and have the student ad-lib the actions of the puppet. As you get to the animal, give the appropriate puppet to the student to help re-enact the story. If you give them all out ahead of time, caution students to not distract the audience by playing with them.

7. End the session by booktalking other Anansi tales. Feature the 398.2 section.

Activity Three: Take a Trip to Africa

Supplies:
Internet computer, animal reference books, writing materials, materials for making dioramas

Evaluation:
Other students can learn about animals from the "zoo plaques" and dioramas that they each make.

Procedure:
1. Students each choose an African animal. They are to make a diorama of the habitat they would provide at the zoo.

2. They are to provide the information sign that accompanies the exhibit to give zoo attendees the facts they need to know about their animal.

3. Provide animal books for student research. Additional help can be found at the Internet site *Shamwari Game Preserve* <www.shamwari.com/europe.asp>. The site includes an extensive list of all animals found in the preserve. For each animal, a chart gives a description, diet, habitat, life expectancy, gestation, and number of young. There are some photos and eight amazing Virtual Preserve Tours. The site provides the download of Apple Quicktime VR Movies if you do not already have it on your computer. The tours are worth the wait involved in loading.

Topic #8 # Anansi and the Moss-Covered Rock

LOGIC LESSON

Activity Four: Counting in Swahili

Supplies:
Writing and drawing materials

Evaluation:
Teacher can check that information for the book is correct as he helps students brainstorm ideas and do their research.

Procedure:
1. Share the book *Moja Means One* by Muriel Feelings (Dial, 1971).

2. Have students write a companion book, beginning with the number 20 and going backward. Have them research other African words to use with each number and write a brief paragraph to go with each. Brainstorm a list of people, places, and things that are African to accompany each number. Students choose a number and research it. Encourage originality, for example, _____ is the number of letters in the name of the largest country in Africa.

3. Provide students with useful African books from your collection. You may wish to bookmark this site or give it to your students on a bookmark: *K-12 Electronic Guide for African Resources on the Internet* <sas.upenn.edu/African_Studies/K-12/AFR_GIDE.html>.

    If you're teaching anything about Africa, this well-researched and incredibly comprehensive site will help. It is collected and maintained by Ali B. Ali-Dinar of the University of Pennsylvania.

Anansi and the Moss-Covered Rock Topic #8

Activity Five: Playing Mancala

Supplies:
An egg carton for every pair of students, pinto beans, transparent mancala board, authentic mancala board (if available), 8 small plastic cups, such as those used for individual servings of pudding, 3 oz. papger cups

Evaluation:
Students can successfully play the game.

Procedure:

1. Make an abridged overhead version of a mancala board by taping six plastic cups together in a 3 x 2 pattern. Add an additional cup to each end, centered between the two rows. This will be your demonstration board.

2. Go to the *Mancala* site <www.imagiware.com/mancala> for instructions on how to play. You can actually play at this site as well.

3. Students come to the library with their egg cartons that already have the lids removed. Give each student a paper cup with six beans in each. These cups will be their "pits."

4. Use the transparent board to teach students how to play. Show them a mancala board and tell them that the one on the projector is abridged to make the game go faster for demonstration purposes.

5. Give students time to play the game. (We played on the floor.) Walk around and check that students are playing correctly.

6. Before they leave, tell them that the actual game of mancala is played with 12 beans per person and that when they feel confident playing with the 6 beans, they can play with 12.

MUSICAL LESSON

Activity Six: Drum Rhythms

Supplies:
Cassette or compact disk of African music, drum for each student

Evaluation:
Students can discuss their experience.

Procedure:
1. Make a set of drums (Activity Seven) and share them with each class.
2. Students use drums to keep the beat of the African music.
3. Students may want to write songs using African facts they have learned.

KINESTHETIC LESSON

Activity Seven: Making a Drum

Supplies:
Large balloon, large rubber band, and a can with both ends removed for each child. Coffee cans work best, but any larger sized can will do.

Evaluation:
Children can use drums to make a beat.

Procedure:
1. Students bring in a can with both ends removed.
2. Provide information on African drums from your online encyclopedia or book collection. Original African drums are made from animal hides for the drumhead.
3. Cut the balloon to provide the largest surface area.
4. Stretch the balloon over the end of the can and secure it snugly with the rubber band.
5. Group students by the size of their drum. Have them play percussion in rounds. Discuss the different sounds between the different size drums.

INTERPERSONAL LESSON

Activity Eight: African Speaker

Supplies:
None

Evaluation:
Students will attend to the speaker's story.

Procedure:
Invite a storyteller of African stories or performers who do African dances. Check with your local theater groups, speakers' bureau, and even parents in your community. One man performed as a Nigerian *griot* to tell stories, and we hired the players of The Express Theatre of Houston to perform *The African Talking Drum.*

INTRAPERSONAL LESSON

Activity Nine: Tasting African Foods

Supplies:
Foods listed, cut into serving pieces, napkins for each participant. **Note:** Be aware that some students may be allergic to coconut.

Evaluation:
Students can complete a ranking sheet developed by themselves or the teacher.

Procedure:
1. Explain the following facts about each food.

2. Have the students taste it.

Facts about African Foods

a. **Coconut**—Probably first used as food in the Pacific islands, now found in all tropical countries. The coconut palm produces about 100 coconuts annually, which take one year to ripen. Inside is milk and coconut "meat." The dried meat is called copra and is sold worldwide. To open one, pierce one of the three "eyes" to drain out the milk. Place the coconut in a bag and smash it with a hammer. Scrape off the meat with your teeth and drink the milk.

b. **Plantains**—Bananas originated in Asia, but are grown in all tropical countries. Uganda, in Africa, is a major banana producer. Some bananas are thumb-sized and red-skinned. Some are large and pulpy and are called plantains. A banana tree is not a true tree—it has no woody trunk or boughs.

c. **Yams**—(Substitute sweet potato for the taste test.) Western Africa produces half the yams in the world. They will not grow in the United States because the weather is too cool and the growing season too short. The United States does produce a cousin of the yam called a sweet potato, which also grows underground. Some yams grow to weigh 100 pounds and are 6 feet long!

d. **Muskmelon**—Muskmelons include cantaloupe and honeydew melons. They were first grown in India, spread to Egypt in North Africa, and brought to America from the town of Cantalupo in Italy. In the United States, Texas grows most of the cantaloupes eaten in this country.

Activity Ten: Taking a CyberTrip

Supplies:
The software programs *CyberTrip: Egypt or Cybertrip: Kenya* (Classroom Connect)

Evaluation:
Each tour stop has a brief hands-on activity for assessing student learning.

Procedure:
1. Have students take a CyberTrip. Each CyberTrip unit consists of a 64-page curricular guide and a resource-rich Web site. Each CyberTrip makes of 18 tour stops that emphasize geography, history, and culture. On the *CyberTrip to Egypt*, tour stops include Web visits to Cairo, the Great Sphinx, the Sahara Desert, and many other locales. Each stop has a corresponding topic, such as hieroglyphics, pharaohs, and Egyptian art to explore. Each tour stop has questions to guide student research. The stops can be done in any order.

2. You might use the detailed teacher notes for each stop to help you to teach about any or all of the trip stops.

Anansi Book List

Aardema, Verna. *Anansi Finds a Fool: An Ashanti Tale.*

_____. *Anansi Does the Impossible! An Ashanti Tale.*

Arkhurst, Joyce Cooper. *The Adventures of Spider: West African Folktales.*

Haley, Gail E. *A Story, A Story: An African Tale.*

Kimmel, Eric A. *Anansi and the Talking Melon.*

McDermott, Gerald. *Anansi the Spider: A Tale from the Ashanti.*

Temple, Frances. *Tiger Soup: An Anansi Story from Jamaica.*

Hello Cat, You Need a Hat

VISUAL CENTER

Activity One: Armor of the Past and Present

Supplies:
Computer with Internet capability, poster board or large drawing paper, drawing supplies

Evaluation:
This activity can be used with your third through fifth graders. Evaluation could be based on posters that should include labeled details of the uniforms of medieval and modern soldiers.

Procedure:
1. Go to the site *Circa 1265: Male Clothing and Knightly Armour of the 1250s* <www.bumply.com/Medieval/Kit/kit.htm>. Drawings and detailed descriptions explain the layers of clothing from the knight's skin out to the clothing of mail.

2. Compare these clothes with what modern soldiers wear to battle. Make two posters to show what knights of the 1250s and soldiers of the 2000s wear. Include weapons.

3. Be prepared to explain the similarities and differences to the class.

Activity Two: Making a Hat

Supplies:
(Per child) two double page sheets of newspaper and masking tape, paint or tissue paper, crepe paper, or other decorations

Evaluation:
Hats can be worn.

Procedure:
1. Place one sheet lengthwise from face to back on child's head. Place second sheet crosswise from ear to ear. Smooth down around head.

2. Use masking tape to wrap snugly around forehead to form the crown of the hat. Circle head twice.

3. Roll up the edges carefully to make a brim.

4. Shape and decorate to look like one of the hats from *Hello Cat, You Need a Hat*. Students might want to take hats home to decorate and return for a special "Hats On to Reading" Day.

Subject: English Language Arts, Social Studies, Math

Grades: K-3

Hardware: computer with Internet capabilities, chart tablet

Software: books, materials, and supplies listed in each activity

Pre-lesson Class Preparation: Gather books and materials listed in activities. Copy worksheets for each student or group of students.

Topic #9 Hello Cat, You Need a Hat

VERBAL CENTER

Activity Three: Writing a Sequel

Supplies:
Books about shoes (see list at end of lesson), writing and drawing materials

Evaluation:
Combine book pages into a class book. Read aloud to the class. What do they think of the story?

Procedure:
1. The class can write a sequel called *Hello Cat, You Need Some Shoes.* Discuss the format of the original story, and note the pattern and the rhyme scheme.

2. Brainstorm a list of all the kinds of shoes people might wear.

3. Partners choose a type of shoe and write a pair of rhyming lines.

4. After students do research to accurately draw the illustrations, have them make pages for a class book.

Activity Four: Creating an Alphabet Book

Supplies:
Suggested books, materials to make books

Evaluation:
Students supply at least one page about cowboy clothing or life for a letter of the alphabet.

Procedure:
1. With older students, you might want to explore clothing of a particular period. Because Texas history is required in fourth grade, study of the cowboy is part of our curriculum. The enduring popularity of this subject makes it useful in any state.

2. Read Jean Greenlaw's *Ranch Dressing* (Lodestar Books, 1993), Bobbie Kalman's *Bandanas, Chaps and Ten Gallon Hats* (Crabtree, 1998), or *Hats Are for Watering Horses* (Hendrick-Long, 1993) by Mary Blount Christian. All three discuss the origin and use of each article of cowboy clothing.

3. Ask students to bring in examples of cowboy clothing to make a labeled display of clothing and artifacts (optional).

4. After reading books and examining artifacts, have students complete a class alphabet book of cowboy clothing. Use these sites to research letters for which students have difficulty thinking of clothing:

   Western Folklife Center <www.westfolk.org>

   Sarah's Rodeo Page <rodeo.miningco.com/msu_history.htm>

Hello Cat, You Need a Hat

LOGIC CENTER

Activity Five: Careers and Uniforms

Supplies:
Copies of Careers and Uniforms worksheet, chalkboard or chart tablet, career books, writing materials. If you are using this unit with younger students, make it more applicable to community helpers.

Evaluation:
Rubric

Procedure:

1. Students research various careers, using the 300s section of the library or interviews with career people to complete the Careers and Uniforms worksheet (page 219).

2. Based on their fact sheets, students write a descriptive paragraph.

3. Students read their paragraph to the class.

4. After papers are read, the class chooses which of the careers reported they like best. They may choose several.

5. Students record their selections by attaching a paper hat to a bar graph made on the board or a chart tablet. Students can use the information to compose word problems or can answer questions from the teacher, based on the facts shown on the graph. Examples of questions are: Which are the top three career favorites of our class? Which career has fewer votes than _____? If each hat represented five votes, how many would _____ have?

reproduce full page at 219

Name_____

CAREERS AND UNIFORMS

Research a career to discover if a uniform is required for this job. Write a brief description of the job and tell about its uniform if one is required.

Job title: _____

Description of job: _____

Description of the uniform: _____

Does the job require specialized clothing? _____

How did you get your information? _____

Name_____

CAREERS AND UNIFORMS Sample Answers

Research a career to discover if a uniform is required for this job. Write a brief description of the job and tell about its uniform if one is required.

Job title: *policewoman*

Description of job: *a woman who is specially trained to prevent crime, catch criminals, protect the public, and enforce the laws. She talks to kids at schools, arrests people, goes to court, helps people in trouble, and is at the scene of accidents and fires.*

Description of the uniform: *A policewoman wears a uniform with a jacket and skirt, or shirt and pants, depending on the occasion. She wears regulation black shoes, a hat with a visor, and a police badge.*

Does the job require specialized clothing? *She wears a gun on a holster belt, a nightstick, handcuffs, shoulder radio, and a Kevlar bulletproof vest if she is going into a dangerous situation.*

How did you get your information? *Interview with Catherine McCarthy, policewoman at the Fort Bend Police Station*

Activity Six: Shoe Graph

Supplies:
Graphing mat, counters

Evaluation:
Class solves student problems, then checks answers together.

Procedure:

1. Compile a list of types of shoes as students brainstorm. Make a graph listing the shoe types down the left side. Have students mark each pair they own. For example:

These Are the Kinds of Shoes We Have

Kind of shoe	Group 1	Group 2	Group 3	Group 4
tennis shoe	XXXXX	XXX	XXXXXX	XXX
ballet slippers	XXXX	XXX		X
cowboy boots	XXX	XXXXX	XXX	XXX
loafers	XX	X	XXX	

2. Use unifix cubes, poker chips, or other markers placed on a large graphing mat.

3. Use the chart to have students develop word problems. Examples: Which group has the most tennis shoes? Which type of shoe has the largest number of pairs? How many?

4. Students must either draw, write a description, or act out their thinking process using manipulatives to represent shoes.

Hello Cat, You Need a Hat

MUSICAL CENTER

Activity Seven: Cowboy Poetry

Supplies:
Computer with Internet connection, TV with VCR, video *The Cowboy Poets: Live at Elko* (Western Folklife Center, 1994)

Evaluation:
Students complete assignments for credit.

Procedure:
1. While you are exploring the lives and times of cowboys, be sure students know that cowboys are still an important part of American life and culture. Cowboys often told stories in verse and created a distinctly American literary form. Take a virtual field trip to the *Western Folklife Center* at <www.westfolk.org> and hear their Cowboy Poets or view the video *The Cowboy Poets: Live at Elko.*

2. At this site, you can see and hear modern cowboys recite their poetry, and tour the Western Folklife Center to learn more about their lives. After becoming familiar with cowboy life, students can try their hand at writing their own cowboy poetry. Or, have students select their favorite cowboy poem, print it, and illustrate it with scenes from western life.

3. Students may want to set their original poem to music or provide music for one of the poems on this Web site.

KINESTHETIC CENTER

Activity Eight: Dress for Success

Supplies:
Tagboard, large sheets of colored paper, copies of person pattern for each child

Evaluation:
Have a style show with student narrating costumes.

Procedure:
1. Use an encyclopedia on CD-ROM, such as *Microsoft Encarta* or *World Book Multimedia*, to research the origin or purpose of one of these uniforms or costumes. You may wish to pair students, and you or the teacher should be available to supply assistance:

   Military: Army, Air Force, Coast Guard, Marines, Navy, or National Guard

   Native costume: from a country in your heritage or your interest

   Native American: tribal dress of a nation

   Careers: astronaut, cowhand, surgeon, police, firefighter, clown

   Religious: habits, vestments, ceremonial or holiday wear

2. Use this information to dress the person pattern (page 235) and display on an appropriately titled bulletin board. Alternately, trace children on large bulletin board paper. Dress figures in one of the uniforms or costumes from the preceding list. Cut out a circle in the face so artist can "wear" the costume. Feature books about the people on the bulletin board to encourage reading.

3. An alternate activity would be to ask students to bring various uniforms or cultural costumes to class to explain and possibly model.

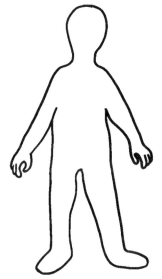

Person Pattern
reproduce full page
at 235

Topic #9 Hello Cat, You Need a Hat

Activity Nine: What's My Hat?

Supplies:
Collection of hats or pictures of hats

Evaluation:
Students correctly guess winners.

Procedure:
1. Use your hat collection or pictures of various hats to spur a discussion of why people wear hats. Make a list of hats children can name and why we wear them.

2. Read *Hello Cat, You Need a Hat.* Pause before turning the last page. Ask students to indicate whether they think the mouse will try to trick the cat or will keep his promise to stop mentioning hats. Then read the surprise ending.

3. Hats listed in the book include helmets, walkie-talkie hats, and bat hats. Use the books listed at the end of this activity to have students identify the "hats to sun in" as a sombrero and a pith helmet, "hats to be the bride and groom in" as a veil and a top hat, and so on for all the unnamed hats.

4. Use the books listed to have students research a type of hat. They bring in either the real hat or a drawing of the hat. Display all hats at the front. Then play *What's My Hat?* by having a child describe what her hat is used for and the material from which it is made. Class tries to guess by using the correct name for the hat, for example, "Is it the sombrero? Is it the bonnet?"

► *Hello Cat, You Need a Hat* is more enjoyable with a large group in the big book format available from Scholastic, Inc., 2931 E. McCarty Street, Jefferson City, MO 65101, 800-724-6527. Scholastic is the source of more than 100 big books at $14.95 each.

Book List

Our classes use these books to research hats and shoes for their own works. See the bibliography at the end of the book for publishing information.

Boyd, Lizi. *Princess, Cowboy, Pirate, Elf.*

Christian, Mary Blount. *Hats Are for Watering Horses: Why Cowboys Dressed That Way.*

Corbett, Sara. *Hats Off to Hats!*

Greenlaw, M. Jean. *Ranch Dressing.*

Kalman, Bobbie. *Bandanas, Chaps and Ten-Gallon Hats.*

Miller, Margaret. *Whose Hat?*

Morris, Ann. *Hats, Hats, Hats.*

Nichelason, Margery. *Shoes.*

O'Keefe, Linda. *Shoes: A Celebration of Pumps, Sandals, Slippers and More.*

Winthrop, Elizabeth. *Shoes.*

Yue, Charlotte. *Shoes: Their History in Words and Pictures.*

Are You My Mother? Topic #10

VISUAL LESSON

Activity One: Match Me to My Mother

Supplies:
Pictures of a variety of birds, drawing paper, drawing materials, small colored feathers—two per student (optional), filmstrip or movie of birds

Evaluation:
Students pin their birds to a class or library bulletin board with the mothers in small groups at the top and the babies in correlated small groups just below them.

Procedure:
1. Use study prints, pictures, and a filmstrip or movie to introduce students to the variety of sizes, colors, and shapes of birds. Students will be drawing a large and a small version of one of the birds, so as they look at the birds, they should be observing them for their physical characteristics.

2. To inspire drawing, make a list of birds. Include birds from hummingbirds to penguins, including distinctive ones, such as peacocks, roosters, turkeys, cardinals, ostriches, and owls.

3. Students draw two birds, making them similar except in size.

4. Color and cut them out. Put them on the bulletin board, perhaps in groups of five, with the idea that a viewer would try to match the mother with the baby.

VERBAL LESSON

Activity Two: Animal Families

Supplies:
Copies of Farm Animal Families chart (page 224) for each participant, helpful books about farm animals, including beginning encyclopedias and children's almanacs

Evaluation:
Check responses against the answer key.

Procedure:
1. Ask students to help you complete the data chart based on what they already know. If you use dog, you'll have to explain that the name for a female dog also has come to mean an unflattering term for a person.

2. Have students use the nonfiction books, a beginning encyclopedia, or an almanac to find the rest of the answers. This might work as a library contest, with all correct sheets being part of a drawing. You can give animal cookies or related books as prizes.

Subject: English Language Arts, Math, Science

Grades: 2-3

Hardware: computer with Internet access

Software: CD-ROM of birds, filmstrip or video of birds

Pre-lesson Class Preparation: Copy data charts for each student of Farm Animal Families.

Are You My Mother?

Name _____ **Date** _____

FARM ANIMAL FAMILIES

Find the names of each of these animal family members.

Animal Family	Male	Female	Baby
cow	bull	cow	calf
horse	stallion	mare	foal
cat	tom	queen	kitten
sheep	ram	ewe	lamb
goat	billy	nanny	kid
turkey	tom	hen	poult
chicken	rooster	hen	chick
pig	boar	sow	piglet
duck	drake	duck	duckling
goose	gander	goose	gosling
rabbit	buck	doe	bunny
donkey	jack	jenny	foal
dog	dog	bitch	puppy

Are You My Mother?

Activity Three: Telling with a Story Apron

Supplies:
Storytelling pocket apron (page 19), flannel board or chalk rail to arrange pictures, pictures of story characters (below), *Are You My Mother?* by P.D. Eastman (Random House, 1960), nonfiction books about farm animals. Refer to page 203-207.

Bird	*Cat*	*Dog*	*Hen*

Boat	*Cow*	*Wrecked Car*

Airplane	*Earth Moving Machine*	*Bird with Mother*

Evaluation:
Students correctly put sequence pictures in order according to story.

Procedure:
1. Use apron (page 19) to tell *Are You My Mother* to the students. Show characters as you tell. The baby bird should say something such as, "Let's see, now I know a dog is not my mother, a cat is not my mother," and so on as you review each character in order from the beginning.

2. Provide a set of sequence pictures based on the preceding figures and encourage stories to arrange them in order. Use the stories to retell the story to a group.

LOGIC LESSON

Activity Four: Compare/Contrast

Supplies:
Computer with Internet access

Evaluation:
Rubric

Step:
1. Have children take notes for a week based on their observations of the birds in their neighborhood. If birds are not plentiful in your area, students can go to the live camera pointed at *Hummingbird Nests* <www.portalproductions.com/h/nest.htm>. Here you can see photos and information about hummingbird nest building and feeding the young.

2. If it is the wrong time of year for the live observation, students can read the log and summarize the data in a short report describing the "childhood" of a hummingbird.

MUSICAL LESSON

Activity Five: Old McDonald's Baby Animal Farm

Supplies:
Photographs or drawings of baby farm animals

Evaluation:
Students can correctly identify the baby animal by name.

Procedure:
1. Provide pictures of each farm animal from data chart in Activity Two. Review names.

2. Use pictures and names to sing a revised version of "Old McDonald Had a Farm." In the baby animal version, for example, the song would be changed to:

   "…and on this farm he had some turkeys, EIEIO. With a turkey poult here and a turkey poult there, here a poult, there a poult, everywhere another poult…"

   You could sing another version that includes only the male animals and another with only the female animals.

KINESTHETIC LESSON

Activity Six: Make a Bird Feeder

Supplies:

Books with directions for bird feeder, such as *Steven Caney's Kids' America* (Workman, 1978), or a Web site that gives instructions, supplies listed in directions

Evaluation:

Project is a success if birds eat at the feeder.

Procedure:

1. Follow instructions in book to make pine cone feeder, suet bags, or strings of berries, nuts, and popcorn.

2. Students can make birdhouses as well. If you have the windows and setting for bird feeders and houses, this is a wonderful activity to help bird mothers and babies.

3. Go to this site for directions on how to make a milk carton bird feeder: <www.dfw.state.or.us/ODFWhtml/Education/BirdFeeder.html>. The Oregon Department of Fish and Wildlife that maintains this site also provides lists of good foods to stock the feeder and the best place to hang it.

Activity Seven: Barnyard Buddies

Supplies:

Computer with Internet connection. Students will need paper, pencil, two pennies, and a small cup to play.

Evaluation:

Self-evaluation

Procedure:

Students can visit *KidsFarm* <www.kidsfarm.com/farm.htm> to learn more about a variety of farm animals, what grows on a farm, equipment, kids' rodeo, and the people who work on farms. Site includes information and games.

INTRAPERSONAL LESSON

Activity Eight: Playing on the Farm

Supplies:
Computer with Internet connection, writing supplies

Evaluation:
Self-evaluation

Procedure:
1. The U. S. Department of Agriculture provides a fun and educational site *Take a New "Spin" on Agriculture* <www.usda.gov/nass/nasskids/games/games2.htm> for a child to become familiar with livestock, crops, and facts about the industry that keeps us in food. While learning, a student can play three different Mad Lib games, hear barnyard animal sounds, and unsnarl a variety of agricultural word scrambles. The site also includes farmyard trivia, jokes, and lots of facts along with the fun.

2. Students compile a scavenger hunt sheet to be answered by navigating and reading this site. The child who is strong in the intrapersonal intelligence especially delights in preparing this type of activity.

INTERPERSONAL LESSON

Activity Nine: Are You My Mother?

Supplies:
One large plastic egg, glued shut

Evaluation:
None

Procedure:
After a reading of the story, extend the fun by playing the game *Are You My Mother?* Students sit in a circle. One student is the lost chick and stands in the circle. One child on the circle has the plastic egg, but hides it behind his back. As the students chant the following, the students all act as though they are passing eggs behind their backs. The chick gets three tries to guess her "mother" (the child holding the egg) at the appropriate time in the song. If the chick is correct, she may stay in the circle. If incorrect, the child with the egg takes her place, and play continues.

"Chick Chant"
Chick, chick, who's your mom?
Can you tell us where she's gone?
Look around, look up and down,
Now, tell us chick, who's your mom? *All stop passing. Chick makes a guess. If wrong, repeat again until third incorrect guess.*

Lilly's Purple Plastic Purse Topic #11

VISUAL CENTER

Activity One: What's Inside?

Supplies:
Writing and drawing materials

Evaluation:
Students ask one another riddles about what they have drawn.

Procedure:

1. Draw a picture of what you would keep in a purse or fanny pack.

2. Write a riddle for two of those things. If students are unfamiliar with riddles, share some with them from your riddle collection. Discuss how riddles are like little puzzles to solve. Model several that you, then students, make up. Then students write their own, either alone or in pairs.

3. Ask your riddles of a friend or of the class.

WRITING CENTER

Activity Two: This Is the Way We Go to School

Supplies:
Writing materials, useful books from your collection, including Edith Baer's *This is the Way We Go to School* (Scholastic, 1990), copies of We All Go to School for each child or pair of children.

Evaluation:
Students correctly color their charts (page 220) to reflect which facts are similar and which are different. Modify We All Go to School as needed for your age group.

Procedure:

1. Work alone or in pairs. If any students have attended school outside your state, ask them to contribute information about their experiences to compare and contrast as an example.

2. Research school information books from the library and the Yahooligans.com search index.

3. Use research to complete the chart. Color similar statements yellow and different statements pink.

4. Share findings with the class. Add details to a class chart that encompasses all the countries researched.

Subject: English Language Arts

Grades: 1-3

Hardware: computer with Internet connection

Software: *Arthur's Reading Race* (Broderbund, 1995)

Pre-lesson Class Preparation: Gather books, materials, and supplies for activities. Duplicate copies of needed worksheets.

reproduce full page at 220

Name _____

WE ALL GO TO SCHOOL

**Choose a country to compare with our own. Complete the chart.
Use library books, the Internet, and encyclopedias.**

**Color the boxes that are the same yellow.
Color the ones that are different pink.**

	In the United States	**In _____**
Getting to school		
Eating lunch		
Hours and days at school		
Subjects studied		

Activity Three: School Customs

Supplies:
Copy of Comparing Two Schools (page 221) for each student

Evaluation:
Students can complete sheet and explain it to the class (may send home for help if needed).

Procedure:
1. Lead a discussion of school customs.

2. Students compare their current school and one they previously attended.

3. If they have never been to another school, they might want to compare this year with last year, comparing two different grades.

Lilly's Purple Plastic Purse

reproduce full page at 221

Name _____

COMPARING TWO SCHOOLS

Write describing words in each box.
Tell how the schools are the same and different.

	This school	My old school OR last year at this school:
Library		
Eating lunch		
Recess		
Teacher		
Friends		

MATH CENTER

Activity Four: Finger Counting

Supplies:
Abacus, computer with Internet connection

Evaluation:
Students can demonstrate or explain use of abacus.

Procedure:
1. Mention that Lilly is very proud of her three quarters. Introduce an abacus to explain how shopkeepers in China used it for thousands of years to record purchases and work with numbers.

2. Access the site *Aloha Mental Arithmetic* <www.alohama.com/index/ shtml> for some lessons in fingering math (Chisenbop) and abacus calculations. This site features a virtual classroom in Malaysia.

Lilly's Purple Plastic Purse

Activity Five: Cause and Effect

Supplies:
Sentence strips with causes written on strips of one color, effects on another.

Evaluation:
Check answers against the answer key.

Procedure:
1. Read the story *Lilly's Purple Plastic Purse* by Kevin Henkes (Greenwillow, 1996).

2. Explain cause and effect.

3. Tell students some causes and effects from the story are written on strips. Read all the causes aloud, then all the effects, asking students to think which go together.

4. Distribute strips to students and have them match them. Then have them read the cause and effect events in story sequence.

CAUSE AND EFFECT EVENTS

1c. Lilly did not wait to show her purple plastic purse.

1e. Mr. Slinger kept it at his desk.

2c. Lilly was sad and missed her purse.

2e. She did not feel like eating her snack.

3c. Lilly got very angry with Mr. Slinger.

3e. She wrote an angry note and put it in Mr. Slinger's bag.

4c. Mr. Slinger gave Lilly a kind note and a tasty snack.

4e. Lilly felt so mean she sat in the uncooperative chair.

5c. Lilly was sorry about the mean note to Mr. Slinger.

5e. She wrote a new story and brought him a tasty snack.

ACTION CENTER

Activity Six: Building an Abacus

Supplies:
Computer with Internet capability, Lego building blocks

Evaluation:
You may want to print instructions for students to complete at home. They bring the completed abacus back to use at school with math activities.

Procedure:
1. Go to *The Abacus: Lego* <www.ryerson.ca:8080/~elf/abacul/lego.

2. Use your Lego blocks to construct an abacus, following the directions on this site.

3. Bring your abacus back to class to learn how to use it. Get directions from a book in our library or go to *The Virtual Abacus* <203.116.95.144/abacusstart.html>. The site gives you interactive instructions on how an abacus works and includes a game for you to practice your knowledge.

4. Demonstrate abacus use to a small group or to the class, or bookmark the preceding site for use as a center.

INTRAPERSONAL ACTIVITIES

Activity Seven: Going to School with Arthur

Supplies:
Computer with CD-ROM drive, CD-ROM *Living Books: Arthur's Reading Race* (Random House/Broderbund, 1996)

Evaluation:
Students keep a log of activities done for credit.

Procedure:
1. The programs begin in a school setting, complete with a show-and-tell session. They include an interactive story with reading and spelling games.

2. Have students keep a log of the activities they complete.

Lilly's Purple Plastic Purse

GROUP CENTER

Activity Eight: Interviewing Kevin Henkes

Supplies:
Costume supplies, copies of Kevin Henkes books, microphone on a stand as if characters were sitting inside a radio news booth (optional), books about authors, such as *Children's Books and Their Creators* edited by Anita Silvey (Houghton Mifflin, 1995)

Evaluation:
Rubric

Procedure:
1. Go to *Carol Hurst's Children's Literature* Web site at: <www.carolhurst. com/newsletters/newslettersld.html>.

2. Find the April 1996 newsletter featuring author Kevin Henkes.

3. An activity for some with an interpersonal strength is for one partner to pretend to be Kevin Henkes. The other is the interviewer. Dress the parts.

4. Student author and interviewer prepare at least five questions and the answers. Rubric should include originality, accuracy, and entertainment.

5. Do an interview in front of the class, using the material in this article and other sources for the answers.

INTRAPERSONAL ACTIVITIES

Activity Nine: Expressing a Feeling

Supplies:
Letter writing materials that include various papers, colored and lead pencils, pens, and other drawing and writing materials

Evaluation:
Give credit if note is written to a book character and expresses at least one feeling.

Procedure:
1. Lilly used a note to tell Mr. Slinger how she felt. Distribute paper and writing materials. The best kind has room for a picture at the top and lines for writing at the bottom.

2. Students write a note from one storybook character to another to explain their feelings. Here are suggestions for notes:

   Mr. Slinger to Lilly after she constantly interrupts him or after he gets her angry note

   Pig to wolf after he blows down its house

   Goldilocks to bears after she damages their things

   Prince to Cinderella after he discovers she has run away from him at the ball

   The giant to Jack after Jack takes his hen that lays golden eggs

   The miller's daughter after the king tells her she must spin a roomful of straw into gold

   Other ideas by your students

3. Older students can write a letter from one of their current book characters to a character in a different book. For example, what if Junie B. Jones compared notes with Ramona Quimby?

4. Demonstrate the proper form for a friendly letter. You might want to feature other letter and note writing books, such as *Dear Peter Rabbit* by Ada Alma Flor (Atheneum, 1994), the Ahlberg's *Jolly Postman* (Little Brown, 1986), Marissa Moss' *Amelia Writes Again* (Tricycle Press, 1996), or Beverly Cleary's *Dear Mr. Henshaw* (Morrow, 1983).

Jan Brett Author Study

VISUAL CENTER

Activity One: A Scavenger Hunt

Supplies:
Copies of three scavenger sheets one sheet for each group (pages 225-227), at least one of each of the books in the bibliography, pencils (optional), computer with access to Jan Brett's Web site

Evaluation:
Students or teacher will check student scavenger sheets against answer keys.

Procedure:
1. Divide students into groups. Each group will have copies of a different scavenger sheet and a copy of the four books related to their sheet. Multiple copies of the books will allow for many smaller groups.

2. Students work as a group to find the answers in the books.

3. Upon completion of the scavenger sheet, group checks its work either with the key or with their teacher.

    Optional: Jan Brett has a brief scavenger hunt on her Web site. Children are asked to look through her books to find a variety of foods listed on the screen. This may be good for an enrichment activity. Go to <www.janbrett.com> and click on the scavenger hunt.

reproduce full page at 225

Name: _____

JAN BRETT BOOK HUNT, PART 1

Use the Jan Brett books to answer these questions:

1. **(The Mitten)** Many animals squeeze into the mitten.
    Write their names from smallest to largest. Two are done for you.
    meadow mouse, _____
    _____, brown bear

2. **(Armadillo Rodeo)** Bo's mother has to search for him.
    Which animals did she ask for help? (Hint: Look in the side pictures.)
    _____
    _____

3. **(Annie and the Wild Animals)** Annie ended up with three new pets.
    What colors were they? _____
    _____

4. **(Comet's Nine Lives)** Write the names of three boats found on the bay.
    _____
    _____

Subject: Language Arts

Grades: 1-3

Hardware: computer with Internet connection, cassette player or CD player

Software: music tapes or CD

Pre-lesson Class Preparation:
Go to the *Jan Brett* site <www.janbrett.com>. Bookmark the various pages used in the following activities. Print the masks from each of the stories. Duplicate copies of needed sheets. Have students bring a small, clean milk carton from the cafeteria if they are in grade 2 or 3 and will be completing the armadillo project. Have a copy of each of her books available.

Subscribe to Jan Brett's online newsletter at her Web site. You will receive notice of the latest additions to her Web site and other interesting developments. Request her teacher/librarian pack by writing to Jan Brett, PO Box 366, Norwell, MA 02061.

Jan Brett Author Study

reproduce full page at 226

Name: _____

JAN BRETT BOOK HUNT, PART 2

Use the Jan Brett books to answer these questions:

5. **(Fritz and the Beautiful Horses***)* What did the beautiful horses crack?

    _____

    The picture of this cracked thing is on which page? _____

6. Many animals got mad at **The Gingerbread Baby**. Which animals were chasing him?

    _____

    _____

7. **(The Trouble with Trolls)** What did the hedgehog eat? (Hint: Look at the bottom of the pages.)

    _____

    _____

8. **The First Dog** saved Kip from three dangerous animals. What were they?

    _____

    _____

reproduce full page at 227

Name: _____

JAN BRETT BOOK HUNT, PART 3

Use the Jan Brett books to answer these questions:

9. **(Christmas Trolls)** What animal is the troll's helper?

    _____

    Name three gifts that the trolls took. _____

    _____

10. **(Goldilocks and the Three Bears.)** Look close! What little animals live with the bears? _____

11. In **The Hat**, the animals are taking the clothes off the line!
    Can you find what each animal took?

Hen	_____	Goose	_____
Cat	_____	Dog	_____
Pig	_____	Horse	_____

12. **(The Night Before Christmas)** Who is riding with Santa in his sleigh?

    _____

    _____

Name: _____

JAN BRETT BOOK HUNT, PART 1 Answer Key

Use the Jan Brett books to answer these questions:

1. **(The Mitten)** Many animals squeeze into the mitten.
   Write their names from smallest to largest. Two are done for you.
   Meadow mouse, mole, hedgehog, rabbit, owl, badger, fox, brown bear

2. **(Armadillo Rodeo)** Bo's mother has to search for him.
   Which animals did she ask for help? (Hint: Look in the side pictures.)
   coyote (or wolf), deer, rabbit, cow (or steer or longhorn), horse

3. **(Annie and the Wild Animals)** Annie ended up with three new pets.
   What colors were they? *gray, white, black*

4. **(Comet's Nine Lives)** Write the names of three boats found on the bay.
   Jean T., Brant Point, Cindi

Name: _____

JAN BRETT BOOK HUNT, PART 2 Answer Key

Use the Jan Brett books to answer these questions:

5. **(Fritz and the Beautiful Horses)** What did the beautiful horses crack?
The bridge
The picture of this cracked thing is on which page? *21*

6. Many animals got mad at **The Gingerbread Baby**. Which animals were chasing him?
dog , horse, pig, dog, goats, cat

7. **(The Trouble with Trolls)** What did the hedgehog eat? (Hint: Look at the bottom of the pages.)
fish, nuts (acorns)

8. **The First Dog** saved Kip from three dangerous animals. What were they?
woolly mammoth (elephant), (cave) bear, (saber-toothed) tiger

Name: _____

JAN BRETT BOOK HUNT, PART 3 Answer Key

Use the Jan Brett books to answer these questions:

9. **(Christmas Trolls)** What animal is the troll's helper?
   Hedgehog
   Name three gifts that the trolls took.
   mittens, treetop angel, Christmas pudding

10. **(Goldilocks and the Three Bears.)** Look close! What little animals live with the bears? *2 mice (give credit for an owl)*

11. In **The Hat**, the animals are taking the clothes off the line!
    Can you find what each animal took?

Hen	*gloves*	Goose	*hat*
Cat	*scarf*	Dog	*sweater*
Pig	*vest*	Horse	*longjohns (or pants)*

12. **(The Night Before Christmas)** Who is riding with Santa in his sleigh?
    2 elves

Activity Two: Observing Authentic Details

Supplies:

Filmstrip viewer or TV/VCR, filmstrip or video of traditional architecture and clothing of selected countries. Match country videos to the following titles:

The Hat—Denmark

Christmas Trolls, Trouble with Trolls, The Wild Christmas Reindeer—Norway

Comet's Nine Lives—Nantucket (U.S.)

Armadillo Rodeo—Texas ranch (U.S.)

Berlioz the Bear—Bavaria (Germany)

Gingerbread Baby—Switzerland

The Mitten—The Ukraine

Evaluation:

Decide on acceptable number of details for a satisfactory, good, or excellent list. Share this rubric with students before they start their project.

Procedure:

1. Select one of Jan Brett's books. Read it to the students, calling attention to the details Brett includes in her illustrations. Brett spends time in the countries that provide background for her stories. She photographs buildings, people, and other details that will enrich her story and provide an authentic backdrop.

2. After viewing the country video or filmstrip relevant to the book, help students list illustration details from the book that reflect that country's heritage.

3. Students contribute to a class chart called "Discovering Details." (page 222)

4. If it is age-appropriate, have students select another book and video/filmstrip and complete a similar activity with a partner or a small group.

Jan Brett Author Study

reproduce full page at 222

Name _____ **Date** _____

DISCOVERING DETAILS

**Look at one of the books below. Watch the filmstrip or movie that goes with it.
Write down a few details from the book that look like the real things.**

Title	Country	Real Details
The Hat	Denmark	
Christmas Trolls Trouble with Trolls or The Wild Christmas Reindeer	Norway	
Comet's Nine Lives	Nantucket, U.S.	
Armadillo Rodeo	Texas ranch, U.S.	
Berlioz the Bear	Bavaria, Germany	
The Mitten	The Ukraine	
Gingerbread Baby	Switzerland	

Activity Three: Correlated Art Projects

Supplies:

For pencil topper—copies from Web page, colored pencils or fine-tipped markers, scissors, glue, yarn, their own pencil

For armadillo—small milk carton, brown craft paper (use paper sack or bag), black fine-tipped markers or crayons, glue, scissors, a model made in advance for students to see;

For sailor's bracelet—three yards of 3-ply nylon or cotton string or cord that is about 1/8 inch in diameter for each student. Make a sample of each project in advance so you will be able to help students and show them a finished model. If your project is successful, word will spread, and the bracelets will become a "must-have." Capitalize on this demand by pairing older bracelet makers with younger students. This is a good esteem builder for both students.

Evaluation:

No subjective grade is given. Completing a project will earn the student a good grade. Projects can be displayed with name plaques to recognize the student artists.

Procedure:

1. On her Web page, Brett has dozens of coloring pages, activities, and things to make. Go to the site to make copies of the directions for each of the following projects.

2. Student chooses one of the following projects and brings supplies:

   Grade 1, 2, or 3: Make a pencil topper. Related to *Trouble with Trolls* and *Christmas Trolls* <www.janbrett .com/make_a_pencil_topper.htm>

   Grade 2 or 3: Make an armadillo. Related to *Armadillo Rodeo* <www.janbrett .com/armadillo_carton_project_page.htm>

   Grade 3: Make a sailor's bracelet. Related to *Comet's Nine Lives* <www.janbrett.com/sailors_bracelet.htm>

3. Students divide into groups by projects with copies of directions and supplies. With some adult assistance, students help each other to complete project.

WRITING CENTER

Activity Four: Send a Postcard

Supplies:
Computer with Internet connection or printed sample of Jan Brett's blank postcards, colored pencils, pens or pencils

Evaluation:
Students will write a postcard to a fellow student. Optional: The receiver will evaluate the postcard based on a rubric established by the group.

Procedure:
1. After having heard or read at least five of Jan Brett's books, each student will choose a postcard to send to a fellow student.

2. Student will select a postcard design (and color if desired).

3. Student will tell partner which book she likes best and why.

4. Student will deliver postcard via computer or by hand.

MATH CENTER

Activity Five: Nautical Flags

Supplies:
Copies of gridded paper from Brett's Web site on nautical flags: <www.janbrett.com/piggybacks/piggybacks_comet_nautical_flag_namespell. htm>, color copies of nautical flags from that site. Make several sets for your activities.

Evaluation:
Students pair up and check one another's flags for accuracy.

Procedure:
1. In *Comet's Nine Lives*, the dog character that runs the lighthouse is using nautical flags to spell something. Use the printed key from the site mentioned to figure out what he is saying on each page.

2. Look at the sample flags, and use the gridded paper and colored pencils to make a set of flags to spell out your name using nautical flags. Discuss reasons for use of flags.

MUSIC CENTER

Activity Six: Background Music

Supplies:
A variety of cassettes or CDs featuring classical music, movie tracks, and other types of music suitable for background music (instrumentals are best), casscttc or CD player

Evaluation:
Project will be acceptable if student can explain why he chose the musical piece he did for his book.

Procedure:
1. Read one of Jan Brett's books.

2. What kind of feeling do you get from this book? (happy, sad, cheerful, depressed, quiet, loud)

3. What kind of instrument would represent this book? Why? **Note:** Jan Brett thinks "Peer Gynt" would make good background for *Berlioz the Bear.*

4. What kind of music would represent this book? (modern, classical, jazzy, stately, calm)

5. Choose a musical selection that would represent this book.

6. Be prepared to bring the music to be played as the teacher rereads the story to the class.

7. Tell the class why you chose this piece.

Activity Seven: Instruments

Supplies:
Several copies of *Berlioz the Bear*, reference books or pictures of musical instruments, copies of page 228 for each child

Evaluation:
Check student's work against answer sheet.

Procedure:
Student compares instruments in the Berlioz book with reference pictures to identify each instrument and the family to which it belongs (woodwind, percussion, stringed).

reproduce full page at 228

Name _____ **Date** _____

NAME THE INSTRUMENT

Use reference pictures to identify the instrument on each of these pages (count pages with the title page as page 1):

Instrument Name	Page #	Instrument Family (woodwind, stringed, percussion)
	3	
	4	
	16	
	28, 31	
	28, 30	
	22	

NAME THE INSTRUMENT Answer Key

Use reference pictures to identify the instrument on each of these pages (count pages with the title page as page 1):

Instrument Name	Page #	Instrument Family (woodwind, stringed, percussion)
Double bass	3	Stringed
Bass drum	4	Percussion
Violin	16	Stringed
Trombone	28, 31	Woodwind
French Horn	28, 30	Woodwind
Oboe	22	Woodwind

ACTION CENTER

Activity Eight: Making Gingerbread

Supplies:

You may request that the classroom teacher or students help with ingredients. If your group is too large to make this activity economically feasible, send home the recipe and a modified version of the parent letter. Children who return a homemade ginger cookie will get credit for the activity.

Recipe ingredients: flour, salt, baking soda, ginger, cinnamon, ground cloves, nutmeg, butter, brown sugar, egg, molasses, vanilla

Utensils: two bowls, measuring spoons for tablespoon, teaspoon, and 1/4 teaspoon, measuring cups for one cup and 1/2 cup, a self-sealing plastic bag for each participant, large spoons for stirring. Optional: sifter, mixer.

This is a good recipe to make in school, since the dough has to rest for several hours before baking. Make it at school and send home parts of the dough in a small self-sealing plastic bag along with the parent note. Also supply commercially made gingersnaps.

Evaluation:

Student brings one of his cookies back to school to get credit for completion.

Procedure:

1. Students have read or listened to Jan Brett's *Gingerbread Baby.*

2. In case students have not tasted gingerbread cookies, let them taste a commercially made gingersnap. Explain to them that ginger is made from the underground stem (rhizome) of the ginger plant. Most preserved ginger is from China.

3. In supervised groups, students will measure and mix the recipe ingredients. Be sure students and utensils are clean. A group of three will get enough batter to make about eight cookies.

Parent note:

Dear Parents,

Today we made ginger cookie dough. The dough needs to rest for several hours, so we are requesting that you help your child to finish the cookies at home.

To make, roll the dough out on waxed paper. When the dough is about 1/4 inch thick, cut it with a cutter. You can use a small glass or jar lid as a cutter. Bake 7 to 10 minutes on a greased cookie sheet at 375 degrees.

When cookies are cool, please send one back to school in the plastic zip bag. This is how your child will get credit for completing the project.

Thank you for your help. We hope you will enjoy this family activity and the wonderful smell that the baking cookies will make in your home.

Sincerely,

Recipe:

from Jan Brett (used with permission)

In a large bowl, sift and mix together:
>   3 cups flour
>   1/4 teaspoon salt
>   1 teaspoon baking soda
>   1 tablespoon ginger
>   1 teaspoon cinnamon
>   1/4 teaspoon ground cloves
>   1/4 teaspoon ground nutmeg

In another bowl or mixer cream:
>   12 tablespoons (1 1/2 sticks) unsalted butter
>   3/4 cup brown sugar
>   1 egg

Stir the dry ingredients into the creamed mixture.
Then add:
>   1/2 cup molasses
>   1 tablespoon vanilla

INTRAPERSONAL ACTIVITIES

Activity Nine: Yourself as a Bear

Supplies:

Hand mirror or photo of self, *Berlioz the Bear,* printout of Brett's Web page <janbrett.com/newsnotes/berlioz_newsnotes3.htm> that shows photographs of several musicians and how Jan changed them to look like bears, drawing paper, drawing pencils, crayons, colored pencils, writing paper

Evaluation:

This is an entirely personal and subjective activity. No outside evaluation will be made.

Procedure:

1. The student will read and study the pages of the Berlioz characters and how they were derived from real life.

2. View the video *How to Draw a Bear* by Jan Brett on your computer. It is found at <janbrett.com/learn_to_draw_a_bear.htm>.

3. Student will study her face in a hand mirror or photograph, and try to draw herself as a bear. Then in a paragraph, she will explain what qualities about herself she brought out in her bear picture.

GROUP CENTER

Activity Ten: Story Re-enactment

Supplies:
Masks from the Jan Brett site for these stories. Students will be in a group, each of which will perform a different story. Print masks from Jan Brett's Web page for these stories: *Gingerbread Baby, The Hat, The Mitten, Town Mouse/ Country Mouse,* or *Hedgie's Surprise.*

Evaluation:
Develop a group rubric for the audience to evaluate the performance of each story.

Procedure:
1. Read the selected story twice to become familiar with the story.

2. Choose a character from the story.

3. Practice the story with each character acting appropriately in the sequence of the story.

4. Perform for the class.

Activity Eleven: A Visit from Jan Brett

Supplies:
Books about authors or illustrators, such as *Meet the Authors and Illustrators, Volume II* by Deborah Kovacs and James Preller (Scholastic, 1993) or *Children's Books and Their Creators* edited by Anita Silvey (Houghton Mifflin, 1995)

Evaluation:
Develop a rubric that includes number of facts, accuracy, and performance.

Procedure:
1. Students will perform as if they are visiting author Jan Brett. Author information can be read from the Web site (click on "About Jan Brett"). At this page, students can hear two audiotapes about Jan and her books. They also can view six videos that show Jan working on her books, cooking, and even flying with The Blue Angels. Or they can get author information from a number of author books.

2. They should tell the class the following: Family information, how she gets her book ideas, pets, where she is from and lives now, and other facts determined by the group.

Bibliography of Jan Brett's Books Used in These Activities

Annie and the Wild Animals. Houghton Mifflin, 1985.

Armadillo Rodeo. G. P. Putnam's Sons, 1995.

Berlioz the Bear. G. P. Putnam's Sons, 1991.

Christmas Trolls. G. P. Putnam's Sons, 1993.

Comet's Nine Lives. G. P. Putnam's Sons, 1996.

The First Dog. Harcourt Brace Jovanovich, 1988.

Fritz and the Beautiful Horses. Houghton Mifflin, 1981.

Gingerbread Baby. G. P. Putnam's Sons, 1999.

Goldilocks and the Three Bears. G. P. Putnam's Sons, 1987.

The Hat. G. P. Putnam's Sons, 1997.

Hedgie's Surprise. G. P. Putnam's Sons, 2000.

The Mitten. G. P. Putnam's Sons, 1989.

Night Before Christmas. G. P. Putnam's Sons, 1998.

Trouble with Trolls. G. P. Putnam's Sons, 1992.

Bibliography of Children's Books

A

A. Nonny Mouse Writes Again! Selected by Jack Prelutsky. Knopf, 1993.

Aardema, Verna. *Anansi Finds a Fool: An Ashanti Tale.* Dial Books for Young Readers, 1992.

_____. *Anansi Does the Impossible! An Ashanti Tale.* Atheneum, 1997.

_____. *The Crocodile and the Ostrich: A Tale from the Akanba of Kenya.* Scholastic, 1984.

Adler, David A. *Cam Jansen and the Scary Snake Mystery.* Viking, 1997.

_____. *A Picture Book of Davy Crockett.* Holiday House, 1996.

_____. *A Picture Book of Eleanor Roosevelt.* Holiday House, 1991.

_____. *A Picture Book of Florence Nightingale.* Holiday House, 1992.

Agard, John. *No Hickory, No Dickory, No Dock: Caribbean Nursery Rhymes.* Candlewick, 1995.

Agee, Jon. *Go Hang a Salami! I'm a Lasagna Hog? And Other Palindromes.* Farrar Strauss Giroux, 1991.

_____. *So Many Dynamos! And Other Palindromes.* Farrar Strauss Giroux, 1994.

Ahlberg, Janet and Allan. *The Jolly Postman or Other People's Letters.* Little Brown, 1986.

Alderson, Sue Ann. *Pond Seasons.* Douglas & McIntyre, 1997.

Alma Flor, Ada. *Dear Peter Rabbit.* Atheneum, 1994.

Andersen, Hans Christian. *The Emperor and the Nightingale.* Troll and Associates, 1979.

Anderson, Laurie Halse. *No Time for Mother's Day.* Albert Whitman & Company, 1999.

Angelou, Maya. *Soul Looks Back in Wonder.* Dial Books, 1994.

Arkhurst, Joyce Cooper. *The Adventures of Spider: West African Folktales.* Little Brown, 1992.

Armstrong, William Howard. *Sounder.* HarperCollins, 1969.

Aylesworth, Jim. *Gingerbread Man.* Scholastic, 1998.

_____. *Teddy Bear Tears.* Atheneum, 1997.

Axelrod, Amy. *Pigs Will Be Pigs.* Simon & Schuster, 1994.

B

Baer, Edith. *This Is the Way We Go to School.* Scholastic, 1990.

Bagert, Brod. *Let Me Be the Boss: Poems for Kids to Perform.* Wordsong, 1992.

Balan, Robert. *Jump, Frog, Jump.* Greenwillow, 1981.

Balian, Lorna. *A Garden for a Groundhog.* Humbug Books, 1985.

Ballard, Robert D. *Ghost Liners.* Little Brown, 1998.

Bancroft, Henrietta. *Animals in Winter.* HarperCollins, 1997.

Barrett, Judi. *Cloudy with a Chance of Meatballs.* Atheneum, 1978.

Bate, Lucy. *Little Rabbit's Loose Tooth.* Crown Publishers, 1975.

Bateman, Teresa. *The Ring of Truth: An Original Irish Tale.* Holiday House, 1997.

Baxter, Nicola. *Winter.* Children's Press, 1996.

Beeker, Selby B. *Throw Your Tooth on the Roof: Tooth Traditions from Around the World.* Houghton Mifflin, 1998.

Beesley, Scott. *"Pizza Hut"* (audiocassette). Bridge Records, 1991.

Berger, Melvin. *What Do Animals Do in Winter? How Animals Survive the Cold.* Ideals, 1995.

Birdseye, Tom. *Air Mail to the Moon.* Holiday House, 1988.

Blake, Robert. *Akiak: A Tale from the Iditarod.* Philomel Books, 1997.

Bowen, Betsy. *Antler, Bear, Canoe: A Northwoods Alphabet Year.* Little Brown, 1991.

Boyd, Lizi. *Princess, Cowboy, Pirate, Elf.* Hyperion Paperbacks for Children, 1995.

Brett, Jan. *Beauty and the Beast.* Clarion, 1989.

_____. *The Gingerbread Baby.* Putnam, 1999.

_____. *Goldilocks and the Three Bears.* Putnam, 1987.

_____. *Hedgie's Surprise.* Putnam, 2000.

_____. *The Mitten: A Ukrainian Folktale.* Putnam, 1989.

Brill, Marlene Targ. *Tooth Tales from Around the World.* Charlesbridge, 1998.

Brimner, Larry Dane. *The Names Project.* Children's Press, 1999.

Brooks, Gwendolyn. *Bronzeville Boys and Girls.* Harper, 1956.

Brown, Marc Tolon. *Arthur's Tooth.* Little Brown, 1985.

_____. *Arthur's Underwear.* Little Brown, 1999.

_____. *Play Rhymes.* Puffin, 1993.

Brown, Margaret Wise. *The Little Scarecrow Boy.* HarperCollins, 1998.

_____. *The Runaway Bunny.* Harper & Row, 1942.

Browne, Anthony. *Willy the Dreamer.* Candlewick Press, 1998.

Brumbeau, Jeff. *The Quiltmaker's Gift.* Pfeifer-Hamilton Publishers, 2000.

Bryan, Ashley. *Sing to the Sun.* HarperCollins Publishers, 1992.

Buehner, Caralyn. *Fanny's Dream.* Dial Books for Young Readers, 1996.

Bunting, Eve. *Smoky Night.* Harcourt Brace, 1994.

Burleigh, Robert. *Black Whiteness: Admiral Byrd Alone in the Antarctic.* Atheneum, 1998.

C

Caney, Steven. *Steven Caney's Kids' America.* Workman, 1978.

Carle, Eric. *Hello, Red Fox.* Simon & Schuster, 1998.

_____. *Very Hungry Caterpillar.* Philomel, 1969.

Carlstrom, Nancy White. *Northern Lullaby.* Philomel, 1992.

Carroll, Lewis. *The Walrus and the Carpenter.* Boyds Mills Press, 1986.

Cassedy, Sylvia. *Red Dragon on My Shoulder: Haiku.* HarperCollins,1992.

Chapman, Gillian. *Winter.* Raintree Steck Vaughn, 1998.

Christelow, Eileen. *Five Little Monkeys Jumping on the Bed.* Clarion, 1989.

Christian, Mary Blount. *Hats Are for Watering Horses: Why Cowboys Dressed That Way.* Hendrick-Long, 1993.

Cleary, Beverly. *Dear Mr. Henshaw.* William Morrow, 1983.

Cole, Joanna. *Anna Banana: 101 Jump-Rope Rhymes.* Morrow Junior Books, 1989.

_____. *Bony Legs.* Four Winds Press, 1983.

Collis, Len. *Card Games for Children.* Barron's, 1989.

Cooney, Barbara. *Miss Rumphius.* Viking Press, 1982.

_____. *Ox-Cart Man.* Viking Press, 1979.

Corbett, Sara. *Hats Off to Hats!* Children's Press, 1995.

The Cowboy Poets: Live at Elko. (videocassette) Western Folklife Center, 1994.

Curtis, Christopher Paul. *Bud, Not Buddy.* Delacorte, 1999.

Czernecki, Stefan. *The Singing Snake.* Hyperion Books for Children, 1995.

D

Dahl, Roald. *Dirty Beasts.* Puffin Books, 1986.

Day, David. *The Walking Catfish.* Macmillan, 1992.

DeFelice, Cynthia C. *The Dancing Skeleton.* Aladdin, 1996.

Deedy, Carmen Agra. *Treeman.* Peachtree Publishers, 1993.

Demi. *Liang and the Magic Paintbrush.* Henry Holt, 1983.

_____. *The Empty Pot.* Henry Holt, 1983.

DePaola, Tomie. *Legend of the Bluebonnet: An Old Tale of Texas.* Putnam, 1983.

DeZutter, Hank. *Who Says a Dog Goes Bow-Wow?* Doubleday Books for Young Readers, 1993.

Dillon, Jana. *Jeb Scarecrow's Pumpkin Patch.* Houghton Mifflin, 1992.

duVoisin, Robert. *Petunia.* Knopf, 1950.

E

Eastman, P. D. *Are You My Mother?* Random House, 1960.

Egan, Robert. *From Wheat to Pasta: A Photo Essay.* Children's Press, 1997.

Ehlert, Lois. *Snowballs.* Harcourt Brace, 1995.

Emberley, Barbara. *Drummer Hoff.* Prentice-Hall, 1967.

Erickson, John R. *The Mopwater Files.* Maverick Books, 1997.

Erlbach, Arlene. *Sidewalk Games Around the World.* Millbrook, 1997.

Evans, Richard Paul. *The Christmas Candle.* Simon & Schuster, 1998.

F

Falls, C. B. *ABC Book.* Morrow Junior Books, 1998.

Feelings, Muriel. *Moja Means One.* Dial Books for Young Readers, 1971.

Ferris, Jeri. *Go Free or Die: A Story About Harriet Tubman.* Carolrhoda, 1988.

The Firebird and Other Russian Fairy Tales. Edited by Jacqueline Onassis. Viking, 1978.

Fritz, Jean. *What's the Big Idea, Ben Franklin?* Paperstar, 1996.

_____. *Why Don't You Get a Horse, Sam Adams?* Putnam, 1996.

Flanagan, Alice. *The Zieglers and Their Apple Orchard.* Childrens' Press, 1999.

Fleischman, Paul. *Joyful Noise: Poems for Two Voices.* HarperCollins, 1988.

Fleming, Denise. *Mama Cat Has Three Kittens.* Henry Holt, 1998.

Florian, Douglas. *Bing Bang Boing: Poems and Drawings.* Harcourt Brace, 1994.

For Laughing Out Loud: Poems to Tickle Your Funnybone. Selected by Jack Prelutsky. Knopf, 1991.

Fowler, Allan. *Apples of Your Eye.* Children's Press, 1994.

_____. *How Do You Know It's Winter?* Children's Press, 1997.

Frost, Robert. *Stopping by Woods on a Snowy Evening.* Dutton, 1978.

G

Gag, Wanda. *Millions of Cats.* Coward McCann, 1928.

Galdone, Paul. *Cat Goes Fiddle-I-Fee.* Clarion, 1985.

_____. *The Elves and the Shoemaker.* Clarion, 1984.

Garcia, Jerry & David Grisman. *There Ain't No Bugs on Me.* HarperCollins, 1999.

Gelman, Rita Golden. *Hello Cat, You Need a Hat.* Scholastic, 1979.

George, Kristine O'Connell. *Old Elm Speaks: Tree Poems.* Clarion, 1998.

Gerberg, Mort. *Geographunny: A Book of Global Riddles.* Clarion, 1991.

Gerrard, Roy. *Sir Francis Drake: His Daring Deeds.* Farrar Straus Giroux, 1988.

Gibbons, Gail. *Deadline! From News to Newspaper.* Crowell, 1987.

Giblin, James Cross. *Thomas Jefferson: A Picture Book Biography.* Scholastic, 1994.

Gilman, Phoebe. *Something from Nothing: Adapted from a Jewish Folktale.* Scholastic, 1992.

Glass, Marvin. *What Happened Today, Freddy Groundhog?* Crown Publishing, 1989.

Gleason, Karen. *Factivities.* Good Apple, 1991.

Gonzalez, Lucia. *The Bossy Gallito.* Scholastic, 1999.

Goodwin, Jude. *Let's Play Cards: Great Card Games for Kids.* Devyn Press, 1989.

Greene, Carol. *George Washington Carver: Scientist and Teacher.* Children's Press, 1992.

Greenlaw, M. Jean. *Ranch Dressing.* Lodestar Books, 1993.

Grimm, Jacob & Wilhelm. *The Bremen Town Musicians: A Tale.* North-South Books, 1998.

Guiberson, Brenda. *Winter Wheat.* Henry Holt, 1995.

H

Hahn, Mary Downing. *Wait Until Helen Comes.* Clarion, 1986.

Haley, Gail E. *A Story, A Story: An African Tale.* Aladdin, 1970.

Hall, Donald. *Ox-Cart Man.* Viking, 1979.

Hall, Godfrey. *Games.* Thomson Learning, 1995.

Hall, Zoe. *The Apple Pie Tree.* Blue Sky Press, 1996.

Hand in Hand: An American History Through Poetry. Selected by Lee Bennett Hopkins. Simon & Schuster, 1994.

Heller, Robert J. *How to Win at Trivial Pursuit and Other Knowledge Games.* Rinehart & Winston, 1984.

Heller, Ruth. *Behind the Mask: A Book About Prepositions.* Grosset & Dunlap, 1995.

_____. *A Cache of Jewels and Other Collective Nouns.* Putnam & Grosset, 1998.

_____. *Fantastic! Wow! And Unreal! A Book About Interjections and Conjunctions.* Putnam & Grosset, 1998.

_____. *Kites Sail High: A Book About Verbs.* Grosset & Dunlap, 1988.

_____. *Many Luscious Lollipops: A Book about Adverbs.* Grosset & Dunlap, 1989.

_____. *Merry-Go-Round: A Book About Nouns.* Grosset & Dunlap, 1990.

_____. *Mine, All Mine: A Book About Pronouns.* Grosset & Dunlap, 1997.

_____. *Up, Up, and Away: A Book about Adverbs.* Grosset & Dunlap, 1991.

Hendry, Linda. *Making Gift Boxes.* Kids Can Press, 1999.

Henkes, Kevin. *Lilly's Purple Plastic Purse.* Greenwillow, 1996.

Hesse, Karen. *The Music of Dolphins.* Scholastic, 1996.

_____. *Out of the Dust.* Scholastic, 1997.

Hewavisenti, Lakshmi. *Problem Solving.* Gloucester Press, 1991.

Hoban, Tana. *So Many Circles, So Many Squares.* Greenwillow, 1998.

Hoberman, Mary Ann. *Miss Mary Mack.* Scholastic, 1998.

Hodges, Margaret. *Saint George and the Dragon.* Little Brown, 1984.

Holland, Gini. *Diego Rivera.* Raintree Steck-Vaughn, 1997.

Home: A Collaboration of Thirty Distinguished Authors & Illustrators of Children's Books to Aid the Homeless. Selected by Michael Rosen. HarperCollins, 1992.

Hughes, Langston. *The Dream Keeper and Other Poems.* Knopf, 1994.

Hurwitz, Johanna. *The Just Desserts Club.* Morrow Junior Books, 1999.

I

I Know an Old Lady Who Swallowed a Fly. Holiday House, 1990.

I Saw Esau: The Schoolchild's Pocket Book. Edited by Iona and Peter Opie. Candlewick Press, 1992.

I Thought I'd Take My Rat to School: Poems for September to June. Selected by Dorothy M. Kennedy. Little Brown, 1993.

Imai, Miko. *Little Lumpty.* Candlewick Press, 1996.

Inner Chimes: Poems on Poetry. Selected by Bobbye S. Goldstein. Wordsong/Boyds Mills Press, 1994.

Irving, Washington. *The Legend of Sleepy Hollow.* Creative Education, 1990.

Isadora, Rachel. *Caribbean Dream.* G.P. Putnam's Sons, 1998.

J

Janovitz, Marilyn. *What Could Be Keeping Santa?* North-South Books, 1997.

Johnston, Toni. *The Soup Bone.* Harcourt, Brace, Jovanovich, 1990.

K

Kalan, Robert. *Jump, Frog, Jump!* Greenwillow, 1981.

Kalman, Bobbie. *Bandanas, Chaps and Ten-Gallon Hats.* Crabtree Publishing Company, 1998.

Kasza, Keiko. *The Wolf's Chicken Stew.* Putnam, 1987.

Katz, Bobbi. *Poems Just for Us!* Scholastic, 1996.

Keller, Holly. *Geraldine's Blanket.* Mulberry, 1988.

Kellogg, Steven. *Chicken Little.* William Morrow, 1985.

_____. *Jack and the Beanstalk.* Mulberry, 1997.

_____. *Johnny Appleseed.* Morrow Junior Books, 1997.

_____. *The Three Little Pigs.* William Morrow, 1997.

Kennedy, Richard. *Song of the Horse.* Dutton, 1981.

Ketteman, Helen. *Bubba the Cowboy Prince: A Fractured Texas Tale.* Scholastic, 1997.

Kidder, Harvey. *The Kids' Book of Chess.* Workman, 1990.

Kimmel, Eric A. *Anansi and the Moss-Covered Rock.* Holiday House, 1988.

_____. *Anansi and the Talking Melon.* Holiday House, 1994.

King, David C. *Colonial Days: Discover the Past with Fun Projects, Games, Activities and Recipes.* J. Wiley, 1998.

Kirk, David. *Miss Spider's ABC.* Scholastic, 1998.

Kline, Suzy. *Herbie Jones and the Class Gift.* Puffin, 1987.

Koscielniak, Bruce. *Geoffrey Groundhog Predicts the Weather.* Houghton Mifflin, 1995.

Kraus, Ruth. *The Carrot Seed.* Harper & Row, 1945.

Krensky, Stephen. *How Santa Got His Job.* Simon & Schuster, 1998.

Krull, Kathleen. *Lives of the Presidents: Fame, Shame (and What the Neighbors Thought).* Harcourt Brace, 1998.

L

Landau, Elaine. *Apples.* Children's Press, 1999.

Lang, Robert. *Origami Animals.* Crescent Books, 1992.

Lankford, Mary. *Hopscotch Around the World.* Morrow Junior Books, 1992.

_____. *Jacks Around the World.* Morrow Junior Books, 1996.

Lasky, Kathryn. *Alice Rose & Sam: A Novel.* Hyperion Books for Children, 1998.

_____. *A Brilliant Streak: The Making of Mark Twain.* Harcourt Brace, 1998.

Lear, Edward. *Daffy Down Dillies.* Wordsong/Boyds Mills Press, 1994.

_____. *Owls and Pussycats.* Bedrick, 1993.

Lepthien, Emilie. *Woodchucks.* Children's Press, 1992.

Levine, Gail. *Ella Enchanted.* HarperCollins, 1997.

Lillegard, Dee. *Do Not Feed the Table.* Doubleday Books for Young Readers, 1992.

Little Rabbit Foo Foo. Retold by Michael Rosen. The Trumpet Club, 1990.

Lobel, Arnold. *Frog and Toad Are Friends.* HarperCollins, 1970.

London, Jonathan. *Froggy Gets Dressed.* Viking, 1992.

Longe, Bob. *The World's Best Card Tricks.* Sterling Publishing Company, 1991.

Lots of Limericks. Selected by Myra Cohn Livingstone. M. K. McElderry Books, 1991.

Love, D. Anne. *Bess's Log Cabin Quilt.* Bantam Doubleday Dell Books for Young Readers, 1996.

Lyon, George Ella. *A Traveling Cat.* Orchard Books, 1998.

M

Macaulay, David. *Black and White.* Houghton Mifflin, 1990.

MacDonald, Betty Bard. *Mrs. Piggle-Wiggle's Won't Take-a-Bath Cure.* HarperCollins, 1997.

Maestro, Betty. *How Do Apples Grow?* HarperCollins, 1992.

Marchon-Arnaud, Catherine. *Gallery of Games.* Tichnor & Fields, 1994.

Marshall, James. *The Three Little Pigs.* Penguin, 1989.

Marzollo, Jean. *I Spy.* Scholastic, 1993.

McCourt, Lisa. *I Love You Stinky Face.* BridgeWater Books, 1997.

McDermott, Gerald. *Anansi the Spider: A Tale from the Ashanti.* Henry Holt, 1972.

McGovern, Ann. *Shark Lady: True Adventures of Eugenie Clark.* Scholastic, 1998.

_____. *Stone Soup.* Scholastic, 1968.

_____. *Too Much Noise.* Houghton Mifflin, 1967.

McKissack, Patricia. *A Million Fish . . . More or Less.* Knopf, 1992.

McPhail, David. *Edward and the Pirates.* Little, Brown, 1997.

Medearis, Angela Shelf. *Too Much Talk.* Candlewick Press, 1995.

Melmed, Laura Krauss. *The Rainbabies.* Lothrop, 1992.

Miller, Margaret. *Whose Hat?* Mulberry Books, 1997.

Miss Mary Mack. Adapted by Mary Ann Hoberman. Scholastic, 1998.

Moore, Eva. *Buddy: The First Seeing Eye Dog.* Scholastic, 1996.

Moore, Lillian. *Sunflakes: Poems for Children.* Clarion, 1992.

Morris, Ann. *Hats, Hats, Hats.* Mulberry, 1993.

Moss, Lloyd. *Zin! Zin! Zin! A Violin.* Simon & Schuster, 1995.

Moss, Marissa. *Amelia Writes Again!* Tricycle Press, 1996.

Moutran, Julia Spencer. *The Story of Punxsutawney Phil, "The Fearless Forecaster."* Literary Publications, 1987.

Murphy, Shirley Rousseau. *Tattie's River Journey.* Dial, 1983.

Musgrove, Margaret. *Ashanti to Zulu: African Traditions.* Dial, 1976.

N

Neitzel, Shirley. *The Jacket I Wear in the Snow.* Greenwillow, 1989.

Nielsen, Laura. *Jeremy's Muffler.* Bradbury, 1994.

Numeroff, Laura Joffe. *If You Give a Mouse a Cookie.* Harper & Row, 1985.

_____. *If You Give a Pig a Pancake.* Laura Geringer Books, 1998.

Neuschwander, Cindy. *Amanda Bean's Amazing Dream: A Mathematical Story.* Scholastic, 1998.

Never Take a Pig to Lunch and Other Poems About the Fun of Eating. Edited by Beatrice de Regniers. Scholastic, 1988.

Nichelason, Margery. *Shoes.* Carolrhoda Books, 1997.

Nixon, Joan Lowery. *Search for the Shadowman.* Delacorte Press, 1996.

Noble, Trinka Jakes. *The Day Jimmy's Boa Ate the Wash.* Dial Press, 1980.

O

O'Connell, Kristine. *Old Elm Speaks: Tree Poems.* Houghton Mifflin, 1998.

O'Keefe, Linda. *Shoes: A Celebration of Pumps, Sandals, Slippers and More.* Workman, 1996.

O'Neill, Mary De Luc. *Hailstones and Halibut Bones: Adventures in Color.* Doubleday, 1961.

Oram, Hiawyn. *Out of the Blue: Poems About Color.* Hyperion Books for Children, 1993.

Over in the Meadow: An Old Counting Rhyme. Illustrated by David Carter. Scholastic, 1992.

P

Park, Barbara. *The Kid in the Red Jacket.* Knopf, 1987.

Parker, Steven. *Louis Pasteur and Germs.* Chelsea House, 1994.

_____. *The Wright Brothers and Aviation.* Chelsea House, 1995.

Parkinson, Kathy. *The Enormous Turnip.* Albert Whitman, 1986.

Pass It On: African American Poetry for Children. Selected by Wade Hudson. Scholastic, 1993.

Paulsen, Gary. *Brian's Winter.* Delacorte Press, 1996.

Peanut Butter and Jelly: A Play Rhyme. Adapted by Nadine Bernard Westcott. Dutton, 1987.

Peet, Bill. *Bill Peet: An Autobiography.* Houghton Mifflin, 1989.

Pelletier, David. *The Graphic Alphabet.* Orchard, 1996.

Perrault, Charles. *Cinderella.* North-South Books, 1999.

Perry, Susan. *A Cold is Nothing to Sneeze At.* Child's World, 1993.

Pilkey, Dav. *The Adventures of Captain Underpants: An Epic Novel.* Blue Sky Press, 1997.

_____. *The Terrible Trouble with Halley Tosis.* Blue Sky Press, 1994.

Pinkney, J. Brian. *Max Found Two Sticks.* Aladdin Paperbacks, 1997.

Poem Stew. Selected by William Cole. Lippincott, 1981.

Polacco, Patricia. *The Keeping Quilt.* Simon & Schuster, 1988.

_____. *Pink and Say.* Philomel, 1994.

Polushkin, Maria. *Mother, Mother, I Want Another.* Crown Publishers, 1978.

Pomerantz, Charlotte. *The Tamarindo Puppy and Other Poems.* Greenwillow, 1993.

Pooley, Sarah. *Jump the World: Stories, Poems, and Things to Make and Do From Around the World.* Dutton Children's Books, 1997.

R

Prince, Maggie. *House on Hound Hill.* Houghton Mifflin, 1998.

Ringgold, Faith. *Tar Beach.* Crown Publishers, 1991

Robbins, Ken. *Autumn Leaves.* Scholastic, 1998.

Robinson, Marc. *Cock-a-Doodle-Doo: What Does It Sound Like to You?* Stewart, Tabori and Chang, 1993.

Root, Phyllis. *One Duck Stuck.* Candlewick Press, 1998.

Rosen, Michael. *Walking the Bridge of Your Nose.* Kingfisher, 1995.

Rosenberg, Liz. *The Carousel.* Harcourt Brace, 1995.

Rylant, Cynthia. *Henry and Mudge: The First Book of Their Adventures.* Simon & Schuster, 1987.

_____. *Dog Heaven.* Blue Sky Press, 1985.

S

Sabuda, Robert. *Cookie Count.* Simon & Schuster, 1997.

Sachar, Louis. *Holes.* Farrar Straus and Giroux, 1998.

San Jose, Christine. *The Emperor's New Clothes.* Boyds Mill Press, 1998.

San Souci, Robert D. *The Faithful Friend.* Simon & Schuster, 1995.

_____. *Sukey and the Mermaid.* Four Winds, 1992.

Sandburg, Carl. *Poetry for Young People.* Sterling, 1995.

Sanford, William R. *Sam Houston: Texas Hero.* Enslow, 1996.

Sattler, Helen Roney. *Recipes for Art and Craft Materials.* Lothrop, Lee & Shepard, 1987.

Saunders-Smith, Gail. *Apple Trees.* Pebble Books, 1998.

_____. *Eating Apples.* Pebble Books, 1998.

_____. *Fall Harvest.* Pebble Books, 1999.

_____. *Warm Clothes.* Pebble Books, 1998.

_____. *Winter.* Pebble Books, 1998.

Schnur, Steven. *Autumn: An Alphabet Acrostic.* Clarion, 1997.

School Supplies: A Book of Poems. Selected by Lee Bennett Hopkins. Simon & Schuster, 1996.

Schubert, Ingrid. *There's a Hole in My Bucket.* Front Street Books, 1998.

Service, Robert. *The Cremation of Sam McGee.* Greenwillow, 1987

Shepard, Aaron. *The Crystal Heart: A Vietnamese Legend.* Atheneum, 1998.

_____. *The Sea King's Daughter: A Russian Legend.* Atheneum, 1997.

Showers, Paul. *How Many Teeth?* HarperCollins, 1991.

Silverstein, Shel. *Falling Up.* HarperCollins, 1996.

Simon, Seymour. *Sharks.* HarperCollins, 1995.

Sing a Song of Popcorn: Every Child's Book of Poems. Selected by Beatrice Schenk de Regniers. Scholastic, 1988.

Singer, Marilyn. *It's Hard to Read a Map with a Beagle on Your Lap.* Henry Holt, 1997.

Sleep Rhymes Around the World. Selected by Jane Yolen. Wordsong/Boyds Mills Press, 1994.

Sloat, Terri. *There Was an Old Lady Who Swallowed a Trout!* Henry Holt, 1998.

Slobodkina, Esphyr. *Caps for Sale: A Tale of a Peddler, Some Monkeys, and Their Monkey Business.* HarperCollins, 1985.

Small Talk: A Book of Short Poems. Selected by Lee Bennett Hopkins. Harcourt Brace, 1995.

Snuffles and Snouts. Selected by Laura Robb. Dial Books for Young Readers, 1995.

Spinelli, Eileen. *Somebody Loves You, Mr. Hatch.* Simon & Schuster, 1991.

Stanley, Diane. *Bard of Avon: The Story of William Shakespeare.* Morrow Junior Books, 1992.

_____. *Cleopatra.* Morrow Junior Books, 1994.

Steig, William. *The Amazing Bone.* Farrar, Straus, Giroux, 1987.

_____. *Doctor DeSoto.* Farrar Straus Giroux, 1982.

_____. *Pete's a Pizza.* HarperCollins, 1998.

Steiner, Joan. *Look-Alikes.* Little Brown, 1998.

Stevens, Janet. *Cook-A-Doodle-Doo.* Harcourt Brace, 1999.

_____. *Tops and Bottoms.* Harcourt Brace, 1995.

T

Taback, Simms. *Joseph Had a Little Overcoat.* Viking, 1999.

Tafuri, Nancy. *Counting to Christmas.* Scholastic, 1998.

Tamar, Erika. *The Junkyard Dog.* Knopf/Random House, 1995.

Tejima, Keizaburo. *Fox's Dream.* Philomel, 1987.

Temple, Frances. *Tiger Soup: An Anansi Story from Jamaica.* Orchard, 1994.

Terban, Marvin. *The Dove Dove: Funny Homograph Riddles.* Clarion, 1988.

_____. *Eight Ate: A Feast of Homonym Riddles.* Clarion, 1982.

_____. *Funny You Should Ask: How to Make Up Jokes and Riddles with Wordplay.* Clarion, 1992.

_____. *Guppies in Tuxedos: Funny Eponyms.* Clarion, 1988.

_____. *In a Pickle and Other Funny Idioms.* Clarion, 1983.

_____. *It Figures: Fun Figures of Speech.* Clarion, 1993.

_____. *Mad as a Wet Hen! And Other Funny Idioms.* Clarion, 1987.

Tolkien, J. R. R (John Ronald Reuel). *Fellowship of the Ring: Being the First Part of the Lord of the Rings.* Ballantine, 1973.

Tresselt, Alvin R. *The Mitten: A Ukrainian Folktale.* Lothrop, 1964.

Troughton, Joanne. *What Made Tiddalick Laugh.* Blackie and Son, 1977.

Tunnell, Michael O. *Mailing May.* Greenwillow, 1997.

Turkle, Brinton. *Deep In the Forest.* Puffin, 1976.

Tzannes, Robin. *Sanji and the Baker.* Oxford University Press, 1998.

V

Vail, Rachel. *Over the Moon.* Orchard, 1998.

Van Allsburg, Chris. *Jumanji.* Houghton Mifflin, 1981.

_____. *The Wreck of the Zephyr.* Houghton Mifflin, 1993.

Viorst, Judith. *Alexander and the Terrible, Horrible, No Good, Very Bad Day.* Atheneum, 1972.

_____. *Sad Underwear and Other Complications: More Poems for Children and Their Parents.* Atheneum, 1995.

W

Wade, Mary Dodson. *Amelia Earhart: Flying for Adventure.* Millbrook, 1992.

Wallner, Alexander. *Beatrix Potter.* Holiday House, 1995.

Wardlaw, Lee. *Punia, King of the Sharks: A Hawaiian Folktale.* Dial Books for Young Readers, 1997.

Watterson, Bill. *Calvin and Hobbes.* Andrews, McMeel & Parker, 1987.

Wegman, William. *Cinderella.* Hyperion Books for Children, 1993.

Wheels on the Bus. Adapted by Maryann Kovalski. Trumpet Club, 1987.

Wick, Walter. *Optical Illusions.* Scholastic, 1998.

Wilcox, Cathy. *Enzo the Wonderfish.* Tichnor and Fields, 1994.

Williams, Vera. *Chair for My Mother.* Greenwillow, 1982.

Winter Poems. Selected by Barbara Rogasky. Scholastic, 1994.

Winters, Kay. *Did You See What I Saw? Poems About School.* Viking, 1996.

Winthrop, Elizabeth. *Shoes.* Harper & Row, 1996.

Wisniewski, David. *Golem.* Clarion Books, 1996.

_____. *Rain Player.* Clarion Books, 1991.

Wood, Audrey. *Bright and Early Thursday Evening: A Tangled Tale Dreamed by Audrey Wood.* Harcourt Brace, 1996.

_____. *The Napping House.* Harcourt Brace, 1984.

_____. *The Red Racer.* Simon & Schuster, 1996.

Y

Yagawa, Sumiko. *The Crane Wife.* Morrow, 1981.

Yolen, Jane. *Owl Moon.* Philomel, 1987.

_____. *Weather Report: Poems.* Wordsong, 1993.

Yue, Charlotte. *Shoes: Their History in Words and Pictures.* Houghton Mifflin, 1997.

Z

Zelinsky, Paul O. *Rapunzel.* Dutton Children's Books, 1997.

Ziefert, Harriet. *The Little Red Hen.* Puffin, 1995.

_____. *A Polar Bear Can Swim: What Animals Can and Cannot Do.* Penguin Putnam, 1998.

_____. *The Princess and the Pea.* Viking, 1997.

Zion, Gene. *Harry the Dirty Dog.* Harper & Row, 1956.

Bibliography of Professional Books

A

Anderson, Dee. *Amazingly Easy Puppet Plays: 42 New Scripts for One-Person Puppetry.* American Library Association, 1997.

B

Bannister, Barbara Farley. *Ready-to-Use Reading Bingos, Puzzles and Research Activities for the Elementary School Year.* Center for Applied Research in Education.

Barchers, Suzanne. *Fifty Fabulous Fables: Beginning Readers Theatre.* Teacher Ideas Press, 1997.

_____. *Readers Theatre for Beginning Readers.* Teacher Ideas Press, 1993.

Bauer, Caroline Feller. *Celebrations: Read Aloud Holiday and Theme Book Programs.* H. W. Wilson, 1985.

_____. *Leading Kids to Books Through Puppets.* American Library Association, 1997.

_____. *Leading Kids to Books Through Magic.* American Library Association, 1996.

_____. *The Poetry Break.* H. W. Wilson, 1995.

_____. *Presenting Readers' Theater: Plays and Poems to Read Aloud.* H. W. Wilson, 1996.

Benson, Allen C. *Connecting Kids and the Internet: A Handbook for Librarians, Teachers and Parents.* Neal-Schuman, 1996.

C

Campbell, Bruce. *The Multiple Intelligences Handbook: Lesson Plans and More.* Campbell & Associates, Inc., 1994.

Campbell, Linda, Bruce Campbell & Dee Dickinson. *Teaching and Learning Through Multiple Intelligences.* Allyn & Bacon, 1998.

Champlin, Connie. *Storytelling with Puppets.* American Library Association. Second edition, 1998.

Children's Books and Their Creators. Edited by Anita Silvey. Houghton Mifflin, 1995.

Cooper, Gail & Garry. *Virtual Field Trips.* Libraries Unlimited, 1997.

D

DeSpain, Pleasant. *Thirty-Three Multicultural Tales to Tell.* August House Publishers, Inc., 1993.

F

Fleck, Tim. *Hyperstudio for Terrified Teachers: Grades 3-5.* Teacher Created Materials, Inc., 1997.

Fredericks, Anthony D., *Frantic Frogs and Other Frankly Fractured Folktales for Readers Theater.* Teacher Ideas Press, 1993.

_____. *Tadpole Tales and Other Totally Terrific Treats for Readers.* Teacher Ideas Press, 1997.

G

Gardner, Howard. *Frames of Mind: The Theory of Multiple Intelligences.* Basic Books, 1993.

_____. *How Are Kids Smart? Multiple Intelligences in the Classroom* (videocassette). National Professional Resources, Inc., 1995.

_____. *Multiple Intelligences: The Theory in Practice.* Basic Books, 1993.

Gardner, Howard & David G. Lazear. *Multiple Intelligences: Developing Intelligences for Greater Achievement* (two videocassettes). The Journal, 1995.

Goldish, Meish. *28 Folk and Fairy Tale Poems and Songs.* (with audiocassette) Scholastic Professional Books, 1995.

H

Handler, Marianne G., Ann Dana & Jane Peters Moore. *Hypermedia as a Student Tool: Guide for Teachers.* Libraries Unlimited, 1998.

Harrison, Annette. *Easy-to-Tell Stories for Young Children.* National Storytelling Press, 1992.

Haven, Kendall. *Great Moments in Science: Experiments and Readers Theater.* Teacher Ideas Press, 1996.

Holden, Greg. *Creating Web Pages for Kids and Parents.* IDG Books Worldwide, 1997.

I

Information Power: Building Partnerships for Learning. American Association of School Librarians of the American Library Association, 1998.

J

Justice, Jennifer. *The Ghost & I: Scary Stories for Participatory Telling.* Yellow Moon Press, 1992.

K

Kagan, Dr. Spencer & Miguel Kagan. *Multiple Intelligences: The Complete MI Book.* Kagan Cooperative Learning, 1998.

Kovacs, Deborah & James Preller. *Meet Authors and Illustrators, Volume II.* Scholastic, 1993.

L

Lazear, David G. & Howard Gardner. *Teaching for Multiple Intelligences.* Phi Delta Kappa Educational Foundation, 1992.

Lee, Carol K. & Fay Edwards. *57 Games to Play in the Library or Classroom.* Alleyside Press, 1997.

Lipman, Doug. *Storytelling Games.* Oryx Press, 1995.

M

MacDonald, Margaret Read. *The Storyteller's Start-Up Book.* August House Publishers, Inc., 1993.

Maguire, Jack. *Creative Storytelling: Choosing, Inventing, and Sharing Tales for Children.* Yellow Moon Press, 1985.

Marsh, Valerie. *Beyond Words: Great Stories for Hand and Voice.* Alleyside Press, 1995.

N

The National Storytelling Association. *Tales as Tools: The Power of Story in the Classroom.* National Storytelling Press, 1994.

O

Oakley, Ruth. *Board and Card Games.* Marshall Cavedish, 1989.

O'Connor, Anna and Sheila Callahan-Young. *Seven Windows to a Child's World: 100 Ideas for the Multiple Intelligences Classroom.* IRI/Skylight Publishing, Inc., 1994.

1001 Rhymes and Fingerplays. Warren Publishing House, 1994.

Orlando, Louise. *The Multicultural Game Book: More than 70 Traditional Games from 30 Countries.* Scholastic Professional Books, 1993.

P

Polette, Nancy. *Reading the World with Folktales.* Book Lures, 1993.

_____. *Readers Theatre Booktalks.* Edited by Nancy Polette. Book Lures, 1994.

R

Roberts, Lynda. *Mitt Magic: Fingerplays for Finger Puppets.* Gryphon House, Inc., 1985.

Rump, Nan. *Puppets and Masks: Stagecraft and Storytelling.* Davis Publications, 1996.

S

Schroeder, Joanne. *Fun Puppet Skits for Schools and Libraries.* Teacher Ideas Press, 1995.

Shepard, Aaron. *Stories on Stage: Scripts for Readers' Theater.* H.W. Wilson, 1993.

Schrock, Kathleen & Midge Frazel. *Microsoft Publisher for Every Day of the School Year.* Linworth Publishing, 1998.

Sierra, Judy. *Fantastic Theater: Puppets and Plays for Young Performers and Young Audiences.* H. W. Wilson Company, 1991.

_____. *Multicultural Folktales for the Feltboard and Readers' Theater.* Oryx, 1996.

Sierra, Judy & Robert Kaminski. *Multicultural Folktales: Stories to Tell Young Children.* Oryx, 1991.

T

Tunnicliff, Myram Forney & Susan Sheldon Soenen. *The Reference Information Skills Game.* Libraries Unlimited, 1995.

W

Williams, Robin & John Tollett. *The Non-Designer's Web Book.* Peachpit Press, 1998.

Wisniewski, David & Donna. *Worlds of Shadow: Teaching with Shadow Puppetry.* Teacher Ideas Press, 1997.

Wright, Denise Anton. *One-Person Puppet Plays.* Teacher Ideas Press, 1990.

Bibliography of Internet Sites

A

Aaron Shepard's RT (Readers' Theater) Page. Aaron Shepard, 1998. <www.aaronshep.com/rt/index.html>

The Abacus: Lego. Luis Fernandes. <www.ee.ryerson.ca:8080/~elf/abacus/lego>

ADA Kids Corner. American Dental Association, 1999. <www.ada.org/public/topics/kids/index.html.>

Aloha Mental Arithmetic. <www.alohama.com/index/shtml>

Ancient Olympic Games Virtual Museum. Dartmouth College and The Foundation of the Hellenic World. <devlab.dartmouth.edu/olympic>

The @rt Room. Craig Roland, 1996. <www.arts.ufl.edu/art/rt_room/index.html>

Association for the Promotion and Advancement of Science Education, 1999. <www.discoverlearning.com/forensic/docs/index.html>

At Home in the Heartland Online. Illinois State Museum, 1996. <www.museum.state.il.us/exhibits/athome>

B

Barnyard Buddies. Cheryl Null & Carol Gad. The Stardom Co., Ltd., 1999. <www.execpc.com/%7Ebyb>

The Bear Den. Don Middleton, 1996. <www.nature-net.com/bears/>

Berlioz. Jan Brett, 2000. <janbrett.com/newsnotes/berlioz_newsnotes3.htm>

Blue Mountain Arts. Blue Mountain Arts, Inc., 1996-1998. <www.bluemountain.com>

C

Carol Hurst's Children's Literature Newsletter. Carol Otis Hurst, 1996. <www.carolhurst.com/newsletters/newsletters11d.html>

Cartoon Corner. Emmett Scott, 1995. <www.cartooncorner.com>

Children's Music Web's Radio Refrigerator. <www.childrensmusic.org/fridge.html>

Circa 1265: Male Clothing and Knightly Armour of the 1250s. Andy Goddard, 1999. <www.bumply.com/Medieval/Kit/kit.htm>

Classical Midi Archives. Pierre R. Schwab, 2000. <www.prs.net/index.html>

Classroom Connect. <www.classroom.com>

Classroom Connect Store. <store.classroom.com>

The Conjuror. Neil Alexander and Magic Happens Productions, 1997-1998. <www.conjuror.com/magictricks>

Cornell Chronicle: Groundhog Day Facts and Factoids. Cornell University News Service, 1996. <www.news.cornell.edu/Chronicle/96/2.1.96/facts.html>

Customs and Traditions of St. Patrick's Day. Jerry Wilson, 1998. <wilstar.com/holidays/patrick.htm>

Creative Kids. <creativekids.ca>

Crossword Puzzles. Mind Fun.com, 2000. <www.mindfun.com/cross2/htm>

Cyberkids. Able Minds, Inc., 1999-2000. <www.cyberkids.com>

D

Dan's Wild, Wild Weather Page. Dan Satterfield, 1997. <www.whnt19.com/kidwx>

A Day in the Life of Thomas Jefferson. Thomas Jefferson Memorial Foundation, 1996. <www.monticello.org/jefferson/sunrise/home.html>

Deep in the Bush Where People Rarely Ever Go. Phillip Martin, 1999. <members.nbci.com/Pmartin/Bush/bushhomepage.htm>

Diamond Jim's Interactive Magic. Diamond Jim Productions.

Dogpile. <www.dogpile.com>

Dr. Rabbit's No Cavities Clubhouse. American Dental Association, 1998. <www.colgate.com/Kids-world/index.html>

Draw a Bear. Jan Brett, 2000. <www.janbrett.com/learn_to_draw_a_bear.htm>

E

Education Central. iVillage, Inc., 1998. <www.parentsoup.com/edcentral>

Etch-A-Sketch. Ohio Art Company, 1998. <www.etch-a-sketch.com>

Evaluating Your Learning Style. Charles Darling, 1988. <webster.commnet.edu/faculty/~simonds/styles/intro2.htm>

F

Fascinating Folds: Cup. Fascinating Folds, Inc., 1997. <www.fascinating-folds.com/diagrams/beginners/cup/cup.htm>

Folkmanis Puppets. <www.folkmanis.com>

From Story to Stage: Tips on Scripting. Aaron Shepard, 1998. <www.aaronshep.com/rt/tips.html>

Fruit Game. 20/20 Technologies, 1999. <www.2020tech.com/fruit>

G

Gallery of Interactive Geometry. University of Minnesota Science and Technology Center, 1993-2000. <www.geom.umn.edu/apps/gallery.html>

The Great Horned Owl. <oz.uc.edu/~verri/jr>

H

Hangman. <www.superkids.com/aweb/tools/words/hangman>

The Hex Agency. <library.thinkquest.org/17932>

Hogtivities. Faculty and staff of West End Elementary, Punxsutawney, PA, 1998. <www.groundhog.org/hogtivities>

Homework Central. Encyclopedia Central. 1997-1999. <www.bigchalk.com>

How To Create Your Own Web Page. Lance Little. <shianet.org/info/create.html>

The Human Skeleton. Columbia/HCA Healthcare Corporation, 1995-2000. <www.medtropolis.com/vbody/bones/index.html>

Hummingbird Nests. Larry & Terrie Gates, 1998. <www.portalproductions.com/h/nest.htm>

I

I Think… Therefore… MI! Walter McKenzie, Jr. <surfaquarium.com/im.htm>

Ideas and Rubrics. Chicago Board of Education, 1999. <intranet.cps.k12.il.us/Assessments/Ideas_and_Rubrics/ideas_and_rubrics.html>

J

Jan Brett's Home Page. Jan Brett, 1996-1999.

Judy and David's Online Songbook. <JudyandDavid.com/Songbook/Songbookcover.html>

Jumping Frog. John Smith, 1995. <www.users.waitrose.com/~pureland/frog.gif>

K

K-12 Electronic Guide for African Resources on the Internet. 1996. <www.sas.upenn.edu/African_Studies/K-12/AFR_GIDE.html>

The Kids Domain. Attitude Network Ltd., 1999. <www.kidsdomain.com/down/index.html>

Kids Farm. KidsFarm, Inc., 1997-2000. <www.kidsfarm.com/credits.htm>

Kids' Place. <www.eduplace.com/kids/index.html>

L

Lemonade Stand. Jason C. Mayans, 1999.
<www.littlejason.com/lemonade>

The Louvre. 1999. <www.louvre/fr/>

Lower East Side Tenement Museum. WNet Station, Kravis Multimedia Education Center, 2000.
<www.wnet.org/tenement>

M

Maine Mammal Information Table (Red Fox). Maine Wildlife Park, 1998.
<janus.state.me.us/ifw/wildlife/mamtable.htm>

Making a Weather Station. Miami Museum of Science, 1996.
<www.miamisci.org/hurricane/weathertools.html>

The Mammal Society: The Hedgehog. The Mammal Society of London, England, 1997.
<www.abdn.ac.uk/mammal/hedgehog.htm>

The Mammal Society: The Woodmouse. The Mammal Society of London, England, 1997.
<www.abdn.ac.uk/mammal/woodmous.htm>

Mancala. <imagiware.com/mancala>

The Marmot Burrow. D.T. Blumstein, 1995-1999.
<falcon.cc.ukans.edu/~marmota/marmot burrow.html>

Mastermind.
<www.javaonthebrain.com/java/mastermind>

The Metropolitan Museum of Art. 2000.
<www.metmuseum.org/home.asp>

Milk Carton Bird Feeder.
<www.dfw.state.or.us/ODFWhtml/Education/ BirdFeeder.html>

The Money Game: World School Investment Challenge. Perpetual Wealth Management, 1999.
<www.moneygame.com>

Mrs. Rose Shows You.
<www.homestead.com/mrsroseshowsyou/ map.html>

Music Adventureland.
<www.netrover.com/~kingskid/cards/ adventure.html>

Music Magic: A Piano Exploration. Think Quest Team 15060, 1998.
<library.thinkquest.org/15060/index.html>

N

The National Educational Technological Standards Project. International Society for Technology in Education. <cnets.iste.org>

National Science Education Standards. National Academy of Sciences.
<www.nap.edu/readingroom/books/nses/html>

Neuroscience for Kids.
<faculty.washington.edu/chudler/neurok.html>

North Carolina Traditional Weather Lore. NCNatural, 1999. <ncnatural.com/wildflwr/fall/folklore.html>

O

Official Groundhog Site, Julia Spencer Moutran, Ph.D., 1997-1999. <www.groundhogs.com/index.htm>

Old Sturbridge Village. 1995.
<www.osv.org/pages/descrip.htm>

Online Class.
<www.onlineclass.com/General/strategies.html>

Oriental Trading Company. <www.oriental.com>

P

Pets Need Dental Care, Too. Hill's Pet Nutrition, 1999.
<www.petdental.com/index.htm>

Pilkey's Web Site O' Fun. Dav Pilkey, 1997.
<www.pilkey.com>

Poetry Writing with Jack Prelutsky. Scholastic, Inc.
<teacher.scholastic.com/writewit/poetwit/index.htm>

The Portrait Gallery of Classical Composers. R. Christian Anderson, 1998.
<www.geocities.com/Vienna/Choir/4004/>

Principles and Standards for School Mathematics. National Council of Teachers of Mathematics.
<www.nctm.org/standards2000>

Punxsutawney Chamber of Commerce. 1997-1999.
<www.penn.com/punxsycc/souv.html>

Punxsutawney Phil. Commonwealth of Pennsylvania, 1998. <www.groundhog.org>

Puppeteers of America Homepage. Puppeteers of America, Inc., 1999. <www.puppeteers.org>

Puppetry Traditions Around the World.
<sagecraft.com/puppetry/traditions/index.html>

Q

The Quiltmaker's Gift. <www.QuiltmakersGift.com>

R

Room 108. <www.netrover.com/~kingskid/>

S

Sarah's Rodeo Page. Prentice, Sarah L. & David A., 1995-1998. <mama.indstate.edu/prentice/sarah>

Shamrock Lane. Franklin Institute Fellowship, 1999. <www.fi.edu/fellows/fellow7/mar99>

Shamwari Game Preserve. <www.shamwari.com/europe.asp>

The Smithsonian Institution. 1995-2000. <www.si.edu>

Snowshoe Hare. Illinois State Museum, 1995. <www.museum.state.il.us/exhibits/larson/lepus_americanus.html>

The Staff Room: Rubrics. Huron Perth Catholic District, 1999. <www.odyssey.on.ca/~elaine.coxon/rubrics.htm>

Standards and Position Statement. National Council for the Social Studies. <www.ncss.org/standards>

Standards for the English Language Arts. National Council of the Teachers of English. <www.ncte.org/>

StoryNet: Your Storytelling Resource on the Internet. National Storytelling Association, 1998. <www.storynet.org/>

Superkids Educational Software Review. Knowledge Share LLC, 1998-2000. <www.superkids.com>

A Symphony of Learning Styles <www.weac.org/kids/june96/styles.htm>

T

The Tokugawa Art Museum. 1995. <www.cjn.or.jp/tokugawa/index.html>

Tom Snyder Productions. <www.tomsnyder.com>

U

The United Nations Cyber School Bus. The United Nations, 1999. <www.un.org/Pubs/CyberSchoolBus>

V

The Virtual Abacus. <203.116.95.144/abacusstart.html>

The Virtual Badger Sett. Paul Butler, 1996. <www.qni.com/~badger/>

Virtual Boston: Freedom Trail. Virtually Boston, 1998. <www.vboston.com/VBoston/Content/FreedomTrail/Index.cfm>

Virtual Field Trips Site. Tramline, Inc., 1997-1999. <www.field-guides.com>

W

Wacky Web Tales. Houghton Mifflin, 2000. <www.eduplace.com/tales/index.html>

Welcome to Shakey's Place! ThinkQuest Team 10502, 1997. <library.advanced.org/10502>

Welcome to Wiarton Willie. Wiarton Willie Organization, 1999. <www.wiarton-willie.org/index.cfm>

Western Folklife Center: Cowboy Poets on the Internet. Western Folklife Center, 1998. <www.westfolk.org/>

Writing HTML for Teachers. Maricopa Center for Learning and Instruction 1994-1999. <www.mcli.dist.maricopa.edu/tut>

Y

Yahooligans! Yahoo! Inc., 1994-1999. <www.yahooligans.com>

Bibliography of Software

Carmen Sandiego Think Quick Challenge. The Learning Company.

Cartopedia. Dorling Kindersley, 1995.

Children's Songbook. Grolier.

Community Construction Kit. Tom Snyder Productions.

Creative Writer. Microsoft Corporation, 1994.

Fizz and Martina's Math Adventure. Tom Snyder Productions.

Fun with Architecture. Grolier.

The Graph Club. Tom Snyder Productions.

Hyperstudio. Knowledge Adventure.

I Spy. Scholastic.

Living Books: Arthur's Reading Race. Random House/Broderbund, 1996.

Louvre Museum for Kids. Grolier.

Making Music. Grolier.

Mask World. Visions.

Memory Challenge. Critical Thinking.

Microsoft Bookshelf. Microsoft Corporation, 2000.

Microsoft Encarta. Microsoft Corporation, 2000.

MiDisaurus. Musicware.

MovieWorks. Interactive Solutions.

Music Loops for Multimedia. FTC.

My First Amazing Diary. Dorling Kindersley.

Slam Dunk Typing. The Learning Company.

Strategy Challenges I and II. Edmark.

That's a Fact Jack! Read. Tom Snyder Productions.

Thinkin' Things. Edmark.

Visual Spanish or Visual French. ABC Clio Interactive.

World Book Multimedia Encyclopedia. World Book, Inc., 1998.

Writing and Reading Poetry. Visions.

Appendices

Appendix A

The Nine Information Literacy Standards for Student Learning

Information Literacy

Standard 1: The student who is information literate accesses information efficiently and effectively.

Standard 2: The student who is information literate evaluates information critically and competently.

Standard 3: The student who is information literate uses information accurately and creatively.

Independent Learning

Standard 4: The student who is an independent learner is information literate and pursues information related to personal interests.

Standard 5: The student who is an independent learner is information literate and appreciates literature and other creative expressions of information.

Standard 6: The student who is an independent learner is information literate and strives for excellence in information seeking and knowledge generation.

Social Responsibility

Standard 7: The student who contributes positively to the learning community and to society is information literate and recognizes the importance of information to a democratic society.

Standard 8: The student who contributes positively to the learning community and to society is information literate and practices ethical behavior in regard to information and information technology.

Standard 9: The student who contributes positively to the learning community and to society is information literate and participates effectively in groups to pursue and generate information.

Appendix B

Learning and Teaching Principles of School Library Media Programs

These principles were identified and developed by the Information Power Vision Committee, reviewed and commented upon by the profession, and approved by the AASL and AECT Boards as the cardinal premises on which learning and teaching within the effective school library media program is based.

Principle 1: The library media program is essential to learning and teaching and must be fully integrated into the curriculum to promote students' achievement of learning goals.

Principle 2: The information literacy standards for student learning are integral to the content and objectives of the school's curriculum.

Principle 3: The library media program models and promotes collaborative planning and curriculum development.

Principle 4: The library media program models and promotes creative, effective, and collaborative teaching.

Principle 5: Access to the full range of information resources and services through the library media program is fundamental to learning.

Principle 6: The library media program encourages and engages students in reading, viewing, and listening for understanding and enjoyment.

Principle 7: The library media program supports the learning of all students and other members of the learning community who have diverse learning abilities, styles, and needs.

Principle 8: The library media program fosters individual and collaborative inquiry.

Principle 9: The library media program integrates the uses of technology for learning and teaching.

Principle 10: The library media program is an essential link to the larger learning community.

Appendix C

Publisher's Web Site

Many publishers include educational activities, book reviews, games, and lesson plans to accompany their books. All include a way to reach them if your students have questions for the publisher or for their authors.

Publishing Company	Address of Parent Company
Bantam Dell Doubleday Knopf Random House	<www.randomhouse.com/kids>
Clarion Houghton Mifflin	<www.hmco.com/trade>
Dial Dutton Penguin Philomel Puffin Putnam Viking	<www.penguinputnam.com/yreaders/index.htm>
Dorling Kindersley	<www.dkflbooks.com>
Greenwillow William Morrow	<www.williammorrow.com/child/main_features.htm>
Harcourt Brace	<www.harcourt.com>
HarperCollins	<www.harperchildrens.com/index.htm>
Little Brown	<www.twbookmark.com/children>
Millbrook Press	<www.millbrookpress.com>
North-South Books	<www.northsouth.com>
Orchard Books	<www.grolier.com>
Scholastic Publishers	<www.scholastic.com/kids/index.htm>
Simon & Schuster	<www.simonsayskids.com>

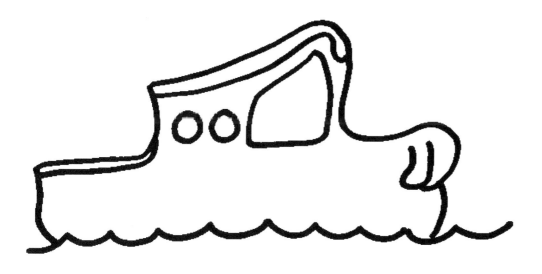

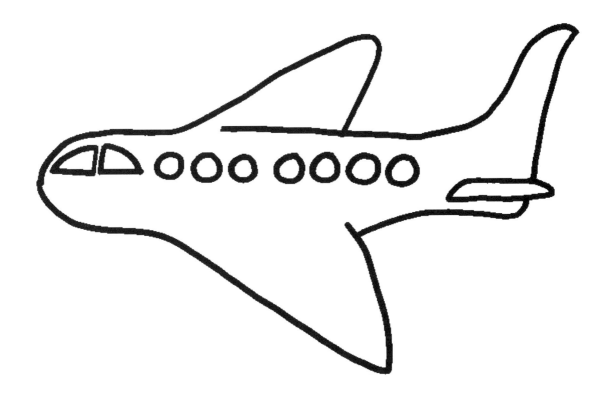

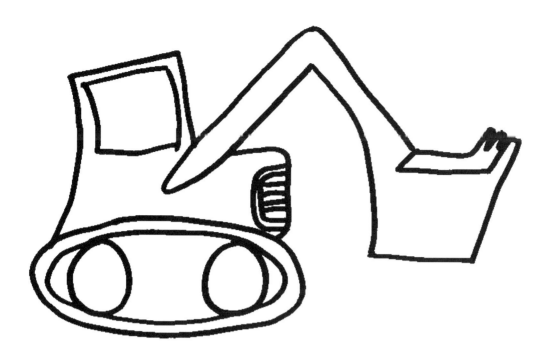

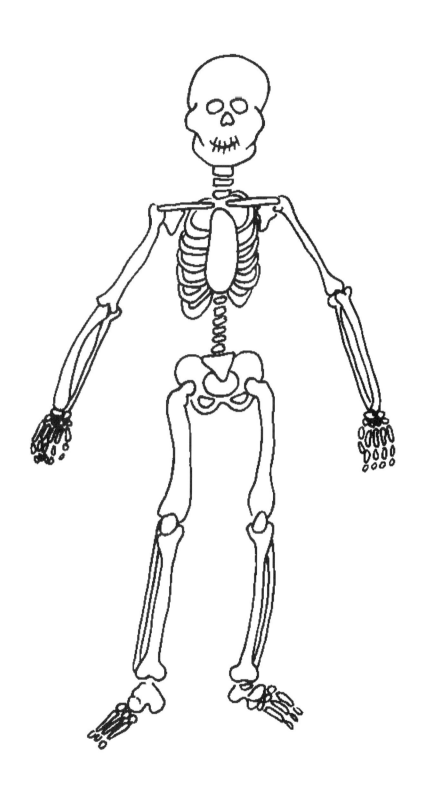

ANIMAL SIZES

Animal	Size	Weight	Page of information source

ANIMALS FROM JAN BRETT'S *THE MITTEN*

Research to complete the chart. For type of eater, write one of these:

C = carnivore, a meat-eating animal
H = herbivore, a plant-eating animal
O = omnivore, an animal that eats plants and meat

Animal	Descriptive Words	Habitat	State(s) in Which Found	Type of Eater
Snowshoe Hare				
Red Fox				
Brown Bear				
Great Horned Owl				
Hedgehog				
Badger				
Mole				
Field Mouse				

Lotto Board

CAREERS AND UNIFORMS

**Research a career to discover if a uniform is required for this job.
Write a brief description of the job and tell about its uniform if one is required.**

Job title: _____

_____

Description of job: _____

_____

_____

_____

Description of the uniform: _____

_____

_____

Does the job require specialized clothing? _____

_____

_____

How did you get your information? _____

_____

_____

Name_____

WE ALL GO TO SCHOOL

Choose a country to compare with our own. Complete the chart. Use library books, the Internet, and encyclopedias.

Color the boxes that are the same yellow.
Color the ones that are different pink.

	In the United States	In _____
Getting to school		
Eating lunch		
Hours and days at school		
Subjects studied		

Name_____

COMPARING TWO SCHOOLS

Write describing words in each box.
Tell how the schools are the same and different.

	This school	**My old school OR last year at this school:**
Library		
Eating lunch		
Recess		
Teacher		
Friends		

Name _____ **Date** _____

DISCOVERING DETAILS

Look at one of the books below. Watch the filmstrip or movie that goes with it.
Write down a few details from the book that look like the real things.

Title	Country	Real Details
The Hat	Denmark	
Christmas Trolls, Trouble with Trolls, or *The Wild Christmas Reindeer*	Norway	
Comet's Nine Lives	Nantucket, U.S.	
Armadillo Rodeo	Texas ranch, U.S.	
Berlioz the Bear	Bavaria, Germany	
The Mitten	The Ukraine	
Gingerbread Baby	Switzerland	

Name _____ Date _____

FAIRY TALE ANALYSIS

Check off the appropriate characteristics for the fairy tales you read or hear.

Title, Author, Copyright	Conflict between good and evil	Conflict resolved	Use of three	Royalty	Happy ending	Magical powers

FARM ANIMAL FAMILIES

Find the names of each of these animal family members.

Animal Family	Male	Female	Baby
cow			
horse			
cat			
sheep			
goat			
turkey			
chicken			
pig			
duck			
goose			
rabbit			
donkey			
dog			

Name:_____

JAN BRETT BOOK HUNT, PART 1

Use the Jan Brett books to answer these questions:

1. (**The Mitten**) Many animals squeeze into the mitten.
   Write their names from smallest to largest. Two are done for you.

   meadow mouse, _____

   _____

   _____

   _____, brown bear

2. (**Armadillo Rodeo**) Bo's mother has to search for him.
   Which animals did she ask for help? (Hint: Look in the side pictures.)

   _____

   _____

   _____

   _____

3. (**Annie and the Wild Animals**) Annie ended up with three new pets.

   What colors were they? _____

   _____

   _____

   _____

   _____

4. (**Comet's Nine Lives**) Write the names of three boats found on the bay.

   _____

   _____

   _____

   _____

Name:_____

JAN BRETT BOOK HUNT, PART 2

Use the Jan Brett books to answer these questions:

5. **(Fritz and the Beautiful Horses***)* What did the beautiful horses crack?

    _____

    _____

    _____

    The picture of this cracked thing is on which page? _____

6. Many animals got mad at **The Gingerbread Baby**. Which animals were chasing him?

    _____

    _____

    _____

7. (**The Trouble with Trolls**) What did the hedgehog eat? (Hint: Look at the bottom of the pages.)

    _____

    _____

    _____

8. **The First Dog** saved Kip from three dangerous animals. What were they?

    _____

    _____

    _____

Name:_____

JAN BRETT BOOK HUNT, PART 3

Use the Jan Brett books to answer these questions:

9. **(Christmas Trolls)** What animal is the troll's helper?

_____

_____

Name three gifts that the trolls took. _____

_____

_____

10. **(Goldilocks and the Three Bears.)** Look close! What little animals live with the bears?

_____

_____

_____

11. In **The Hat**, the animals are taking the clothes off the line!

Can you find what each animal took?

He _____   Goose _____

Cat_____   Dog _____

Pig_____   Horse _____

12. **(The Night Before Christmas)** Who is riding with Santa in his sleigh?

_____

_____

_____

NAME THE INSTRUMENT

Use reference pictures to identify the instrument on each of these pages (count pages with the title page as page 1):

Instrument Name	Page #	Instrument Family (woodwind, stringed, percussion)
	3	
	4	
	16	
	28, 31	
	28, 30	
	22	

Name _____ **Teacher** _____

PICTURE BOOK ILLUSTRATION EVALUATIONS

1. Title of book: _____

   Art media used (look on copyright page): _____

   _____

   Scale of realism (Circle one, 1 is least, 5 is most):   1   2   3   4   5

2. Title of book:

   Art media used (look on copyright page):

   Scale of realism (Circle one, 1 is least, 5 is most):   1   2   3   4   5

3. Title of book:

   Art media used (look on copyright page):

   Scale of realism (Circle one, 1 is least, 5 is most):   1   2   3   4   5

4. Title of book:

   Art media used (look on copyright page):

   Scale of realism (Circle one, 1 is least, 5 is most):   1   2   3   4   5

5. Title of book:

   Art media used (look on copyright page):

   Scale of realism (Circle one, 1 is least, 5 is most):   1   2   3   4   5

   The illustration I like best is _____

   because _____

   _____

   _____

Name:_____

SKELETAL COMPARISONS WORKSHEET
Complete the chart by examining the graphs of our class.

Animal	Number of Bones	Rank by number of bones

Name:_____

SKELETAL COMPARE/CONTRAST

Have a partner measure you for each of these measurements: Record the inches next to the part of the skeleton.

Measurement	Bone Name	Comparison (circle one)	Student Name
	Skull (Cranium)	less same more	
	Thigh bone (Femur)	less same more	
	Thumb	less same more	
	Hand (from wrinkle at wrist to tip of longest finger)	less same more	
	Height	less same more	

Name:_____

WHAT DO WE WEAR IN THE SNOW?

Use a thesaurus to find synonyms for different types of winter wear:

Winter Clothing Type	Synonym	Synonym
gloves		
boots		
coat		
scarf		
cap		
sweater		
pants		
shirt		
underwear		

Leaves grow

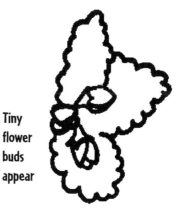

Tiny flower buds appear

Petals blow off

Small green apples appear

Apples get bigger

Apples are ready to pick

cookie

milk

straw

napkin

mirror

scissors

broom

book

papers/crayons

pen

tape

pillow

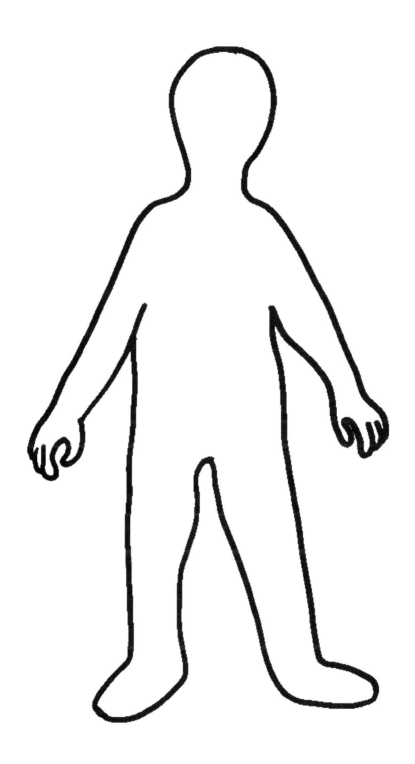

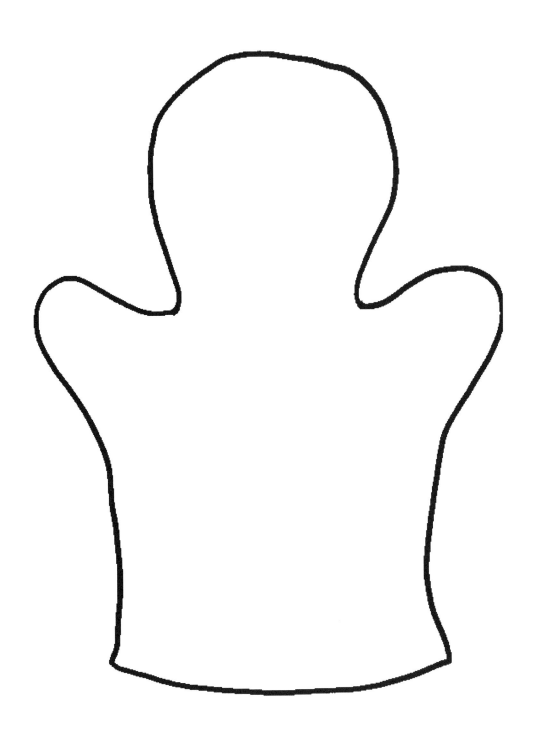

Index

Index of Activities

Musical Activities

compose
> a healthy habits song, 86
> a hygiene song, 85
> a tooth song, 85
> a wish song, 115
> a work song, 92, 107
> an animal song, 154

learn
> a state song, 92
> body parts with song, 98

listen to a musical performance, 141
play musical instruments, 130, 140
record a story with music, 98
select background music for a book, 174

Reading and Writing Activities

adaptations, 106
almanac usage, 107, 118, 129
alphabet book, 144
animal research, 119, 127, 137
cause and effect, 20, 160, 161
clothing synonyms, 104
counting book, 138
country research, 170
cowboy poetry, 148
dental writings for an E-zine, 88
descriptive paragraph, 121
details, 170
disaster plan, 109
evaluative paragraph, 121
heritage hunt, 112, 114
how-to paragraphs, 90
interrogative paragraph, 83
interview questions, 87, 94, 163
letter writing, 8, 20, 164
participate in children's chat line, 88
persuasive paragraph, 116
play script, 94, 111
readers' theater script, 94
recipe, 90
research, 9, 83, 92, 104, 109, 114, 119, 121, 122, 126,
> 127, 133, 137, 138, 144, 145, 149, 151, 157, 174-
> 175, 178
riddles, 37-38, 157
scavenger hunt, 42, 133, 156, 165-169
sequel, 106, 144
tall tale, 109
tooth customs, 83
Traveling Poem Day, 22
write a play, 94
write and address a postcard, 173

About the Author

Pat Miller's professional experience includes teaching grades 2-5 for 15 years, and 13 years of experience as a school library media specialist. She currently works at Walker Station Elementary in Sugar Land, Texas.

Her education includes a bachelor's degree in elementary education and English from St. Edward's University (Austin), a master's degree in reading and reading specialist endorsement from the University of Houston, and a library resources endorsement from Sam Houston State University.

Her tips and articles have appeared in *Library Talk, Technology Connection, The Book Report,* and *School Library and Media Activities Monthly* magazines. She is also a book reviewer for Linworth Publications.

Pat has given workshops and presentations at colleges, library districts, school districts, puppetry guild conferences and her school. As a storyteller, she has told stories at the George Memorial Library's *Christmas Tales,* at the George Ranch's *Texian Days,* at Beeville College, and in her own library.

She and her husband John, a school principal, have been married twenty-eight years. They have three readers in college and two illiterate dogs.